Friends for Life

The Story of a Holocaust Survivor and His Rescuers

LOUIS GOLDMAN

FOREWORD BY
DONNA KANTER

Paulist Press
New York/Mahwah, NJ

Cover design by Trudi Gershenov
Cover photo supplied by Adina Goldman. Used with permission.

Book design by Lynn Else

Library of Congress Cataloging-in-Publication Data

Goldman, Louis, 1925–
    Friends for life : the story of a Holocaust survivor and his rescuers / Louis Goldman ; foreword by Donna Kanter.
        p. cm.
    ISBN 978-0-8091-4534-8 (alk. paper)
    1. Goldman, Louis, 1925– 2. Refugees, Jewish—Italy—Biography. 3. Holocaust, Jewish (1939–1945)—Italy—Personal narratives. 4. Righteous Gentiles in the Holocaust—Italy. 5. World War, 1939–1945—Jews—Rescue—Italy. 6. Italy—Ethnic relations. I. Title.
    DS135.I9G648 2008
    940.53'18092—dc22
    [B]
                                                                2008028214

Published by Paulist Press
997 Macarthur Boulevard
Mahwah, New Jersey 07430

www.paulistpress.com

Printed and bound in the
United States of America

To my parents
and to my brother Harry

And for my children
so they know
and forever remember

~

I am most grateful to
editor Donna Kanter for her
dedication to the story and
her unfailing encouragement
since the day she
"found" me.

Let love and faithfulness never leave you;
bind them around your neck,
write them on the tablet of your heart.

Then you will win favor and a good name
in the sight of God and man.

—PROVERBS 3:5

Friends for Life is a tribute to a group of young Catholic priests who, for two years, from 1943 to 1945, risked their lives to save Jews from the Nazis. The priests acted entirely on their own initiative, and I am one of many alive today thanks to them.

The friendship born in those dark days between priests and their protégés has continued and deepened over the past fifty-three years.

The following events are a true account based on my own experiences and those of all involved.

Foreword

~

When Louis Goldman was eighteen years old, he was one of several hundred Jews who were captured in a brutal Nazi SS raid that swept through Florence, Italy—birthplace of Dante and cradle of Italian culture. It was November 6, 1943.

Twenty five years later, nearly to the day, I took the first step in a labyrinthine journey that led me inevitably to Goldman's studio in New York. While I did not realize it at the time, I had already begun looking for Louis in 1968.

On that crisp November morning of '68, I joined my fellow American graduate students in Florence's Piazza della Repubblica to pursue advanced degrees at the University of Florence. It was a time of social upheaval, similar to my recent experience on the Berkeley campus at the University of California.

Thirty years earlier, in 1938, Italy's King Victor Emmanuel III had issued laws which decreed that Jews could not attend public schools. Yet on enrolling in the Facoltà di Lettere e Filosofia, I found no courses on World War II, Fascist Italy, the Italian Holocaust, or the Italian Resistance—to teach us what author Primo Levi would later term "paradoxical Italy, officially anti-Semitic."

The academic year abruptly ended when our Florentine classmates went on strike for free speech, in solidarity with their Parisian counterparts. My dean then whisked me off to private tutoring with a Dantean who railed against another Inferno: America's *maledetta* Vietnam War. As university classes alternately resumed and halted, we students immersed ourselves in the glory of the city which the young Louis Goldman, hidden in its outskirts, had dared to explore under the noses of the Nazi Gestapo.

In February 1969, as some of my disenchanted classmates trickled home to the States, I read newspaper reports about Don Enzo Mazzi, a forty-two-year-old priest who had been suspended from his parish in nearby Isolotto. He had taken a stand against threatened layoffs by the Galileo Optics Factory, where many of his parishioners had labored since childhood. It stood next door to Madonnina del Grappa, the orphanage in which priests had hidden Louis Goldman during the Holocaust.

Intrigued by events swirling about me, I went to Isolotto to learn about the schism between Mazzi's working-class parish and Cardinal Ermenegildo Florit. Isolotto was built on Florence's former garbage dump, paved over after World War II to create public housing for desperately poor families. I arrived at the church to find its doors locked by the police on Florit's orders until Don Mazzi agreed to resume tending to the souls of his flock instead of its politics. However, when the cardinal sent police to collect the church keys from Don Mazzi, over a thousand people greeted them, loudly jingling their own keys midair in rebellious glee.

In 1943, at the height of World War II, Mazzi had been a seventeen-year-old seminary student, chosen by his mentor, Florence's earlier cardinal Elia Dalla Costa, to distribute parish funds. Cardinal Dalla Costa, against tacit church policy, was hiding and assisting refugee Jews fleeing the Germans. He, too, had once ordered church doors shut: against Adolf Hitler, who had come to view Florence from atop Piazzale Michelangelo. Dalla Costa's diocesan priests later would hide Louis Goldman at the Madonnina del Grappa.

Mazzi had joined his cardinal's clandestine operation through workers' parties that organized a partisan movement that dealt the penultimate blow to Italy's alliance with Nazi Germany. Isolotto's Gino Tagliaferri, ninety-three (when I met him), nearly blind but still vital, had led the partisan "troops" in northern Tuscany, speeding to his dangerous tasks on a bicycle.

When I went home to California to complete my studies toward a doctoral thesis on the Italian Resistance, my professors discouraged me from the subject. I later discovered why: During the war two of them had been young partisans—two soldiers in Il Duce's army.

I returned often to Florence for additional research. Then in 1993, I met one of Florence's former mayors, GianCarlo Zoli, and his wife Gabriella. As a law student fifty years earlier, Zoli had forged Italian identity cards for refugee Jews streaming into Florence, the Germans at their heels. Initially he had done it to impress fiancée Gabriella, whose Aunt Lisa had already begun to hide Jewish families in her home. But after witnessing the horror of the German raids on Jews hidden in his city, Zoli was impelled by his own convictions to stand with his cardinal, Dalla Costa.

August 11, 1994, was the fiftieth anniversary of Florence's liberation from the Nazis by partisan snipers—and the day GianCarlo presented me with *Amici Per La Vita* ("Friends for Life"), a book by Louis Goldman. It was the true story of a family that survived the Holocaust in Italy, and the Italian clergy who had saved them.

The story enthralled me, transcending my expectations as subject matter for the simple interviews I had first contemplated for a series of articles. The book had been translated into Italian from its original English by Goldman's friends in Treviso.

From my reading of his nagging precision and love of order, I knew that Louis Goldman was uncharacteristically late for our meeting in New York the following September. The bellman had already hailed me a cab for JFK when Louis at last appeared in the hotel lobby, only moments before my departure.

We had our first cappuccino together, but not nearly as exuberantly as when we drank the ones Louis would later make in his kitchen. We discussed his manuscript's haunting images—many night-permeated—which only young Louis, a future photographer, could have committed to memory. His story of how a peasant woman on a train pressed a red-kerchiefed basket of food— the only gift she had to offer—on the Goldmans after Louis's father barely escaped arrest caused Louis to weep in the telling, a luxury he could not have indulged in at that time of terror.

That moment, a "still frame" capturing the memory of Louis's father and the peasant woman, seemed a metaphor for an innate Italian humanity and the "divine disobedience" that would later guide Louis's writing—also the reason for his lateness that afternoon. He had almost broken our appointment because he did not trust that he could reveal his historic pain to a stranger.

Two years later, I feel privileged to have edited Louis Goldman's *Friends for Life,* at a time when Italian cultural institutes around the world are sponsoring "Shalom, Italia" symposiums for Italians and Jews to remember together that which must never be allowed to happen again. Many Italians in the years since the Holocaust have yet to understand that their anti-Fascism must include also an abhorrence of anti-Semitism.

To the righteous Italian priests on Louis Goldman's pages and to those we will never know—gunned down beneath the old walls of Lucca, starved at Mauthausen, and murdered by lethal injection at Dachau—I am grateful as much as to Louis Goldman for bringing me home.

—*Donna Kanter, Sherman Oaks, California, July 2008*

Preface

On September 8, 1943, pandemonium broke out in Saint-Martin-Vesubie.

That day, Marshal Pietro Badoglio, head of the Italian government—after replacing the ousted Benito Mussolini (Il Duce) on July 25—capitulated to Allied forces invading southern Italy. Mussolini remained imprisoned by his own people.

Since France's surrender to Germany and Italy in June 1940, the Italian 4th Army occupied a sizable chunk of southern-French territory. It had designated Saint-Martin-Vesubie, a placid resort town in the Maritime French Alps above Nice, as one of several forced-residence areas for Jews. Although Italy was Germany's ally in a war that had raged since 1939, it did not accede to the Nazis' genocidal policy against Jews. Consequently, its Italian zone became a haven for thousands of Jews who fled from the German-occupied zone of northern France, where they had lived in fear of the daily deportations to concentration camps. Of those, eight-hundred Jews took refuge in Saint-Martin-Vesubie. They were forbidden to leave town except in medical emergencies and had to register each day at the Italian police post. However, there were no persecutions and, above all, no deportations.

Most of the Jews were refugees for the second and third time. Hunted by the Germans, they had come from Poland, Belgium, Holland, Germany, and German-occupied France. Among them were my parents, Polish-born Pinkus and Mina Goldman, my twelve-year-old brother Harry, my aunt Sonia

Rosenstrauch, and her fourteen-year-old daughter Sylvia. I, the other Goldman son, aged eighteen, was living and working in Nice on a temporary French police permit.

In time, the relationship between Italians and Jews became harmonious and friendly. Each daily registration procedure evolved into a rendezvous for neighbors and acquaintances. Many of the refugees and Italians got to know each other by sight and name. My father was hired as gardener at the mayor's villa, and Harry, Sylvia, and the other Jewish children were allowed to attend school again. In warm weather, the Italians authorized a boxing club and use of the swimming pool and tennis court. On weekends, Italians and Jews played spirited soccer matches while army brass and refugees cheered wildly for their respective teams. My father, a soccer champion during his youth in Poland, was one of the most enthusiastic fans.

This idyll came to an abrupt end on the evening of September 8, 1943. With news of Italy's capitulation, there was great rejoicing among the refugees and even among the Italian soldiers, never at heart great friends of Nazi Germany. But there was also confusion and apprehension. What would happen next?

The following morning the Allies who had occupied Sicily landed in southern Italy near Salerno, not far from Naples. The Italian units in Saint-Martin-Vesubie received orders to return home immediately. An officer told the panic-stricken Jews, "We can't protect you anymore, but follow us to Italy. You have nothing to gain by staying here. The Germans will probably take over our zone in a few hours."

The Italian units' own haste to make it across the border and avoid contact with the Germans was contagious. The refugees scrambled home, flung together a few essentials, packed some victuals, and rushed out into the streets again. Only a small percentage of the Jewish population decided to remain and take their chances.

PREFACE

A long column of refugees, including old and sick people, children and pregnant women, and my parents, brother Harry, and cousin Sylvia, streamed out of town in the wake of the retreating Italians.

Chapter One

On the morning of September 9, 1943, I received an urgent cable from my parents to come to Saint-Martin-Vesubie. I was living alone in Nice, having been caught there four weeks earlier with a fake French identity card while en route to visit my parents from Montpellier, where I'd been hiding and working in a photography studio. I'd had to remain in Nice and report to the police precinct twice a week.

My parents' cable also asked me to bring my Aunt Sonia. She had broken her arm and was getting it set in a cast at a hospital in Nice. The doctor had just applied the plaster before we rushed to catch the last bus of the day to Saint-Martin-Vesubie.

By the time Aunt Sonia and I arrived, it was late afternoon. The streets were deserted, shops closed. In the distance, on the road leading up into the mountains, we saw a long, straggly line of refugees carrying suitcases, bundles, and their small children.

My parents' home looked as though it had been turned upside down, very unlike my mother's neat housekeeping. Clothes spilled out of half-open drawers, and cold soup and coffee were still on the table. Mother's apron lay on the floor by the door.

We knocked on the apartment door of the landlord, Mr. Roux. "They left at two and took your cousin Sylvia along. They'll wait for you at the sawmill up toward Col de Fenestre. Just follow the crowd," he said.

Aunt Sonia and I dashed to her place to get a few belongings. As we packed, someone in the street yelled, "Hurry up! Germans

are on the road to Nice!" We rushed out into the gathering darkness and joined the swelling migration of refugees.

To get from Saint-Martin-Vesubie into Italy, we would have
to climb some of the Alps' most formidable peaks. If we could
just stay ahead of the Germans, we would arrive behind Italian
troops in an Italy occupied entirely by Allies, free of the war. To
avoid oncoming Germans, the column of refugees followed a
narrow inside path away from the main track.

It wasn't long before suitcases became unbearably heavy.
Some older people said they couldn't continue and would go
back down to Saint-Martin, come what may. Most of the
refugees were from urban environments and had seldom been
near mountains, much less climbed one, and years of persecution had affected their health.

As the incline got steeper, it became difficult to breathe,
and our pace slowed considerably. Night fell. Only a few people
had flashlights, and families found it hard to stay together. The
darkness echoed with shouts in French, German, Polish, and
Yiddish. To fall behind meant getting lost.

My aunt's cast hadn't hardened yet and kept getting caught
in low-hanging branches. She was also afflicted with asthma,
and even with me carrying her luggage we had to make frequent
rest stops. Two years earlier she'd suffered a greater misfortune.
The French Vichy police had seized her husband Jacob, who was
Mother's brother, and deported him to Germany. Not a word
had been heard from him since. Nor had we heard from Aunt
Sonia and Mother's other eleven brothers and sisters and their
families in German-occupied Poland in four years.

Shortly before midnight we finally came within view of the
sawmill. Bonfires projected gigantic shadows of human shapes
onto the surrounding trees and cliffs. I could see why many
refugees had chosen that spot for respite. It was high and isolated, and safe from Germans, at least for the moment.

CHAPTER ONE

Whistling the family's special signal, a repeated syncopation of a high, then low note, I circulated through the mass of weary people and their crying children: some unpacking and repacking their meager belongings, others wandering about anxiously calling out names of relatives they'd lost on the way. I overheard men pleading with their exhausted families to proceed without stopping. Most, though, were sprawled out on the ground, fast asleep.

Suddenly, I heard Papa's answering whistle. A cry of "Ludi!" (my nickname), and in the next instant my brother Harry jumped on my back. I stumbled forward, bumping against Aunt Sonia's suitcase. Harry was a scrawny kid, not yet five feet tall, weighing seventy-five pounds at the most. I turned around. "Gingel!" I yelled, my name for that elf who was too bright, too shrewd, too wise, and too old for his age. Born twelve years before, and bred in troubled times, he was both high-strung and stubborn. Aunt Sonia and Sylvia rushed to embrace each other. Nearly the height of her tall mother, Sylvia had chestnut hair and sad, blue-gray eyes. "Hi," I said, hugging my cousin, the only girl who didn't make me feel awkward. I blamed the war for my lack of a normal adolescence and my extreme shyness. My parents were relieved to finally see us, and, despite the circumstances, it was a happy family reunion.

Papa had a small fire going, his handsome face glowing, ruddy. His thinning hair, even after the exhausting climb, was neatly combed and parted. With a sweeping gesture, he said, "Welcome to the picnic!" They'd been anxiously waiting for several hours, afraid we would miss each other. Aunt Sonia and I slumped down, wanting nothing better than to catch our breath, but Mother insisted we have sandwiches and fruit.

"We'll stay here for the night," Papa said, "and continue at dawn. Some people have gone on, but it's a *mishegas*. You can break your neck climbing mountains in such darkness."

I stretched out; my head propped up on a rucksack, and stared into the velvet canopy of the sky.

Here we go. Refugees again! And yet I didn't see this latest reversal in our lives as a calamity. For me, at eighteen, it even held the thrill of adventure. Climb the Alps and on the other side, perhaps as soon as tomorrow afternoon, freedom!

My parents had a different perspective. Both in their early forties, they had lived through a long succession of setbacks. The day after they were married, August 18, 1923, Pinkus and Maniush—as they affectionately called each other—had fled to Germany from their native Poland (Lodz) to avoid his conscription into the anti-Semitic Polish army. Papa had left behind a promising bank career to start from scratch in Frankfurt. Working hard, he eventually became a representative of a textile firm. Their first child, a girl, died at nine months. I arrived on June 8, 1925, and Harry, almost six years later on March 10, 1931.

In September 1933, after Hitler came to power, one of Mother's brothers was killed by the Nazis in his apartment in Wiesbaden. A silk importer, he was victim of the SA ("Brown Shirts") organization's first official acts of brutality against Jews. We fled to Paris, but Papa had no official permit to work or stay. For three years, every few months he had to return to the indignities of the Châtelet prefecture, where bureaucrats made him plead all day before finally granting another extension: *"Mais après ça, vous foutez le camp, hein?"** Undaunted, he worked harder, traveling without papers into industrial suburbs to sell fabrics.

In 1936, Leon Blum became prime minster, and for a few short years our family enjoyed a peace of sorts. During that golden period, my parents often had as many as fifteen friends for dinner, with Mother fussing about and Papa teasing everyone. When riding the Metro, Papa, mimicking demonstrative

---

*"But after this, you'll scram, right?"

CHAPTER ONE

Parisian lovers, would even corner Mother in a crowded car and smooch all over her, mumbling passionate nonsense in pseudo-French. Even later, when our home consisted of one room, there were always people to join us for *kiddush* and the holidays. However, in June 1940, we were forced to flee again, escaping just hours ahead of the Germans approaching Paris. In late 1940, the pro-German Vichy government interned us in the Agde concentration camp near Montpellier.

I was able to liberate my family the following June by pleading with the prefect to allow Harry and me to resume school. The prefect had come to inspect the camp, and I stepped forward, risking punishment. But he was swayed, on the condition that we would provide for ourselves. Since then, it had been two years of fear and persecution: running from one place to another; hiding in forests, cellars, attics; attempting unsuccessfully to cross the Swiss border. Finally, the Italian zone in France had given us a short reprieve. But now the Germans were at our heels again.

Papa was still awake, fanning the fire. Mother opened her eyes. She was dark and petite, with delicate features. "Pinkus, are you out of your mind? Get some sleep!" If Worry had a protector carrying its torch on earth, it was my mother.

"All right, all right, soon." He snapped some branches in half and spread them on the fire. With the glowing end of a twig he lit a cigarette and lay back. His family was together, safe, and warm. For now, all else was secondary.

Unable to sleep, I watched the fire, its flickering lights bringing back memories of Friday-night candles and Papa's blessing on our heads during *kiddush*. When would we enjoy a normal family life again?

Chapter Two

The dawn came up, leaden and misty. A half hour later the view cleared. Everywhere in the thin air were layers of tall mountains. And looming straight ahead, the jagged peak we would have to climb next, the nearly ten-thousand-foot Col de Fenestre! I wondered how many of us would make it.

Like the thread that unravels a sweater, a long line of people began moving out of the sawmill compound. I joined a youth squad organized to help the old and sick. For a good stretch the terrain wasn't too difficult, but as the slope rose sharply, some people faltered or just gave up. They sat by the wayside and sobbed, begging me not to bother with them anymore, while I cajoled and pushed. Mother took the baby from a woman who'd given birth three days before and carried it for her until she could catch up.

I was laden down with parcels like a mule. Even so, I was one of the first to reach the peak at about 11:00 a.m. Panting, I looked back down and saw a modern version of the Exodus out of Egypt! Several hundred refugees, in a single line that seemed to stretch for miles, were slowly creeping across the plateau and up the mountain. Tackling obstructing boulders, some lost their footing and slipped, falling on people behind them. Rocks loosened and rolled, dislodging more in a snowballing tumble down the mountain. Some of the refugees hurled belongings from the peak to inch upward, unencumbered. Some pathetically held on to a dishpan, an electric heating-plate, or some other item which seemed to them indispensable.

6

My family was managing quite well, buoyed by Harry's and Sylvia's youthful optimism, each of us guiding Aunt Sonia along. Our youth group went down to help, amazed that many older people had been able to keep up the pace while we were at the end of our own strength. Only despair spurred them on, and eventually across.

We started the descent midafternoon. Although less exhausting, this trail was treacherously slippery. Ignoring numbing fatigue, our group spirit was light. We were in Italy now!

The trail led down into an inhabited valley, and we would reach the nearest village before sundown. I told my parents I planned to move to the head of the line, to be among the first to find accommodations. Papa objected, but I insisted, afraid there would be no room left. About a dozen other men had the same idea. Some outdistanced me, and I begrudged them their stamina. The soles on my sneakers had worn thin and, with every step, sharp stones cut into my feet. Every bone in my body screamed for rest. Halfway down the Col de Fenestre I suddenly saw an armed Italian soldier with an officer, barring the way. Who were we and what were we doing? he demanded.

One of our men answered, "We're the refugees from Saint-Martin-Vesubie. Didn't your troops tell you we were coming to Italy?"

"None passed here. They wouldn't take this trail, anyway."

"We only want to escape the Germans."

"What? Germans are in the Italian zone?"

"Not when we left yesterday at noon, but by now, probably."

He pondered for a moment, and then said, "I'm not sure what to do with you. You can't go crossing borders just like that without a visa, you know."

A visa! Was the man insane?

More refugees caught up and grouped around to listen. The officer looked up the trail. People were still coming. "How many of you are there?"

"About five hundred."

He blanched and stared upward again in dismay. Then suddenly, with a show of authority, he turned back to us. "All of you follow me to our barracks. We'll have to investigate this situation."

Ten minutes farther down we found ourselves in a camp of a half-dozen wooden barracks surrounded by barbed wire. The soldiers, from the elite Alpine Corps, gave us curious but friendly looks. The officer told us to wait and called them aside. He briefed them animatedly as more refugees streamed into the camp.

He returned and stood before the crowd with his feet apart in a martial stance. "You will spend the night here. Tomorrow I will have further instructions. In the meantime, don't get any ideas of escaping. I have guards all around and the wire is electrified."

Few took the warning about the wire seriously. There didn't seem to be more than two dozen soldiers in the compound. Still, we kept away from the fence, just in case.

The sun disappeared behind the mountain range, giving the tallest peaks a last brushstroke of lingering pink. Who would have wanted to roam a strange countryside at night, anyway? All I could think of was rest. Things would be straightened out in the morning. After all, we were safe in Italy! Everyone stretched out across the wooden floor of the empty barracks. Although jammed together, we fell asleep quickly.

At about 3:00 a.m., I was awakened by a man's shrill voice, "Hey, the Italians are gone! No more guards!"

Men gathered their families and made hastily for the door, stumbling over complaining shapes just awakening. In the ensuing panic no one paused to wonder whether the Italians had merely deserted or were fleeing approaching Germans. We were obeying collective Pavlovian conditioning: when Italian troops moved, we followed. But in which direction? The only sensible one was continuing the trail with the vanguard down the mountain, though the night was still pitch-black. Caution stands little chance against the herding instinct of people in distress.

It was so dark we could barely see. One man kept striking matches, holding them until the flame reached his fingers, then swirling glowing arcs around him. Mother followed Papa, gripping his coat.

By dawn we eased into the flat of the valley approaching the Italian village of Valdieri. At every turn of the road I anticipated seeing British or American troops. We arrived in the village square, exhausted and hungry, our clothes dirty and torn.

A revolution seemed to be in progress. Italian soldiers were throwing away their uniforms, frantically changing into civilian clothing. Those who had none pleaded to guide our march in exchange for shirts, slacks, jackets—anything that didn't look military. They were abandoning their garrison, while villagers ransacked its vast food supplies. Since our own provisions were depleted, we joined the melee. But as nomads, we had to forgo sacks of flour and cans of pure olive oil and take whatever we could carry: chocolate bars, sugar, biscuits, and cans of meat.

The village swirled in hysterical madness. When we regrouped in the square, the inhabitants took a long and startled look at us. They probably had never seen strangers like us. With the few words we knew, we inquired about the Allied troops. They shrugged, but replied that they expected the Germans to arrive soon.

What a blow! There was nowhere to go. Any direction might take us straight to the Germans. We began to split up. Some groups proceeded on the march while others fanned out in the countryside. Many, like our family, decided to remain and get some rest. Some villagers brought us to an empty school building, where, together with dozens of other refugees, we settled down.

A few days later, standing in the square with a group of men listening to rumors and opinions, I was startled to see two German soldiers in an army car pull up to the bakery. One of them affixed a poster on the wall. It ordered all foreigners to assemble in the square at 6:00 p.m. for registration. Anyone hiding or helping people evade registration would be shot. It was signed by the German SS district commander.

I stared at the two Germans. They seemed so arrogantly sure of themselves, even among hundreds of potentially hostile Jews and Italians. An Italy liberated by the Allies, indeed!

As we read the poster's words over and over, one of the Germans warned, "No use running away. A company will comb the entire area later." Jews darted around like mice in a maze. We knew what registration meant—deportation and the same "disappearances" as that of our relatives. Yet the general reaction was not the one of immediate escape I'd expected. After years of fleeing Germans, many had run out of hope. The march from France over the Alps, which had started with a promise of liberation, was ending in bitter disappointment and resignation. The Germans caught up with us anyway, every time, and everywhere.

I was shocked when Mother refused to leave, too. She just shook her head tiredly, "Where to now, when we have no knowledge of the area and nobody to guide us?" Her legs, always a source of trouble since she was a young girl, were swollen and painful.

I pleaded with her, "Look, even Aunt Sonia with her asthma and broken arm hasn't given up. There are only two Germans in the village so far. Later there will be many more. As long as we're moving, we stand a chance, but staying can only mean disaster." Finally, we prevailed. About an hour before registration time we fell in with a group of about thirty refugees sneaking up to a mountain called Madonna del Colletto.

The road, a narrow mule track through dense woods, was difficult and steep. At one point, when we came around a bend, Valdieri came into view again. I could see refugees gathering in the square, seemingly resigned to surrendering their lives to fate. One of the two Germans supervised them with a submachine gun. The other, on a horse, dashed about the village, rounding up stragglers trying to get away. I could see every detail of the scene, and it filled me with revulsion. I thought of those refugees as conceding to their own rape.

After more than three hours of hard climbing, we were still only halfway up Madonna. The sky darkened. A light drizzle rapidly developed into a cloudburst. The path became so slimy, we grappled tree trunks and hanging branches to keep from slipping, and took turns helping Mother and Aunt Sonia, as torrents of mud washed over our feet. There were gaping holes in the soles of Sylvia's shoes, and she pointed her feet upward, advancing on her heels. Our clothes were sopping sponges. I felt water trickling down my spine.

It was evening when we finally reached the peak of the Madonna. A chapel stood in a clearing of the woods, where several refugees had already taken cover. It served as headquarters for a group of Italian partisans, who made a great show of their weapons. They were ready to make a stand and fight, they said, and kept reassuring us the Germans wouldn't dare come up the mountain. We dozed off on the chapel floor, cold, wet, and miserable, but at least not in German hands.

Chapter Three

At four thousand feet, the peak of Madonna del Colletto was as high as we could go for safety. There were higher mountains on the other side of the valley, but we would have to pass through Demonte, a town heavily garrisoned with Germans. For strategic reasons, the partisans could shelter us for only one night. It was still raining the next day when we set out to find sleeping accommodations for what looked like a long stay on the mountain.

Six acquaintances who wanted to stay together joined our family. Our group of now twelve included two bachelors, Gerard and Marc, and two couples, the henpecking and henpecked Kohns, and the Wallachs. Mrs. Wallach was a gentle and kind lady with crippled legs. Her husband often had to carry her. She was the only one among us who spoke some Italian.

At a little distance from the chapel, down the other side of the mountain, several peasant homes were scattered through the woods, a hamlet called Bau. We sent Mrs. Wallach ahead with Harry as we cautiously approached each door, hoping that the combination of an invalid and a child would move the local folks to give us shelter. Limping up to a door, Mrs. Wallach would ask, *"Scusate prego, avete forse una stalla per dormire?"** We didn't ask for much, any empty shack with a roof to keep us out of the rain, which still hadn't let up. But the peasants didn't know what to make of the haggard strangers suddenly appearing, speaking unfamiliar languages, and maybe bringing trouble. With their armies in collapse, Mussolini a prisoner, the Germans in com-

---

*"I beg your pardon. Would you perhaps have a stable for us to sleep in?"

mand, and the Allies advancing on their soil, in this chaos their safest policy was to trust no one, especially once they learned we were Jews—those people responsible for the death of Christ!

We slept in the woods, taking shelter from the torrential rains and thunderclaps under piles of cut tree trunks. A sympathetic farmer allowed us to spend one night in the stable with his cows. It was warm and dry. Nobody minded the stench. We spread the thin straw along the wall out of reach of the cows' hoofs and huddled together. In the dim light of early morning, we made the startling discovery that all of us had suffered an eruption of freckles overnight, the cause apparent a few minutes later when the next cow's dung flopped to the ground, splashing in all directions.

Finally, a peasant allowed us to move into an abandoned stone shed, which once held farm machinery. It was half in ruins, with neither water nor electricity. Refugees who couldn't find shelter moved on throughout the mountains and valley until they found some sort of abode.

Our most pressing problem was food. Every major item— bread, sugar, fats, meat—was strictly rationed and, of course, we had no ration cards. The peasants had extra food supplies, and for a little while we could buy a few things with our French money. Now and then we sent Harry or Sylvia to Festiona, a small village a little farther down from Bau, where there was a grocery store. Whenever he could, the owner let us have sugar, a bar of soap, or a pound of rice, which Harry and Sylvia carried triumphantly up to our mountain retreat. I went down there at times, too. The fear of capture marking each trip— although the village had no resident police or Carabinieri—was balanced by the joy of returning safe with some food. Stirring a soup of whatever she could put into it on an open fire, Mother sighed wistfully, remembering the recipes in her German cookbook, always starting with *Man nehme* ("One takes"), then listing the recommended amounts of eggs, flour, meat. "But, to take," she commented with irony, "first you've got to have!"

Our money was running out. Not knowing how long we would have to hold out on the mountain, we set aside some pennies for an emergency. We began to eat *castagne,* the wild chestnuts that grew all around and seemed the main staple of the area. The peasants ground, roasted, cooked, and mashed them, and we, too, soon subsisted on almost nothing but chestnut concoctions. But we had to limit our harvesting when the peasants began to make pointed remarks: "We store them for the winter, you know," and, "Did you eat that many in France, too?"

Fresh water, on the other hand, was no problem. A brook about halfway down the mountain relieved us from imposing on the villagers' wells. It was tedious dragging up water each day for twelve people in only pots and pans. But taking turns in groups of twos or threes gave us some sense of daily routine.

In the evening, as we sat around a candle, a wonderful coziness permeated the room. We talked about the good things before there was a Hitler. We never forgot that we were still free, the family together and in good health.

There was a lively zigzagging of refugees from their dugouts across the mountain, dropping in on us for a chat and cup of tea. The stories they told! One girl's parents had repeatedly denied her the pleasure of eating the jam she carried in her rucksack during the march. She loved jam so much, they wanted her to save it. When they finally gave in, the jam had leaked all over; she had walked twenty miles for the privilege of licking it off her spare shoes. A man quartered in a chicken coop complained that the chickens were using his head as a platform to hop in and out. Another was sharing a barn with a goat attached to a rope, but one night, while he was sleeping, the goat tore itself free and swallowed his precious last reserve of sugar. A family told us of the peasant who explained proudly, "This hut is my summer residence, but I also have a winter home in Valdieri. There's a switch on the wall. You flip it and—*tac*—there's light. It's something of another world!" And there was the Yom Kippur service we attended on October 8 in a hayloft. A visiting partisan was so overcome by emotion during the chanting of the soul-stirring *Kol Nidre,* he fainted.

Besides enlivened companionship, such visits also brought the latest rumors. Rumors were as important to us as food and water. Someone always knew someone who knew "for sure" that Hitler's bunker had been hit, or that the end of the war was near—that Jews were being exterminated by the thousands in concentration camps such as Auschwitz and Dachau, or that the Germans had a terrifying secret weapon. Such rumors ran wild daily, but there was no way to verify them in our helpless situation. We accepted the bad ones and didn't dare believe the good ones. I often heard that the Germans were coming up the mountain to search for us. Then we scurried off to hide in the woods all day, listening for steps or shouts. When none came, we cautiously returned to our shed. But at the next rumor, we ran into hiding again. We could never tell when one might prove true.

News of the front in Italy was depressing. The Germans seemed to have it consolidated against the Allies' advance. And Mussolini, daringly rescued by the Germans from prison four days after Marshal Badoglio's capitulation, now put Italy back into the war alongside Germany.

After more than a month on the mountain, our last francs were gone. Desperate, we decided to sell some of Mother's jewelry. In nearby Demonte people bought personal items from hard-pressed refugees, but Demonte was also full of German troops and Carabinieri. I spoke no Italian and wouldn't be able to bluff my way out of a difficult situation. But I put the jewelry in my pocket and kissed my family good-bye.

I stopped in Festiona for help. On one of my trips there to forage for groceries I'd met Viviana, an Italian girl who lived with her family on a farm. She was about twenty-five, very attractive, and tall, with a proud bearing. In a friendly way, she had inquired where I was from and seemed trustworthy. When I told her of our odyssey she expressed genuine concern and thereafter occasionally helped me with food. She agreed to accompany me to Demonte.

"Non parlare!" Viviana admonished when we boarded the tramway. She kept up a constant chatter while I interjected only a *sì, no,* or *grazie* here and there. German soldiers were everywhere. Some sat in cafés under the arcades, their gear and rifles neatly stacked up against the wall, the dreaded SS patches on their uniforms. My stomach churned. What would I do if one of them got fresh with Viviana? Surely they knew there were several hundred Jews hiding in the mountains. How come they were loafing around in cafés? Or were they preparing for action?

Viviana led me to a watchmaker she knew, and he bought the items for a fair price. When I returned to our hideout in the evening, I realized from my parents' welcome that the trip had been a much greater strain on them than on me.

The first week of October had passed, and the prospect of a brutal winter on the mountain loomed large. Mrs. Wallach translated the Italian newspapers for us: "The Allies have succeeded only in taking Naples."

"It's so far south! Nothing else?" I asked.

We listened avidly for signs of hope that somehow never transpired in official communiqués. So, when the Germans boasted they had downed fifty Allied airplanes and only three of theirs didn't return, Mr. Kohn knowingly pointed out that a confession to three losses might mean the actual number was more likely thirty.

Gerard analyzed the matter more reassuringly. "Even assuming what they say is true, what of it? While German factories are being bombed day and night, America goes on producing undisturbed. So, those fifty planes the Allies supposedly lost hardly matter to them—while three downed German planes constitute a tremendous loss. *Voilà!*" I fed hungrily on my companions' reasoning. In the absence of actual good news, it revived our sagging spirits.

Chapter Four

Papa awoke in the night, moaning from sharp pains in his lower abdomen. The constant dragging of wood and other supplies up and down the mountain must have been too much of a strain. The others got up, too, trying to be helpful, but nobody really knew what to do. Terrified, we knelt around Papa, who was writhing on the floor. Mr. Wallach was sure he'd suffered a rupture. The area was so swollen, Papa wouldn't let Mother apply compresses. She nursed and soothed him until daybreak, when he fell asleep from sheer exhaustion.

The nearest doctor or hospital was in Demonte. Exposure to any authority could lead to our arrest and deportation, and Papa was in no condition to be moved down the rough mountain road.

We asked how he felt about the risk involved. With his eyes half closed he murmured weakly, "I don't care anymore." That frightened me even more. We washed and dressed him, and put some lire in his pocket. It was a chilly 5:00 a.m. I took one of Papa's arms, Gerard the other, and we half-carried, and half-dragged him down the path to Festiona. It took hours. He bit his lips with every step and was sweating profusely in the cold. Every few minutes we had to prop him up against a tree. He couldn't sit; the pain of getting up again was too excruciating. When we reached Festiona, I left Papa and Gerard and rushed to Viviana. I explained our dilemma, and she ran to speak to her father.

They would take Papa in their horse wagon to Demonte, where they knew a doctor who could be relied on not to talk. If anyone asked, they would say they found Papa unconscious on the road. It was too dangerous for me to come along. I was to return to their house in the afternoon for news. I raced back to tell Papa. He was ashen, his hands pressing against his abdomen. When Viviana's father arrived with the wagon, we hoisted Papa gently into it, helped him onto the wooden bench, and closed the rear gate. I kissed him good-bye and told him not to worry, for he was with good people. The wagon pulled away. I walked alongside for a little while, talking to him. With every brusque jolt on the rough road, he twisted in agony. The tears in his eyes were not from pain alone. Finally, I stopped and stood looking after the wagon until it disappeared. I had often heard Mother say, "No human being should be punished with having to find out how much he can suffer." I had the feeling I'd suddenly grown up to the meaning of those words.

Viviana and her father were already back when I arrived at their home. They had stayed with Papa while the doctor, in collusion with his surgeon-friend at the hospital, arranged for Papa to have a hernia operation under an assumed identity; then they stayed until the surgeon told them all had gone well and that he would look after Papa until he was discharged in about ten days. He insisted there be no family visits. It would be difficult enough to concoct a plausible story for the hospital staff and the other patients. Neither doctor mentioned payment for services or hospital. Viviana and her father related the details of their trip with particular relish, as though they were Papa's family, not us. As they were telling me their story, the iron walls of the tight little world I'd carried around me—trusting only myself and my own kind, suspicious and afraid of everyone else—suddenly evaporated. I began to feel for the first time the full dimension of the warmth and kindness of the Italian character.

During Papa's recuperation, Mother sent him baked apples—which he loved—through Viviana and her father. A few days later, when Aunt Sonia went to Demonte to have her arm cast removed, the surgeon told her apologetically that Papa would have to leave as soon as possible. The hospital administrators were afraid to keep him much longer.

The next day Papa returned to us. His wound had not yet healed, but the surgeon had given him a supply of bandages and shown him how to apply a new one every few days. He told him if he rested properly, the incision would close without complications. It was good to see Papa smile again as he began walking gingerly, leaning on the cane we'd made from a tree branch.

It was mid-October; howling winds made us doubt we could last much longer. Our resources were gone, and the Germans remained in solid control over most of Italy. In our remote northwestern corner, there was little chance of our liberation for a long time, even if we warded off cold, famine, and Germans until then.

Some families had already left to seek shelter and work in Genoa, Florence, or Rome. While it seemed certain they would be apprehended en route, they preferred danger and uncertainty over their present misery. We began debating a number of our own schemes. Looking for work in the valley's more populated communities and being denounced made us give that up instantly. I felt it indecent to ask Viviana and her family for help again and submit them and us to the embarrassment of a refusal. The logical solution was to go as far south as possible and hide in a large city closer to the Allies. But we had no money, papers, or connections. And we didn't speak Italian.

A few enterprising people in Demonte must have sensed our hopeless predicament. They began to appear on the mountain, hunting for jewelry someone might need to sell. An acquaintance even removed the gold caps from his teeth when he had no other valuables left. They gave him a few bills and went looking for more desperation. It was frightening to see those people circling like vultures around wounded animals. Worse, if they wanted, they could reveal our hiding places.

Eventually, our parents had to sell the last of their valuables: wedding rings, Papa's watch, and Mother's small diamond ring. When two Italians reappeared, Mother slowly removed her wedding ring from her finger. Never taking her eyes off it, she handed it to one of the men. To me, there was something sacrilegious about it. As one examined Papa's watch, Harry took his partner aside. They then bought the watch, but gave flimsy reasons why they weren't interested in Mother's diamond ring: it was too small, they'd never find a buyer, didn't have enough cash for it. Finally, they admitted Harry had pleaded with them not to buy it, Mother's only remaining gift from Papa.

One of the men asked, "What will become of you?" I said we'd thought of going south to a big city but were afraid of the dangers.

"We have to go to Florence," he said. "We'll inquire for you there. Maybe we can help. Be at Borgo San Dalmazzo's station the day after tomorrow at 11:00 a.m."

Two days later, when the train that shuttled between Cuneo and Demonte stopped in Borgo San Dalmazzo, a few people got off, but not the two Italians. Disappointed, I started on the road up the mountain. A man of about forty walked behind me. I'd noticed him at the station because he wasn't dressed like the locals. He wore a suit, tie, and overcoat, and had seemed to be looking for someone. Slightly hunched, he kept both hands in his pockets. I became suspicious and started walking away. He followed faster. To see what he would do, I stopped by a bush and relieved myself. He waited. As I continued to walk, he caught up. "Are you a Jew?" he asked, looking in my eyes.

"Me? The idea!" I answered in shaky Italian, continuing on my way. But he stuck to me.

"You don't have to be afraid," he said. "I'm Jewish myself."

Elementary trick, I thought. "Leave me alone," I snapped.

"Look," he said impatiently, "you don't talk like an Italian. I've come from Florence to speak to Jews hiding in the mountains about a rescue plan. I brought money, too. So, please take me there. I have little time."

I wanted to trust him badly. But what if it were a trap? Then again, he was alone, and any of the jewel hunters could have led the Germans to our hiding places long ago. "All right," I finally agreed.

There was consternation when my family and friends saw me arrive with a stranger, but the man quickly came to the point. His name was Raffaele Cantoni, a Venetian, an accountant by profession, and a member of Florence's and Rome's Jewish Committees.

"Some Italians here told us of your plight, and we spoke about it to Florence's archbishop. He's doing all he can to help rescue Jews. If you come to Florence, Catholic authorities will try to hide you in their institutions. The trip would be dangerous, so decide if you want to risk it. However, remaining on the mountain is equally risky. It will be a long war, and you would have a difficult winter up here. My mission is to find out how many of you want to leave. I have money for the neediest, and will bring more for those who decide to stay when I return in a few days. The first group that wants to go to Florence can leave with me then."

Mrs. Wallach translated our questions until late into the night. Cantoni slept with us. The following day I roamed the mountain with him, into caves, holes, shacks, barns, woods, wherever I knew of Jews. They breathed a little easier; Cantoni had brought them hope. He distributed money here and there to families. At the end of the day, embarrassed, I mentioned my own, but by then he had nothing left. The next morning he returned to Florence.

Few people wanted to stick it out on the mountain. Because Papa's incision was still open, we wanted to be in the first group to leave. The other six in the stone house—the Kohns, Wallachs, and the two bachelors—resolved that they, too, would come with us.

Chapter Five

In a few days, Cantoni returned and briefed us on our journey, to begin that afternoon. First, we would take the rural train to Cuneo, then a train to Turin. In Turin, another transfer to Genoa, where we would have to wait a few hours. To avoid unwanted attention, we would spend that interval in a convent. From Genoa, there would be a last train to Florence. "Never stick together in one group," he lectured. "Split up in threes or fours, but stay within sight of each other. Don't talk, but if you must, speak French. I'll buy the tickets. Follow a few steps behind me as you board or leave trains. I won't sit with you, but I'll be in the vicinity, on the lookout. If you're stopped by Italians, I'll try to help. But if Germans question you, you're on your own. Say you're French refugees who've lost your passports. Stay calm, but whatever happens, don't call out for me. You'd only get us arrested."

We stopped in Festiona. Viviana and her father were visibly touched by our expressions of gratitude as we said good-bye. Watching Papa hobbling about with his stick, Viviana said, "Maybe you should stay here."

Perhaps, but who could say what might happen? Any decision in this stay-alive game might turn out to be either the right or wrong one. The most terrifying aspect was that there were no rules, and no shrewd or stupid gamblers, only gamblers. Jews who'd found the perfect hideout with foolproof papers got trapped. Others, who did something utterly foolish in defiance of all logic, survived. Day-to-day life on the edge of disaster was

24

our predicament. Now, we were betting our lives on Florence. *"Buona fortuna!"* our Italian friends shouted after us.

Cantoni went ahead to see if there were any Germans or Carabinieri hanging around the shuttle stop at Borgo San Dalmazzo. He motioned that all was clear. The train stopped and we piled in through separate doors. It was nearly empty, and there were no uniforms.

As the train began to move, I cast a last glance at the road leading up to and beyond Festiona. For a moment, I actually longed to be back in the familiar surroundings of our stone house, with people we knew. But the mountain that had sheltered us from the Germans for seven weeks was already receding into the past. I felt naked and exposed on the train. I focused on the passing landscape to distract me. It felt good to roll by fields, houses, and roads after our confinement. We were moving deeper into Italy. I was eager to see what the country looked like.

We arrived in Cuneo without incident and took a tramway to the main railroad station. It was slow and claustrophobic. I was hanging onto a strap and had someone's shoulder lodged in my armpit when, in distorted close-up, a red, round-faced, middle-aged man breathed heavily past my ear. I felt his hand grope me. I tried to wriggle free, but his hand made it impossible to move in any direction. Nor could I be absolutely certain it was he; his face was expressionless. I wanted to scream and kick him, but what if he created a commotion and the police came? I was condemned to silence. Feeling trapped and wet with perspiration, I suddenly saw Papa push toward the door. I clutched at his sleeve. The fiend threw me a look as if to say, "The two of us know, don't we?"

It was early evening when we reached Turin. I felt the oppressive war atmosphere: dimmed lights, talk of *bombardamenti*, loudspeaker announcements of train delays, German and Italian uniforms everywhere. We had an hour to wait in the crowded station for the train to Genoa. Our eyes never leaving Cantoni, we scattered ourselves in the crowd, hardly blending in. Our clothes were shabby—shabby Jewish, not shabby Italian—patched hand-me-downs rather than worn, fine fabrics. And by strange coincidence, all our women carried hatboxes, ludicrous objects for people who didn't want to attract attention.

When the train to Genoa was finally announced, Cantoni moved out. We got caught up in the rushing crowd. I didn't notice a corpulent man pressing from the opposite direction. He stepped on my foot with such force, I let out a cry. He stopped and apologized so remorsefully, I felt I had to reply. I quickly translated from the French, *"Il n'y a pas de mal,"* and graciously said, *"Non c'è male."* His puzzled look was disconcerting to me. He continued to watch as I ran to catch up with the others. Amused, Cantoni later told me that what I'd said meant, "Not bad. Not bad at all!"

The train was packed and our family was squeezed into one end of a car's passageway. People lay slumped over their suitcases trying to sleep, as the train rolled through the black night in steady rhythm. I was still too much on edge. I knew that as we moved deeper into the more densely populated areas of Italy, controls and checkpoints would multiply. Papa was in pain. So many people had bumped into him that his wound had reopened. We were looking forward to our stopover at the convent to dress it properly.

I didn't mind being stuck in the corridor. Seated in a compartment with sliding doors closed would be a trap. At least standing outside would allow me to notice and assess approaching danger and take action, although what action, I had no idea. Harry was leaning with his shoulders against the windowpane, his forehead wrinkled. His eyes darted nervously, always alert to stay one step ahead of the next threat to survival. His apprenticeship in that fine art had started at the age of three, when, in the middle of the night, Mother had hushed his cries as we illegally crossed the German border into France. He had been thoroughly trained, experiencing the vise around his chest and the icy fingers of fear so often that he'd long ago become a fully qualified member of the clan: an old Jew at the age of twelve.

The train rolled into a large station and stopped. A few lights pricked the darkness outside. The crowd in the corridor came alive. Someone said we were in Savona, the last major town before Genoa, our destination. I made out a mass of people on the platform, but no one moved to board the train. Sporadic cigarette lights appeared like glowworms in dense foliage. A loudspeaker blared instructions, and everyone pushed toward exit doors. We tried to move aside to let them through. A passenger wildly gesticulated to us to move. "The track's been bombed!" he shouted. We had to get off the train and wait for rails to be repaired.

My family and I found a place on the platform and sat down. I had no idea where the others had gone. A unit of Germans in full military gear milled around behind us, near the waiting room. Our anonymity in the thick crowd, surrounded by darkness, gave me a sense of euphoric security, however precarious. Two German MPs patrolled up and down the platform edge in slow, measured steps. Now and then they stopped, pointed a flashlight into the crowd, and then moved on.

Hours passed and still no train. The friendly night gave way to dawn, and as the first rays of sun grazed the platform I felt naked again. An hour later, the train finally pulled in. We grabbed empty seats in a compartment. One long ride standing in a packed corridor had been enough, though it had been safer than sitting. A line of people piled up outside our compartment. Two German soldiers came to a stop right in front of our door. One peered through the glass at the luggage racks over

our heads, trying to find room for his gear. He opened the sliding door for a closer look. His buddy called over, *"Ist da Platz?"**
His eyes swept across everyone in the compartment, and he yelled back, *"Mensch, da stinkt's nach Italiener,"†* then slid the door shut. We exchanged looks. The Italians hadn't understood, but Mother's cheeks flushed.

When we got off the train in Genoa, Cantoni was on the platform in conversation with a priest. He motioned us to join him. None of us had ever had contact with a Catholic priest. He spoke in an excitable, high-pitched voice full of compassion: "Oh, *buon giorno*. You poor *bambini*, so tired. Come, follow me." He was a wiry little figure, and his black cape and wide-rimmed black hat made him look even smaller. He led us through the ticket control at the exit and out into Genoa's crowded streets, walking ahead to show the way, chatting and smiling, exhorting Harry, "Be brave, *bambino*." Although we were exhausted, unwashed, and hungry, to me every step was fascinating. We passed through a bustling market district crowded with people buying, selling, and shouting, and came upon rows of stores and sidewalk displays heaped with food and delicacies. I'd forgotten their existence. With Europe at war, for years we could get only bare essentials. But here were big fat chickens roasted golden brown, eggs by the basketful, long thick salamis hanging in dense clusters, fine cuts of bologna, tubs of fresh butter, cheese, fruit, fresh vegetables, and more. The sights and smells hypnotized us and, now and then, with a smile, the priest had to urge us forward.

He stopped in front of a convent and rang the bell. A nun opened the heavy wood door a slit, but when she saw us, swung it wide open. Nodding to her, the priest showed us where to freshen up and apply a new dressing to Papa's incision. Then he

---

*"Is there room?"
†"Man, the stench of Italians in there!"

led us through a paneled oak door into an elegant dining room. There was a long table covered with a sparkling white cloth. Each of us had a setting of several dishes, fine silverware, and a folded linen napkin with a fresh crusty brown roll resting on it. Ah, the delicious ecstasy of it all! Perhaps because it was a shock to be made to feel like human beings again, I felt as though I'd entered Shangri-la.

Chapter Six

After our meal, the priest took us back to the station. The special warmth of our temporary oasis kept the edge off my nervousness as my thoughts turned to the trip ahead. We boarded the train to Florence and spread out in different cars. My family sat on two benches facing each other in a wide open coach. Papa and I shared a bench, with two Italians between us. Mother and Harry sat opposite us, near the window. A portly peasant woman, dressed in black and holding a large straw basket covered with a red checkered cloth, took up the rest of their bench. Cantoni stood by a window at the other end of the car, looking unconcerned.

As the train sped through the hills and valleys of Liguria, I gazed at the changing landscape. Over the wheels' rhythmic clanking I heard a wail of sirens in the distance. The train began to slow. When it stopped, I looked out the window to read the name of the station. All I saw was a helmeted German soldier, rifle at the ready, standing below me. I glanced up and down the track. A tight cordon of armed soldiers was spaced every few feet.

Everyone else had gotten up, asking questions and leaning out the windows, but the four of us huddled together. Papa told us that if there was to be a passenger check, and they hauled him away, we were not to indicate we belonged together. He didn't say so, but I knew he thought that if he were seized and led away, his capture would divert attention from the rest of us. But if the whole family got arrested, the SS would separate us anyway.

"Keep this, Ludi," he said, and quickly scribbled the address of the Kupfers, friends from Frankfurt who'd emigrated to Tel Aviv. "If we should be torn apart and survive, we'll have a common point of reference," Papa said. Cantoni strolled by, casually dropped a *"Stiate calmi,"* and moved back to his window.

Now and then the soldier outside our window took a few steps, his boots making a crunching sound on the gravel. The heavy steam engine idled and waited, hissing, *"puishh-tum, puishh-tum, puishh-tum."*

What was happening? Had the track ahead been sabotaged? Were the Germans trying to protect the train against a partisan attack? Improbable: they would be watching the fields, not standing facing the train. Perhaps there were some high-ranking Germans or important political prisoners who had to be escorted off the train? No good either: the Germans would be huddling around one particular wagon. An air raid? That would account for the sirens, but then why didn't they let us take cover in the ditches and fields? Ultimately it boiled down to the most common probability, the one that never required explanation: they were after Jews. However, even that didn't make sense. Why would they go to the trouble of such a military display and stop a train in the middle of nowhere when they could just as well pick up everybody at the station? As minutes ticked by, I grew alternately relaxed and tense. Whatever the reason for the stop, the Germans weren't going to let a nice opportunity like this go by without an identification check. If it were only a spot check, we stood a chance of slipping through. But a person-to-person screening? That would be the end of us.

Then I saw them. They were at the other end of the car. A German officer, flanked by two members of Mussolini's Black Brigades, held someone's ID in his gloved hands. The Italians asked questions and translated the answers for him. The German handed back the paper and the trio moved on slowly, scrutinizing each face carefully. Every few steps the German demanded identification papers.

Papa, of course, had seen all this. I could sense his nervousness by the familiar, involuntary up-and-down tensing of his jaw muscles. Since their seats faced the opposite direction, Mother and Harry were unaware of what was going on. I whispered, "They're coming." Mother's face turned burning red and she gasped for air. Harry casually got up from his seat and sat on my lap, covering my face with his back. He brought my two hands in front of him and started a childish clap-hands game to some tra-la-la tune he sang in a soft voice. I understood what he had in mind: ID checks usually concentrated on men. There was nothing he could do for Papa. Mother, perhaps, wasn't in immediate danger. Harry was a child, and they wouldn't ask anything of him. But I was an adolescent, and by improvising his little game he hoped to make me appear younger, too.

I could clearly hear the voices of the approaching German and his lackeys. Mother looked out the window, trying to conceal her torment, but one could have lit a match from her cheeks. Papa leaned on his cane, looking straight ahead. The large Italian woman with the big basket looked at us and smiled. They stopped at our benches. The German studied everyone, then, in Italian, said to Papa, *"Documenti, prego."* Papa reached inside the breast pocket of his jacket, produced a large wallet, and pulled out a piece of paper. It was a Paris Gas & Electric Company receipt. He handed it to the German. I thought he would slap Papa for such effrontery. Papa did carry his alien ID card from France with JUIF stamped over it in large letters, but he must have thought there was still time to show that. The German examined the receipt with a quizzical look, then handed it to the Italians. They just shrugged their shoulders, nonplussed. "Do you speak German?" the officer asked.

"Yes."

"Do you have any other papers?"

"No."

"Where were you born?"

"In Poland."

"Where are you going?"

"To Florence."

He handed the silly receipt back to Papa. "Come with me. This matter must be checked further."

Papa pulled himself up on his cane, threw us a glance, and followed. We had no idea whether this new checking would take place here or at some remote *Kommandantur,* a military office, while the train pulled away. I realized this moment might be the last I ever saw of my father.

I pushed Harry off my lap and caught up with Papa at the exit door. The German was waiting outside. There were four steep steps down from the wagon. At each one Papa winced in pain. All I could do was prop him up a little under his arm.

"What's the matter?" the German asked.

"I've recently had surgery," Papa answered.

The officer pondered for a moment, looked down the track, then said, "Don't move until I return." He walked briskly away, and I sat down with Papa on the bottom step. We watched the officer walk alongside the train, then, some hundred feet past the engine, climb down an embankment and enter a small wooden hut.

Papa whispered furiously, "You're compromising yourself by staying with me. Go back!"

"Maybe we can talk him into letting you go," I ventured.

"Ludi," Papa said, "if they take me, you must be the one to look after the family." Then he sighed. "Who knows if we'll see each other again?" It was the first time we'd fallen into German hands. The officer came out of the hut and walked back toward us. I looked the other way, blood beating at my temples. He seemed to take ages. Finally, he stopped in front of Papa. "You may continue," he said. "You're lucky. We're not looking for Polish Jews today, but escaped British prisoners of war." We climbed back into the wagon. Cantoni had observed it all, but his face remained impassive. The peasant woman smiled as we sat down. Mother grabbed Papa's hand. One of the two Italians on our bench greeted us with the remark that it was pretty senseless of the German to drag a sick man out. He should have seen right away that his papers were in order.

A few moments later I heard a shrill whistle, followed by a command, and the soldiers left their stations. The engine breathed more heavily and the train moved again, picking up speed rapidly. The peasant woman suddenly jumped up from her seat. She hugged Papa, me, and the whole family, with tears in her eyes. *"Poverini, poverini, come ho avuto paura per voi tutti!"** she exclaimed. Other Italians in the car stood up and applauded. They had sensed all along the danger we were in. Never before had complete strangers, with whom we hadn't exchanged a single word, reacted to us with such empathy. At the next stop, the peasant woman got off. She wished us Godspeed and insisted on leaving us all her food in the basket with the red cloth.

---

*"Poor dear ones, how I feared for you all!"

Chapter Seven

The train pulled into Florence in the late afternoon of October 21, 1943. On the platform I was glad to see that no one was missing. In small groups again, we followed Cantoni through the city's streets and soon emerged on Piazza Duomo, the main square, with its beautiful *Duomo, Campanile,* and Dante's *Battistero*— its cathedral, bell tower, and the baptistery where Dante himself was baptized. God must have blinded our enemies. There was no other explanation how foreigners conspicuously lugging hatboxes could have made it safely across Florence's busy *centro.*

Cantoni rang the bell at the archbishop's palace. As the huge gate shut behind us I exploded with the story of what had happened. Cantoni shook his head in amazement. "What luck!"

Matilde Cassin, a Jewish girl of about nineteen, arrived to take charge of us. She was a member of the Italian Jewish Committee coordinating rescue operations with Catholic authorities. Born in Florence, she had been working since the outbreak of war with Raffaele Cantoni and the DELASEM organization *(DELegazione ASsistenza agli EMigranti Ebrei),* helping Jewish children who'd escaped from Germany, Czechoslovakia, and Austria. As the Germans began taking control of Italy, Matilde started hiding Jewish families in Catholic institutions with the help of a reliable priest named Padre Cipriano Ricotti.

Matilde took us to La Pietra, a suburb of Florence on the road toward Bologna, to stay in a parochial school until permanent hiding places became available. Several families who'd come down from the mountains before us were already there. I recognized only Mr. Hartmayer and his two sons, Sigi and Willy. Their mother was in the Gurs concentration camp in France.

School desks had been moved out of the classrooms, and beds for refugees crammed in. As I stretched out on one of them, I thought of all that had happened since we left the mountain. Had it been only the morning before? For us, lying on a mattress between two white sheets for the first time since we'd fled France, sleep came swiftly.

The Committee provided us with food and pocket money. We had the building to ourselves, and although we were not really in hiding, we were told not to be seen outside too often. So the thirty-odd refugees spent most of their day indoors, playing cards and retelling their adventures. It was sheer boredom for Willy, Sigi, and me. We wanted to go out and immerse ourselves in the city. It was a reckless idea because we looked of military age, had no papers, and spoke little Italian. But we felt confident that by going together and being careful, we would be able to handle any situation. We pestered our parents until they finally gave in.

Sigi was seventeen, with jet-black hair, blue eyes, and a magnificent set of pearly white teeth. Hoping for a miracle, I brushed mine precisely the way I saw him do it, twice a day. He was serious-minded but always ready for a practical joke. Willy, fifteen, blond, and blue-eyed, was thin and sickly. A large scar from a glandular operation ran down the side of his neck behind his right ear, and in cold weather it became beet red and reinfected. He was a great mimic, a young Danny Kaye. His family had nicknamed him *Sauspieler,* an unflattering distortion of the German word for performer. The odd thing about the two brothers was that Sigi spoke only Berlinese slang, while Willy preferred Yiddish.

We did nothing spectacular on our few trips into town, but it was exhilarating just to be there. We went to movies. They were presented in three acts, like an opera. A panel of electric signs hung at the cashier's window: *Attualità* (a newsreel), then *Atto* I, II, and III. Patrons could tell how far the show had progressed by the sign that was lit. To us, it was immaterial. We couldn't follow the dialogue anyway, but that didn't stop us from sitting through a whole show again. Afterward, we would roam the streets, peeking into store windows or strolling through open market stalls. With the few remaining lire cadged from our parents, we splurged on some fancy *nascherei*. If our money ran out, we walked the long way back. It took more than an hour, but the trip was worth it.

We instinctively pooled our "sixth senses" for collective safety. A blink from any one of us, a casual scratch on the neck, or certain facial expressions would immediately warn the others of impending trouble. The paranoia of living through centuries of persecution bequeathed to Jews a finely honed sensitivity, a kind of built-in JEWS radar (Jewish Early Warning System), which picks up threats to survival.

Somehow we sensed where to go in the city, where to make a detour, when to linger, and when to disappear. If we had to split up fast, we found each other again through our own whistling signal. We were once coming out of a movie when Sigi said calmly, "That light raincoat in back of us, I don't like it." We couldn't suddenly take off, so we proceeded at the same slow pace. I could see the man's reflection in the store windows, his eyes riveted on us. We rounded the street corner. Action! Willy disappeared in a doorway. Sigi and I dived into a crowded bakery. Pretending to have a hard time deciding what to buy, from the window we observed the man looking fretfully for us up and down the street. After several minutes, he gave up and started running in the opposite direction. Sigi and I left the store. Willy fell in step as we passed his doorway, and we jumped on the first trolley car that rolled by. The close call sobered us. We didn't venture out again.

Chapter Eight
WHAT I DIDN'T KNOW AT THE TIME

The trickle of foreign Jews into Italy had increased in proportion with the Nazi hegemony over Europe. The first ones had found shelter in northern Italy. Later arrivals came down to Bologna and Florence. As their numbers began to swell, and the Germans took control of Italy, the refugees were once again in great danger.

Among those streaming into Florence in October 1943, was the Ziegler family. Joseph Ziegler was a wealthy tanner from Brussels, fluent in several languages. Earlier, he, his wife, two children, and mother-in-law had escaped to France just ahead of the invading Germans and wound up in Nice with five valises containing a fortune in jewels, diamonds, and furs.

Having already assisted refugees in Brussels, Ziegler continued to make substantial contributions for the needy through the leader of Nice's Jewish community and director of the Banque France-Italie, Angelo Donati. Ziegler also ingratiated himself with the commander of the Carabinieri, Colonello Bodo, with expensive gifts, including a golden crucifix.

At Italy's capitulation, Bodo facilitated the Zieglers' escape to San Remo. One recommendation leading to another, the family ended up in Turin and settled in the house of a Mr. Scassa, a noted industrialist and anti-Fascist. However, Ziegler's mother-in-law kept urging the family to proceed south to Rome, and ultimately Ziegler decided to undertake the perilous trip. Not speaking Italian, he asked nineteen-year-old Marco Ischio, a gentile, if he would accompany them and give any needed help along the way. Jews in Turin knew Marco from his work in the Resistance and had recommended him to Ziegler as being trustworthy. Mr. Scassa gave Ziegler a card identifying him as a Fiat engineer and a glowing letter of recommendation to present to the Vatican. The Zieglers took four of their valises, leaving the fifth behind in Scassa's home, just in case. They nearly made it to Rome without a hitch, but a bombed railroad bridge forced them back north to Florence.

Ziegler immediately sought accommodations for his family. He rushed to Rabbi Nathan Cassuto's office at the synagogue in Via Farini. About two hundred refugees were milling about the courtyard and hallways, their suitcases and bundles heaped everywhere. "Why are all those people exposed out in the open?" Ziegler asked.

"Our small assistance committee is ill-equipped to deal with this sudden flood of refugees," Rabbi Cassuto said. "There may be a thousand in Florence now, perhaps even more. New ones arrive every day. They need help, places to hide, and money, and we don't have nearly enough of either."

Ziegler opened his briefcase and handed a million lire to the startled rabbi. "This solves only part of your problem," he said. "Have you approached the church authorities to help get these refugees off the streets?"

The rabbi shook his head. "Matilde Cassin, one of our Committee members, has been working privately with Padre Cipriano Ricotti, and they've succeeded in placing a few people here and there. What we need is a massive operation, but that would be fraught with greater dangers. We dare not ask the Church to get in trouble for us. It's not even worth asking and later disappointing our people."

"Maybe," Ziegler said. "I understand that it puts you in an embarrassing position on both sides. But what if there's a one percent chance of success? What's there to lose? Let me try."

Ziegler went to the archbishop's palace and met with Monsignor Meneghello, the cardinal's secretary. He showed him Scassa's envelope with the letter of recommendation to the Vatican and asked if he could provide shelter for his family. The monsignor said he could not take the responsibility upon himself and asked Ziegler to wait. Fifteen minutes later he returned to say that Cardinal Elia Dalla Costa would see him. Ziegler again presented the envelope, but the cardinal refused to open it because it was addressed to the Vatican. Ziegler ripped it open and took out the letter. After reading it, the cardinal asked, "How large is your family?"

"Three adults and two children, Your Eminence."

"I think the best place for you would be the Seminario Minore in Via Santa Marta," the cardinal said. "Three hundred priests and nuns live there, but for everyone's safety let no outsiders come to visit you. Do you have means to live on? If not, we can help you."

"That's very kind, but I have all I need," Ziegler answered. "We won't be a burden to the Seminario. On the contrary, I can help you to help others." He took out 60,000 lire.

The cardinal reacted in surprise. "But for whom is this money intended?"

"You be the judge, Your Eminence. And when it's spent, I'll replenish it." The subtle hint was that the money was not meant exclusively for Jews.

Ziegler rose. "I do have another important request. At the synagogue earlier today, I saw about two hundred foreign Jews who have nowhere to go. Many others are wandering aimlessly through the city, and more keep arriving hourly. I fear for them. Any day the Germans could round them up and deport them. They don't speak the language, have no papers, and most, no money. They're the human wrecks Nazism has created. The Jewish Committee doesn't have the contacts or means for this emergency. I said to myself, only the Church can help on such a large scale. Rabbi Cassuto can give Your Eminence a precise report. Safe shelter is the most urgent need. We'll provide the rest."

The cardinal had listened attentively. "We're aware of much misery among our brethren of the Jewish faith, and we'll assist them in every way we can. However, such an operation shouldn't be handled by us directly. The archdiocese is too conspicuous. We'll think of a solution after we speak to Rabbi Cassuto."

The next morning Rabbi Cassuto had a lengthy audience with Cardinal Dalla Costa. Later, the cardinal called in Don Leto Casini, whom he knew for his social work and beneficence assisting Italian war victims. "Would you consider running an operation to hide the Jews who've come to Florence?" he asked Don Casini. "The personal risks could be enormous, but we must help."

"Gladly, Your Eminence," Don Casini answered without hesitation.

That same night the Jewish Committee met with Don Casini in the Curia, the ecclesiastic tribunal in Piazza Duomo. The Committee consisted of Rabbi Cassuto, Raffaele Cantoni, Matilde Cassin, a Mr. Kahlberg, and Joseph

Ziegler. Ziegler introduced Marco Ischio as reliable, someone who could be of valuable assistance. Msgr. Meneghello, designated as the cardinal's personal representative in the rescue operation, also attended. They shaped a plan for the systematic hiding of refugees in various Catholic institutions and private homes. Don Casini felt that food would be their biggest problem. Institutions and individuals barely had enough rations for themselves. Rabbi Cassuto said that by pooling all its resources, the Committee could probably come up with a minimal but regular supply of food. Ziegler added that he would think of ways to make up the difference. His lifestyle had taught him that money and connections bring results.

Almost fifteen-hundred Jews in Florence needed to be hidden. Raffaele Cantoni handed Don Casini the money the Committee had collected for the rescue operation. Ziegler, the biggest contributor, also gave Don Casini a personal sum of 15,000 lire. On three subsequent occasions the Committee gave him more: 200,000, then 20,000, and finally, 500,000 lire.

Don Casini crammed the 500,000 lire in his briefcase and took the tram back to Varlungo. When the conductor came around for the fare, Don Casini realized he had forgotten his wallet. He could not give the man a thousand-lira note. Worse, if the passengers saw his briefcase stuffed with bills of such large denominations, they would become suspicious. Italian banknotes were ridiculously large in size, jokingly called lenzuoli *(bed sheets). Casini apologized and said he would get off at the next stop, but a lady intervened, "No, Padre, please allow me," and paid his fare, unaware that this kindly round-faced priest without money was carrying a fortune.*

Casini went to work tapping his and Msgr. Meneghello's connections. Padre Cipriano Ricotti and Contessa Marucchi, a member of the old Florentine aristocracy, assisted his day-to-day efforts. They arranged for hiding places in institutions, begged and cajoled trusted Catholic families to take in Jews, paid for all their living expenses, bought beds and whatever else was needed, and pleaded in each instance for their cooperation and secrecy. Casini hid an old Jewish couple in his own home.

While the main obstacle the rescue team faced was people's fear of retaliation from the Germans, there were many instances of spontaneous support.

When Don Casini needed to hide three men, he went to the Cento Vecchi, an old-age home run by French nuns. "Impossible," said the mother superior. "We're full."

Don Casini sighed, "What am I going to do with these three Jews?"

"Jews? We'll find room! They can work in the kitchen."

Ziegler ferreted out where to buy food on the black market and distributed it personally to the neediest. With his Fiat card identifying him as working in a vital industry, he could take some chances. However, the card's validity was doubtful. He needed a genuine Italian identity card. He found out that the commander of the local Carabinieri was a Captain Bodo. He quickly phoned the Questura, police headquarters, to find out if the captain was related to his friend in Turin. An adjutant answered, "Who wants to speak to him?"

"It's personal."

Bodo took the phone. "Pronto?"

"Capitano, my name is Ziegler, but it probably won't mean anything to you."

"Ziegler? Yes, yes, my father told me about you. Where are you staying?"

Not wanting to reveal his hiding place, Ziegler asked, "May I come to see you?"

In Captain Bodo's office, Ziegler asked for help in getting a false ID card.

"You were very nice to my father," Captain Bodo said. "Yes, I can arrange that for you." He instructed his adjutant to accompany Ziegler to the Prefettura, where he testified that Ziegler was Italian, born in an obscure village already occupied by the Allies. The official card was issued under the name of Giuseppe Ziegler. Through his new connection with Bodo, Ziegler subsequently met a high official in the city's food administration, a man with strong anti-Fascist feelings. Thus Ziegler was able to obtain a substantial quantity of coupons, which further alleviated the refugees' food shortage.

Safely installed at the Seminario Minore, Ziegler judged the time was right to retrieve the valise of valuables he had left with Scassa. He asked Marco, who had taken a room in town, to travel to Turin and bring it to him. Marco came back a few days later, very upset. He said the train had been bombed on his return trip. The valise got lost in the panic.

Don Casini held three meetings a week in the Curia with the Jewish Committee to coordinate and organize the rescue work. Since the Jewish members had to avoid attention, Don Casini was the direct and ongoing liaison between nuns, monks, Catholic families, institutions, and the mass of Jewish refugees.

Don Casini made the rounds distributing money to Jewish families, even to Italian and foreign Jews who had found hiding places on their own. In addition, he arranged medical care for the sick, found doctors who could be trusted, and paid their fees and for their prescriptions. He managed to get the seriously ill hospitalized under assumed names. He had a lively traffic going with the Finzis in Bologna, a Jewish-Italian family who worked with the underground, and who were a source of fake ID cards at one thousand lire each. Padre Cipriano also had friends among the partisans, who sometimes supplied him blank cards and forged official seals. Thus, Don Casini transformed dozens of local and foreign Jews into natives of Sicily or other areas no longer accessible for verification in the Allied-occupied south.

The Varlungo convent, in Don Casini's parish and a short walk from his rectory, had room to shelter several of the women who had arrived from Saint-Martin-Vesubie. However, the convent was a cloister and under **clausura papale**, *the Church's strictest form of seclusion. He needed the cardinal's permission as well as the abbess's consent to admit those who were not nuns or Catholics. Beyond the departure from immutable regulations, Don Casini's plan also entailed tremendous risk. The Germans considered the hiding of Jews an act comparable to treason. Those caught often paid with their lives.*

Don Casini felt confident about the cardinal, but unsure of the abbess's reaction. As the supreme authority in the convent, if she refused to help, not even the cardinal could force her to cooperate. Don Casini consulted with the convent's young chaplain, Don Giovanni Simioni. He was the only male permitted to enter the nunnery because he heard confessions and administered last rites. Both were diocesan priests wearing severe, black, ecclesiastic attire. They belonged to no specific Catholic order and reported only to the cardinal.

The abbess was hesitant when the two priests came to tell her of their plan, but was swayed by their urgent pleas as well as by the gravity of the times.

Chapter Nine

On October 26, 1943, Dr. Nathan Cassuto, the thirty-four-year-old chief rabbi of Florence and a prominent ophthalmologist, came to tell us that raids against Jews were imminent. His urgency frightened us. We would have to go into hiding immediately.

"It's difficult for the priests to find safe places for everyone," he told us. "To hide the maximum number of people, families will have to split up. Women will go to convents, men spread among monasteries and some private Catholic homes, and we'll take the children to schools or orphanages. Today I've come for the first group of women. In the next few days we hope to transfer the rest of you to other places as they become available."

He then called out a few names, Mother's among them. Her group would go to the Convento dello Spirito in Via Varlungo, Don Leto Casini's parish. The sixty nuns cloistered there in *clausura papale* spent their lives in silence, never leaving except in an emergency. Only a few had contact with the outside world and other human beings, and then only in connection with duties necessary for the convent's functioning. No outsider, man or woman, was allowed inside the nunnery's confines.

"Don Casini is waiting for us. Please pack your belongings quickly," the rabbi urged.

Harry began to cry, begging to stay with Mother. Rabbi Cassuto explained that the separation was better for everyone's protection, and that convents were for women only. Harry went on sobbing. It was heartbreaking to watch. During all our tribulations, our family had managed to stay together. Papa, Mother, and I assured him that we would soon be together again. Harry finally calmed down when Rabbi Cassuto promised to ask the convent if he could visit Mother each day. And so, the group left, the rabbi walking a little distance ahead to a bus.

The next day, Aunt Sonia was transferred to a Catholic institute for women in Via Gioberti, and Sylvia to a Catholic boarding school for girls.

Papa, Harry, and I were moved into an abandoned movie theater with about forty other men, Mr. Wallach and Mr. Kohn among us. I didn't know where their wives or the two bachelors Gerard and Marc had been sent. The theater was an interim arrangement while we waited for permanent hiding places. Rabbi Cassuto told Papa he would soon be hidden with a Catholic family in Livorno, while we boys would be sent to a youth center in Viareggio, near Pisa.

Theater seats had been removed and stacked upstairs in the balcony, and the main floor had been covered with straw mattresses. Papa, Harry, and I made our "home" near steps leading to the balcony. The Hartmayers installed themselves next to us. A gaping hole was at the other end of the auditorium, where the screen used to be. The Dresners, a Jewish orthodox family, settled on the stage. The mother, the only woman in our midst, had refused to leave her husband and six small children. The stage's isolation offered them a little privacy, and its wooden planks were warmer than the auditorium's stone floor.

The theater's side exit-doors opened onto a large courtyard surrounded by a wall. We had access to the street through both the wall's gate and the main entrance by the screen-end of the theater. The men spent most of the day in the courtyard under a pale sun, playing cards or standing around in knots, endlessly discussing politics, the war, and the outlook for Jews. Harry,

Willy, Sigi, and I found a gym horse among the theater's paraphernalia and exercised on it for hours. A field kitchen had
been set up in the courtyard to feed us.

All this was open to the neighbors' puzzled observation from
their apartment windows overlooking the courtyard. They were
told that we were Italian refugees. I don't think they believed it
for a moment, even considering the many unusual dialects spoken throughout the country. To people needing anonymity,
this arrangement made no sense.

At night, the theater became alive with its own show. While
some men sought sleep in vain, others harmonized *"Shteitele
Bels,"* a nostalgic song replete with Yiddish heartbreak. A few
blankets were strung up on cords, a pathetic attempt at privacy
in the cavernous hall. Frayed nerves, irritations, and worry
caused flare-ups and quarrels. For those who found it impossible to sleep until the lights were out, there was no alternative but
to sit and talk. The Hartmayers always told amusing stories.
Willy's improvised Hitler speeches in faultless German, with a
straight face, caused everyone to double up in laughter. And, of
course, there were reminiscences about the peaceful days with
wonderful meals and the comforts of home.

Inevitably, conversation veered to fears about the unknow-
able tomorrow. "If only we had forged papers," Mr. Hartmayer
said. "Look, I've got something here, but I can't use it." A French
identity card had been issued to him by the Vichy government,
priceless since it didn't have the word JUIF stamped on it. Fake
data had been filled in, making him a pure Frenchman, with
even a smiling photograph glued to its proper space. But to be of
any value, the document required an official rubber stamp and
the police commissioner's signature.

"Ludi," Mr. Hartmayer said, "you're a wizard at drawing.
You could make this card look genuine." I was only fair, but my
family imagined great talent in me, especially after my appren-

ticeship at the photographer's studio in Montpellier where I'd learned the art of retouching portrait negatives.

"I could never duplicate a rubber stamp," I said. "That's a job for a professional forger. And it needs special ink."

"Try anyway, just for fun," he urged. "If the result isn't good, I won't use it."

It became a game. I had an ink pencil which, when wetted, wrote in a lilac color close to the ink commonly used on rubber pads. I took some cigarette paper from Papa and traced an official stamp from another document. After much refining, I managed to graft a fake stamp onto Mr. Hartmayer's card and a signature that could have passed a superficial check by someone with poor eyesight on a dark night. But Willy snatched the paper, examined it, and let out a long, approving whistle.

We visited Mother often in Varlungo. In a setting of prison-like austerity, we sat in opposite rooms on wooden benches, speaking through a double-screened partition, two nuns ever in attendance. A little turnstile allowed the passing of gifts. But physical contact with Mother wasn't permitted. Neither Harry nor I could kiss her.

The number of women brought to the convent had grown to eleven. Besides Mother, there were five married women with the surnames Adler, Schwartzwald, Wolf, Forscher, and Ashübel. There were also two women with daughters: Mrs. Glatt and seventeen-year-old Ruth, and Mrs. Grunewald with five-year-old Diane. And there was a lone, thirteen-year-old girl, Renée Czopp, who, like my family, had emigrated to France with her Polish parents. Two years earlier, she had witnessed Germans dragging away her mother and sister. Her father had been moved to the theater with me, Papa, and Harry.

Mother asked Don Casini if it would be possible to transfer Aunt Sonia from the institute where she was hidden. He said he would try. The second bed in Mother's room had remained unoccupied. Harry clamored for it, but Don Casini, patient and good natured, explained that it was out of the question for men to live in this convent.

"All three of you are still out in the open!" Mother said apprehensively as we were leaving. "Have you heard anything about your new hiding places yet?"

"They told us any day now," I said. We promised to visit again on Sunday.

The movie theater's doors were shut against the cold night. I followed the rising smoke of Papa's cigarette and watched it melt into the thick air. He was a heavy smoker, always hungry for another. In such times of strict rationing his craving could never be satisfied. In desperation he once cut and ground a dried leaf into tiny specks. He rolled them into a cigarette paper, moistened the edge, then lit and inhaled his special blend with great relish.

He was stretched on the mattress next to me, his head propped up by an arm, gazing at the ceiling. An incident concerning his smoking came back to haunt me: As we crossed into Italy, I'd been certain there would be no room left if we weren't among the first to reach the village. I'd suggested dashing to the head of the column and running to secure a room for the family. Papa wouldn't hear of it, his argument being that in such dangerous times we had to stay together. I resented his cautiousness and lack of daring and insisted on going. Papa still refused. Something in me snapped and I snarled, "All right, if I get you a cigarette, will you let me go?"—as one would treat a child with, "Here, have a lollipop and stop being a pest!" My cruelty and contempt were immediately apparent to me, as was the pain they caused. Papa said nothing. He merely looked at me in disbelief. But Mother had one of her rare, angry outbursts. I was ashamed, but the damage was done. I wasn't even humble enough to say, "Sorry, Papi, forgive me."

I looked at him now as he lay absorbed in his thoughts, surely worried about when he would be able to offer his family a decent life again. Harry was jackknifed under his blanket. It was late, but his eyes were open, his mind still churning away.

The lights went out amid coughs and sighs as people settled down for the night. I heard Mr. Hartmayer and another man arguing: "What you don't understand, Hartmayer, is that Hitler is in trouble. The Allies are standing still because they want to tie down as many Nazi divisions as possible."

"*Chochem!*"* Hartmayer yelled impatiently. "If the Allies are so strong, why don't they break Hitler's neck?"

The other fellow's voice soared and glided slowly through the darkness, "Ahaaaa....Politik!"

Silence now, except for an occasional creak from the ceiling beams. They had once known happier crowds.

---

*"Smart aleck," or "Genius" (Yiddish).

Chapter Ten

Pounding penetrated my sleep. I jumped up. Others were looking about, startled, too. It was about 5:00 a.m. The obstinate
and ugly pounding persisted. A man in pajamas near the
screen-end of the theater got up and hurried to the door. It
burst open before he could reach it. Turning on his heels, with
his arms outstretched, he gave an anguished cry: "Yeckes!"*

A flood of SS soldiers poured into the theater in a big
swoosh and spread out across the auditorium. We were dumbfounded, but some men instinctively ran to the exit doors leading to the courtyard. Too late! Every exit was blocked. Germans
pointed their submachine guns at us and screamed, *"Alle aufste-
hen und sofort raus, schnell, RRRAUS!"*† Gripped by fear, the crowd was
silent.

It didn't take long to dress—most of us slept clothed or in
underwear, anyway. I threw on the gray suit Mother had sewn
from blankets and took as long as possible to pack my few things
so I could collect my racing thoughts. The SS kicked rabidly
into mattresses to see if anyone was hiding underneath and
roughed up those whose speed in getting ready was not to their
liking. One found a man under a pile of mattresses and hit him
with the butt of his gun as the hapless victim tried to protect his
head. Carrying bundles, refugees began to file out of the theater hurriedly. Papa, Harry, and I said nothing. What could we

---

*"Germans!"
†"Everybody up and out, right away, quick! OUT!"

do but obey? I helped Papa get his things together. He was still hampered in his movements from the surgery.

We joined the others filing toward the main exit, flanked on both sides by SS who hurried us on with, *"Vorwärts, los, vorwärts!"** The beaten man shuffled along, eyes closed, leaning his bleeding head to one side. The crowd slowed in the corridor just before the exit. The double cordon of SS funneled us directly into the back of a big army lorry parked at the door. Plainclothesmen on the sidewalk kept an eye on us, as well as on the neighbors watching from their windows across the street. When our turn came, I hoisted myself into the truck and pulled Papa up by his arms while Harry pushed from below.

As soon as everybody was in, two SS banged the rear half-door shut. A sharp whistle and the motors started up. The officers stepped into a black staff car. Soldiers jumped on the truck and motorcycles, and the convoy was off. Our truck was covered with a tarpaulin, but the back remained open. The staff car was following us. Motorcycles rolled along both sides of the truck. The one with the SS soldiers was probably ahead of us.

Caught! The painful, undeniable reality sank like lead in my heart. Several times in the past we'd been cornered, yet always wriggled free. Now our capture brought into sharp focus the stories I'd heard of the Germans' bestial treatment of Jews. A fear of the worst took hold of me, yet all I could do was keep a sharp eye open for any chance to escape.

The officers' faces in the car behind us were impassive. As the convoy proceeded through deserted streets, I caught fleeting glimpses of the city coming to life: a man rolling up the iron curtain of a tobacco shop, people lining up in front of a meat store. Sigi squeezed his way through to me. "Do you have any idea where Willy is?"

---

*"Forward, let's go forward!"

51

"No. Wasn't he with you when the Germans burst in?"

"Yes. Maybe he escaped," Sigi said, hopefully.

The raid had been so swift and well-planned, I couldn't imagine how anyone could have succeeded in escaping, but I kept that thought to myself. Still, where was he?

After a fast fifteen-minute drive, the convoy came to a stop near the Arno River. I heard someone shout orders, and the convoy slowly moved on. Through the rear of the truck, I saw the river and street recede. Enormous walls of a military garrison appeared. My view of the outside world ended as heavy iron gates clanged shut behind us. The truck stopped. An SS guard ordered us off. We were in a huge square courtyard flanked on all sides by large gray buildings. Signs in German indicated various military departments. There was brisk activity: cars, motorcycles, soldiers dashing in and out of buildings with papers and dossiers.

An earlier catch of Jewish families waited nearby. We hadn't been the only ones trapped while asleep. Three soldiers sat behind a long table. An SS officer stood by, hands folded behind his back. He ordered us to line up near the table in four rows. "One family at a time. Hand over your passports, money, jewelry, watches. Anyone found hiding anything will be shot. Is there anyone who doesn't understand?"

The threat of being shot had blared from loudspeakers on German army vans moving through the darkened French towns of Florac, Cahors, and Lons-Le-Saunier after a daring coup by the Maquis. I'd read it on the *Kommandantur*'s posters, always signed by that bombastic Teutonic name, General Karl Heinrich von Stuelpnagel. Even so, it again hit me with great force.

Silence.

"No? Very well, first family forward!"

A man, his wife, and little girl stepped meekly up to the table. I watched intently from our position in the second row.

A clerk took their passports and wrote their names on a list. The father answered a few questions and then the officer directed the family to an arch in the building behind the table. An armed guard stood at its entrance.

Harry was crying surreptitiously. He stood just a step to my right, his head buried in his shoulders. Uncertain of the Germans' reaction, I hesitated to put my arms around him. "Be good, Harry," I whispered. "Be good, stop crying, we're still together." Papa's face was livid. I could tell the emotional turmoil inside him by his jaw spasms, that nervous tic I'd come to know so well lately.

The Dresner family stood before the table. The father had a beard, the archetype of the Nazis' venomous caricatures of orthodox Jews. His wife's hair was covered with a scarf in religious tradition. Of their brood of six, the four boys had the *peyes* (sidelocks) and pallid looks of *yeshiva* youngsters studying the Torah and Talmud from their earliest years. As preoccupied as I was with our own fate, I feared an ugly, humiliating outburst against this family, the kind that Nazis were known to reserve for the orthodox.

The three clerks were in consultation over a document Mr. Dresner had given them. The officer approached, examined it, and interrogated him. After a few minutes he called for a guard, who snapped to attention. "This family can go. They're Hungarian nationals."

Hungary had taken sides with Germany in the war, but since when did such camaraderie apply to Jews? My eyes followed the Dresners with undisguised envy and, shamefully, resentment as they were escorted out.

It was our turn at the table. I approached with a stubborn lump in my throat that no amount of swallowing could relieve. I emptied my pockets quickly, keeping only a comb. Papa handed over his *accordeon,* the long, green, folding identity card that French authorities gave to foreigners. JUIF was stamped across it. He removed his tie clasp and cuff links and put them on the table with the few lire he had. That was it. There was nothing left in the world to call our own. Harry rubbed his red, tear-filled eyes and surrendered the sweet junk he carried in his pockets. He caught the officer's attention. *"Ja, warum weint denn der Kleine?"** the officer inquired in a solicitous tone.

Leaning on his cane, Papa put his arm around Harry and said, *"Er hat Angst, er ist ja noch ein Kind."* By mentioning that Harry was still a child, and understandably afraid, did Papa hope to soften the German's heart? Was this a last-ditch belief that Nazis were still capable of compassion toward Jews?

"Ach, but there's nothing to be feared," answered the officer in a tone meant to sound reassuring. "You'll all go to a work camp and be treated well."

"You see, Harry, you see," Papa said, meekly faking a jovial tone.

I don't think Harry was fooled, but I wanted to believe what I'd heard. Nothing dies so stubbornly as hope.

We passed the guard and found ourselves under the high, dark archway. A second armed guard stood at the other end, silhouetted against daylight. There were two large, empty horse stables on each side. A third one was roped off. The guard directed us to a fourth, near the opposite arch. We sat down and joined the anguished talk. I guessed it was now 8:30 a.m.

After three years of successfully evading the Nazis, to finally get trapped while asleep! On what caprice freedom depended. If only I'd been in the toilet when they arrived, I would have been able to escape. Or if some insomniac was out for a walk in the early dawn, he would have seen them coming and alerted us in time. Foolish thoughts.

---

*"Well, why is the little one crying?"

Mother! Did she know? How *could* she? How heartbroken she'll be! But was she safe? Had the Nazis nabbed only us, or were there raids all over town? Somehow, the possibility that she, too, might be in the hands of the Nazis was even more distressing, perhaps because even in captivity, Papa, Harry, and I at least still had each other.

More prisoners arrived. The stable got crowded. Astonishingly, my stomach growled. It reminded me I hadn't had breakfast.

Harry was crying softly. He worried about Mother and wanted to be with her. He was tough and courageous for his age, but his deep attachment to Mother had always seemed excessive to me. I tried to console him. I explained there was nothing we could do. Our only hope was that the convent hadn't been raided. But he kept rubbing his swollen eyes, tears glistening at his cheeks. Feeling helpless, I went to Sigi and his father to inquire about Willy. They thought he might have been hustled into another truck, but by now all the people from the theater were in the stable. Had they caught him trying to escape and shot him?

I went back to Papa. His wound was causing him pain again. He leaned on his cane and smoked a cigarette, one of several he'd daringly kept. He looked at me with an expression of love and helplessness. "*Nu*, Ludi," he sighed.* "What will be with us?"

"I don't know, Papi." I was glad he had the solace of a cigarette.

As the morning dragged on, more Jews kept arriving. The Germans had obviously launched their netting operation everywhere. Enough people had already been brought in to fill three stables. There was a hum of anxious conversation under the archway and much milling about from one stable to the next.

---

*"Well, Ludi," he sighed.

Everyone was trying to find out if there had been raids in other parts of town where relatives were hidden. Some families found themselves in bittersweet reunions. I kept looking apprehensively at the entrance to the archway, fearing I would discover Mother in every new batch of captives.

Noon. Guards handed out two bread rolls per person. We quickly swallowed them. That was lunch. Still, the nourishment helped me think more clearly. I decided to try and see what was going on beyond the confines of the stables. Slowly, I walked toward the entrance of the archway we'd entered. The guard saw me approach. I stopped and looked out past him to the big courtyard. After the dimness in the stables, daylight seemed very bright. Jews were still being processed. A tall brick wall surrounded the entire complex of massive, unadorned gray buildings. It was called La Zecca, a Florentine Jew among us had said, and was headquarters for an Italian cavalry regiment. I saw only Germans. "Why do you do this to us?" I suddenly heard myself asking the guard.

The soldier stared ahead. I noticed he wasn't much older than I. After a long moment, he hissed, "The Jews started this war. They wanted it. It serves them right."

"Couldn't you let my little brother go? He's just a kid!"

"No." He shifted his rifle and walked away a few paces.

I went back to Papa and to Harry, who was still obsessed with the idea of being with Mother.

The slow afternoon wore on agonizingly. By now, all four stables were crowded with Jews who'd been rounded up throughout the city (I estimated nearly five hundred). Fortunately, Mother wasn't among them. No new transports had been brought in for awhile. I hoped the sweeping operation had ceased. What were the Nazis going to do with us now? A concentration camp, no doubt. What if the Allies were making tremendous advances from the south? Wouldn't the Germans urgently need large labor forces to build fortifications around Florence? I thought about escaping, but the formidable German presence and the enclosing fifteen-foot wall topped by barbed wire were discouraging. Even going to the toilet meant being escorted by an armed guard.

I stayed close to Papa. Harry walked aimlessly back and forth in our vicinity, a fixed look of something specific on his mind. He disappeared for a short time. When he came back he took me aside: "I got past the guard into the courtyard. Some Italians were collecting garbage in large pails and hoisting them onto a truck. They saw me but didn't say anything. They even turned away deliberately but I couldn't hide inside a pail without a German spotting me. I'm going to look for some other way to escape. Don't tell Papa."

Excited, he walked away. I thought of holding him back, of the punishment he'd get if he were caught, but was it safer just to sit and wait? As a child, perhaps he had a better chance of finding a way out. If caught, the Germans might do nothing worse than drag him back into the stables.

Harry approached the guard at the exit leading to the courtyard. The setting November sun threw a pale sliver of light into the archway. He slowed down and started playfully kicking a little stone in front of him, this way and that, inching closer to the exit. The guard was yawning. The stone rolled past him and Harry nonchalantly went after it. A few kicks, and he was in the courtyard, then out of sight.

I went back to Papa. He was puffing on a cigarette, the burning end nearly touching his lips. He stamped it out on the ground. "That was my last one," he sighed. "Be glad you're not a smoker." Then he looked around. "Where's Harry?"

"I saw him a minute ago. Wandering around, probably." It had grown dark. I watched the archway, fearing the sudden appearance of a German yelling, "Who are the relatives of Harry

Goldman?" After more than an hour had passed, I told Papa that Harry had left to find a way of escaping. I said we hadn't wanted to tell him earlier and upset him. To my surprise, Papa took the news calmly. "I hope he made it. Don't tell anyone else."

Chapter Eleven

Around eight in the evening an officer walked briskly into our stable. Three soldiers followed, carrying large baskets of bread rolls. "There'll be four rolls for each one of you," he said. "Two for tonight; two for tomorrow morning. No pushing, no cheating. Then I'll need volunteers to bring in more straw for you to sleep on tonight."

Papa and I got our rolls. I stepped forward for the straw detail with a dozen other men. It was an opportunity to look over the complex. Sigi sidled up to me. While we waited, I heard a man ask the soldier giving him his rolls, "Why do we have to keep two for the morning?"

"Because," the German answered, "the transport leaves early for Auschwitz, and there won't be time for distributing bread then." His emotionless explanation had the effect of an announcement over a loudspeaker. The four stables, never quiet at any time during that day, were suddenly at fever pitch. Every Jew somehow knew it meant a camp where people were either worked to death or killed. Sigi and I looked at each other. This marked the official end of hope.

The three soldiers divided the volunteers among them. Sigi's and my group stepped out through the rear arch. It was dark, and the German walking at our side lit the way with a flashlight. He led us past the toilets to another stable a hundred feet beyond, pointing his flashlight down. "Pick up all the straw you can and march back to your stable."

We headed back, straw spilling from our arms, the guard waiting while we retrieved it. The courtyard was still active with military personnel coming and going. The throb of city life beyond the wall, reaching us intermittently during the day, had grown faint. I could hear the clear clink-clink-clink of a tramway's bell nearby. Auschwitz! That impatient, tinkling bell started urgent thoughts of escape.

We dumped the straw and went back for more. As we passed the toilets, I was struck by their proximity to the wall. In the darkness, with its barbed-wire topping, the wall looked even more forbidding than during the day. I'd noticed a section almost opposite the toilets where some protruding metal rungs ran from the bottom nearly to the top. We picked up new straw and walked back in a relaxed and undisciplined fashion. Our guard was walking far ahead. I whispered to Sigi, "Damn it, there must be a way of getting out of here. Over the wall, what do you think?"

"You're crazy! With all those Germans around?"

"Once we're on the train it's going to be nearly impossible," I said. "Oh, I think Harry got away."

"He did?"

"I haven't seen him in a couple of hours."

"Over the wall? Are you joking?" Sigi asked, but he looked back at the wall.

There was great activity at the entrance to our stables: groups of volunteers fetching and bringing back straw; others waiting to be escorted to the toilets; a few coming back from them alone, their guards having lost track of them or still waiting for the last ones. The confusion suddenly strengthened my resolve to try escaping that night. Soon there might be a roll call and tightened security. I'd rehearsed imitating a small boy's voice to cover up for Harry, but had no idea what to do if each individual called had to step forward.

I laid down my last bundle of straw. "Papi," I said, "Harry probably got away. I'd like to try, too. I think this is the right moment."

Alarm mounted in his face as I talked. I looked away, remorse-ridden. After a moment he said, "All right, try and get to Mother. Take care of her and Harry. But it's dangerous, Ludi. Do nothing reckless. What if they catch you?"

"I don't know, Papi. I just know I have to try. I'll be careful, don't worry." I gave him the two bread rolls I'd kept for the next morning. "If I don't come back, and you have to make the trip alone, tell them you've just had surgery. Maybe they'll let you go. Who knows, the departure may even be delayed. If I make it, I'll ask the priests at Mother's convent if they can intercede for you."

I looked into his eyes for a moment. With that, I went. No embrace, no farewell kiss, no tears. I was propelled by my instinct for self-preservation and survival. Still, pangs of guilt gnawed at me as I walked away. There was no sense in taking him with me since I had no specific plan, and he was unable to run, crouch, or climb. Yet, shouldn't I stay with him and find another way for both of us to escape later? No. My apprenticeship in the art of survival had taught me that later is a less propitious time—more uncertain and dangerous—than the present.

I went to the archway exit. A few other people, including Sigi, were waiting for a German sentry to escort them to the toilets, and I joined them. The feverish activity in the courtyard had quieted down. A pale moon was trying to break through the clouds. I didn't tell Sigi I'd decided to try to escape. The toilets were the French kind: a hole in the ground between two footrests. I opened my pants and squatted down. The German waited outside. I raised myself and peeked left and right over the swinging half-door of my cubicle. I couldn't see our guard. He was probably at the other end, behind the toilet shack. I examined the wall carefully. It was no more than twenty-five feet away. Several large garbage cans stood against it, directly opposite my cubicle. To the right of them a metal plate covered the ground. Again, I noticed the metal rungs protruding every few feet from the wall, leading almost to the top. The bottom of the wall in the closest area was painted white to a height of about seven feet. Four lines of barbed wire ran along its crest. The odds against my succeeding were astronomical.

I went back to my squatting position to mull it over. From other cubicles came sounds of coughing and shuffling feet. The others had finished. Any second the German would walk us back to the stable. It seemed neither the right time nor the right way to escape. I peeked over the swinging door again, my pants still unfastened. Men were coming out of their cubicles and walking to the other end, where the sentry was probably waiting. I didn't move. I could always be the last one, I thought. Who said we all had to finish at precisely the same instant? Perhaps someone else was still left in the toilets. A moment passed. No one else came out. My heart was pounding in my ears. The guard would count the group and realize somebody's missing. What to do? Should I quickly join them? No, my burning desire to escape had already started me on a reckless course and switched off all rational thinking. I heard the group walk back to the stables. I waited. Complete silence around me. "Sigi," I whispered. No answer.

I told myself, *"Go!"* I quickly buttoned up and stepped out of the cubicle. No one. I strained to hear whether another group was coming. Nothing. I dashed across to the garbage cans and started climbing up the iron rungs. I hadn't given a thought to how I would get through the barbed wire should I reach the top unnoticed. At the fifth rung my foot slipped. I lost my balance and came crashing down on the metal plate. Perhaps an empty pit lay beneath it, as a loud, hollow sound followed my fall, waves of noise reverberating. I thought it could be heard all over Florence. I lay there, frozen, then jumped up, darted back to my cubicle, tore open my pants, squatted, and waited in hysterical fright for all hell to break loose.

Sirens wailing, heavy boots running over the cobblestoned courtyard, flashlights poking, orders being barked. I knew the scenario in advance. When they came and dragged me out, I'd say I had a terrible bellyache and ran to the toilets without waiting for the guard. The noise? What noise? Not around here.

I waited second after second, all my nerves bristling. Nothing happened. It wasn't possible that the sentries and guards hadn't heard the crash. Were they lurking in the shadows, waiting for me to try again and shoot me? Why not call it quits, Louis? Button up and walk back to the relative safety of the stable, back to Papa. Still nothing. My knees were beginning to hurt from the prolonged squatting. I straightened up and looked around. It was as normal as when I'd started out a few minutes before. The commotion was all in *me*!

Up that wall! Should I? Should I not?...*Up that wall!* I ran and started climbing once more. I was nearing the spot where I'd slipped. Careful now. Hold on tight with your hands until you feel both feet on a rung...fine...up another one...up...go on! I was shaking. The height was dizzying. I grabbed the next rung and hoisted myself still higher, obsessed by my goal of reaching the top undetected. The time to consider the foolishness of my action had passed. Midheight I glanced over my left shoulder. I could see the top of our stable. The bottom was hidden by the toilet shack, so the guard at the stable entrance couldn't have seen me yet. So far, so good! I looked behind me. I was staring directly into the offices on the first floor. I'd never thought about what was above the stables. The offices were brightly lit, windows open. I saw and heard uniformed women soldiers typing at their desks, and officers and soldiers making phone calls, handling papers, and entering other offices through connecting doors. I was a mere forty feet away, impaled on the middle of the wall by the light from the offices. Then the moon decided to come out from behind the clouds. It felt like a searchlight had zeroed in on me. I feared my slightest movement would immediately be noticed. My God, how was it possible that no one had spotted me either coming up against the whitewashed part of the wall or in front of all those people? My fists gripping the next rung started to cramp. Should I quit now while I was still ahead? No, climbing down would attract just as much attention.

Up with you! I was moving again. A rung, and another one—my ears bursting with the blood rushing to them. Any second I expected to hear a shout. Would I stop? Silly question. Where would I run? There probably wouldn't even be time to answer. A precise burst from a submachine gun would leave a dotted line of little holes in the wall, interrupted only by the width of my body. I was coming to the top. Two more rungs. Above me, starting very close to the wall, ran the four parallel lines of barbed wire. With both feet on the last rung, my head just reached the wall's crest. I slid one arm under the wires and gripped the top. It occurred to me that the wires might be electrified and that I should have thought about that a bit earlier. But I was in a frenzy. With my other hand I slipped the three wires closest to the wall over my head one by one, and then, with both hands clutching the top, pulled myself up to it. The barbs got stuck in my suit and ripped it. Every few inches I had to let go with one hand and pluck them out. Finally, I hoisted myself up and straddled the wall like a horse. The stables, toilets, offices, all seemed far away, and I suddenly felt an exhilarating whiff of freedom. I looked down the other side. It was dark but I could make out a wide street with apartment houses along the opposite sidewalk. People rushed about. Cars. Tinkling tramways. The most beautiful sight on earth.

It was a fifteen-foot drop to the sidewalk. Only a few pedestrians were using it. Two German sentries paced back and forth along the entire length of the wall. I would have to wait for the moment when there were no pedestrians in sight and the sentries were the greatest distance from me. I didn't want to remain exposed on top of the wall. Yet, I hesitated. Jumping into the void onto concrete made me feel sick. I swung my right leg to the outside of the wall, now facing it, gripped the top with both hands, and let my feet dangle. That way, I was gaining nearly six feet.

No pedestrians on the sidewalk. A quick glance to the left and right. The sentries were at their farthest point. I let go. I didn't clear the wall enough and the stone bricks ripped flesh from my wrists. I hit the sidewalk and, thrown backward by the impact, braced myself with outstretched palms. I got up, darted across the street through traffic to the opposite sidewalk, and slipped into a dark building entrance to catch my breath. I leaned against the door, everything in me drumming, panting, spinning, wheeling, bursting. I was free, alive, looking at the Nazi garrison and the wall from the *outside!* A dizzying wave of hysterical joy swelled up inside and nearly choked me.

I gave a last glance to the garrison, so menacingly near, thinking of Papa in the stable just behind that wall, guilt and exhilaration surging within me. If only I could let him know I made it, if only I could get him out, too. I started walking, sure that any second Germans on motorcycles would burst forth looking for me. I rounded the corner. A tramway to Varlungo came by but I didn't have a lira in my pockets. I kept walking at the fastest speed that wouldn't attract notice. I tried to project nonchalance by whistling the first tune that came to mind.

The streets were dark but still fairly alive with cars, civilians, and, occasionally, German or Italian soldiers. I was positive anyone could see that I'd just escaped the Germans, but the pedestrians I encountered were engrossed in their conversations. Still, I felt that every car coming up behind me carried secret police. In a cold sweat, I followed the long, straight Via Aretina, keeping my bloodied wrists hidden in my pants' pockets, whistling. Two German soldiers came down the street. The sidewalk was too narrow for all three of us. I stepped aside slightly, whistling all the time. *"Du!"* They were speaking to me. I had to turn around. I was annoyed at my knees for shaking. One of the Germans pointed to the ground and said, *"Hast Dein Kamm verloren!"**

"Grazie, grazie tanto!" I picked it up and continued on my way.

Half an hour later I neared the Varlungo convent. I paused before entering the little alley that led to it. What if the Germans had raided the convent and left one of their men behind? Or someone had tailed me? But no one seemed to be following me. The tall, massive, iron gates blocked the view of anything beyond.

I waited, listening for noises that would reveal anything unusual inside. Everything seemed normal. I pulled the handle which rang the bell in the keeper's house across the courtyard. No answer. Perhaps two minutes elapsed, during which I thought I heard some whispering. Finally, footsteps approached the gate. Clanking noises at the lock. The gate swung open. In the darkness I saw a figure clad in black. He grabbed me, jerked me inside, shut the gate, and threw his arms around me in a tight embrace. "Thank God you're safe!" He released me. His penetrating eyes stared through rimless glasses; his fine, chis-

---

*"You've lost your comb."

eled face was overcome with emotion. It was Don Giovanni Simioni, the convent's twenty-nine-year-old chaplain.

He shouted over his shoulder, "Come down quick. It's Ludi!" Someone in the shadows jumped down from a tree and ran toward us. Harry!

"Ludi! Have they let you go? Where's Papa?"

"Let me go? Heck, no! I escaped, but Papa's still inside." We hugged each other, too bewildered by all that had happened to say anything more.

Don Giovanni told me Aunt Sonia had arrived earlier in the evening. Don Leto Casini had been able to arrange for her transfer and, as a result, she'd been the only Jewish woman to escape the Catholic Institute in Via Gioberti a few minutes before it was raided. Harry had met her at the gate and told her the whole story of our capture.

Don Giovanni said the convent hadn't been raided, and Mother and the other Jewish women were unaware that the Germans had rounded up all their families. He hadn't let Harry inside yet, cautioning him to climb up into the tree if anyone rang the bell. He also had asked Aunt Sonia not to say anything to Mother and persuaded me, too, to wait until the morning before seeing her and breaking the news.

Papa! If only he could be told that both his sons had escaped. It would give him new hope and courage. Would the transport actually leave for Auschwitz in the morning? Perhaps the deportation order had been rescinded?

I asked Don Giovanni if he could go to the garrison in the morning and find out. In case he couldn't get in, I wrote a note telling Papa that Harry and I were both safe. I explained to Don Giovanni precisely where our stable was behind the wall. Could he wrap the note around a stone and throw it over the wall? He promised to try.

Harry and I stayed up with Don Giovanni and Don Casini until very late, reliving the day. Harry told us how he'd gotten away. He'd kicked his stone past the guard at the archway without arousing his suspicion and got inside the large courtyard. He slowly went on with his game, skirting the stable building until he reached the garrison wall, but in a sector considerably removed from us and much quieter. He climbed the wall, but once on top he couldn't bring himself to jump. He'd called out to a passing cyclist. Puzzled, the man looked up, got off his bicycle, and leaned it against the wall. Then, when he was standing directly under him, Harry said, "Catch me," and jumped. Instinctively, the man opened his arms and braced Harry's fall. He started to yell at Harry and gave him a slap in the face for his rowdy prank, but Harry begged in halting Italian, "Please, Signore, get me out of here! I just escaped from the Germans!" His expression and voice convinced the man that he was not a mischievous boy playing a naughty game. He put Harry on his bike, and they rode to a quiet side street. "Where will you go now?" the man asked.

"To my mother. She's in a convent."

"Come, I'll take you there."

"No, thank you, it's not necessary."

"But I'll gladly do it. Come on...."

"No," Harry persisted, not wanting to reveal Mother's hideout to a stranger. "I know how to get there. Thank you very much."

The man backed off, and Harry took the tramway to the Varlungo convent, paying his fare with a ten-lira note he'd kept from the Germans.

Chapter Twelve

The next morning Don Giovanni returned from the garrison, disheartened. He told Harry and me that the captives had been sent off from the railroad station at 5:00 a.m.

Ruth Glatt was chosen to tell Mother that her sons were here to see her. Flanked by Don Casini, Don Giovanni, and Rabbi Cassuto, Harry and I stood white-faced before Mother. She looked from me to Harry, blood rushing to her cheeks, then cried out, "They took Papa!"

I tried to console her, pointing out that our presence was a miracle of sorts. "Perhaps Papa will be just as lucky." I didn't say I thought he would be needing all our prayers. Shaking, Mother wrung her hands, her face bathed in tears.

Don Casini said he'd contacted a Catholic boys' orphanage that was willing to hide us. The Orfanotrofio Madonnina del Grappa was located at the other end of town, in the northeastern suburb of Rifredi. Don Giovanni would take us there immediately. Harry's eyes welled up, but he came along without further protest.

The three of us took the tramway. It was both thrilling and frightening to be out in broad daylight so soon after our terrifying ordeal. I kept expecting a sudden identification check to bring my precious liberty to an abrupt end. However, Don Giovanni's ecclesiastical garb, a long black cassock buttoned all the way down to his shoes, gave me a feeling of security.

I'd met Don Giovanni briefly during a visit to Mother and had taken an immediate liking to him. He'd come to Florence from Treviso, a city in the north near Venice, where he'd been assistant rector at the Collegio Pio X. He had a calcified knee, and after an unsuccessful operation the rector at the Collegio hinted that his effectiveness was impaired. So when Don Giovanni heard the position of chaplain had opened in the Varlungo convent, he took it, continuing his studies at the Magistero, the teacher's college of the University of Florence. He lived on the convent's premises in a separate house, which he shared with a gardener/handyman and a housekeeper.

The tramway rounded a curve in front of the Zecca garrison. It seemed to be screaming, "There he is! Grab him!" I glanced at the wall, then quickly looked away.

When we arrived at the orphanage, Don Giovanni asked to see the director, Monsignor Giulio Facibeni. We were shown to a parlor where several people were waiting. A few minutes later a young priest appeared introducing himself as Don Nello Pecchioli, the monsignor's assistant. He was a handsome man of about thirty, tall, with black hair, bushy eyebrows, and a pleasant smile. He took us into an office, closed the door, and said he knew why we had come. He talked with Don Giovanni for a short while, then excused himself to bring in another Jewish boy who'd arrived that morning. Monsignor Facibeni would see three of us together. Don Nello reappeared with the boy.

Willy!

All of us started babbling at the same time until Willy interrupted, "What happened to my father and Sigi?" I told him I'd seen Sigi just before I climbed the wall, and that he and their father were probably in the transport with Papa.

Willy said soberly, "At least they're together."

"How did you escape?" I asked.

Willy said that in the panicky moments after the SS burst into the theater, he remembered the balcony upstairs, stacked ceiling-high with rows of removed seats. He had filed out of the theater toward the truck with everybody else. But as he passed the stairs, an SS man barking at the crowd to move faster looked away for a split second. Willy bounced up the stairs and wriggled himself under the seats. He heard the commotion below, Germans screaming, *"RRRAUS!"* and commanding, *"Fluchtversucher erschiessen."** Through the balcony railing he'd seen Germans beating up the hapless Jew who'd tried to hide beneath a pile of mattresses. Willy knew he would be beaten or shot if they discovered him. But he couldn't bring himself to join the others. Suddenly, he'd felt an urge to urinate. Petrified to make the slightest move, he let it flow through his pants, praying it wouldn't trickle down through a crack in the floor. He heard the people being loaded into the truck, noises in the theater gradually decreasing. Then a terrifying thumping of boots came up the stairs. He watched them pause. A light flashed around in the darkness, and then the boots went down again. A few minutes later there was complete silence. He remained where he was, too frightened to reveal himself, afraid of a trap.

A half hour passed. Again he heard the sound of boots below and fear gripped him anew. He ventured a peek and saw that a commission of SS officers had arrived. The skull-and-bones insignia was on their caps. Officers clustered around their commander, who stood with arms folded on his chest, shaking his head. "So, this is where they were housed, eh?" A junior officer described the raid. "And where was that Jew family with the six children?" He was shown the stage. "Well! What do you say to that impudence?" The junior officer offered to give him a tour of the facility and proceeded to guide everyone

---

*"Shoot anyone who tries to escape!"

71

into the courtyard. After a quarter of an hour all was quiet again. Willy waited a little longer and was about to leave when he heard lone, unhurried footsteps below. An Italian workman was rummaging through the piles of abandoned belongings. Willy tiptoed down slowly. "Pssst, are they gone?"

The man whirled around, startled. "Who? No, there's no one here."

A furtive glance through the rear door, and Willy slipped outside. He'd found his way to the archbishop's palace, where he spent the night. In the morning the cardinal's secretary, Monsignor Meneghello, arranged for him to be brought to the orphanage.

A boy entered and told Don Nello that Monsignor Facibeni would see us.

The monsignor's office was spacious, but the atmosphere stuffy, as though it had not been aired recently. Subdued daylight filtered in through high windows onto simple furniture and glass-fronted book cabinets. A large, bronze crucifix hung on the wall and near it a portrait of Pope Pius XII. Monsignor Giulio Facibeni leaned from his high-backed fauteuil, scribbling in an open notebook wedged between books and papers stacked on his large desk.

Don Nello closed the door and approached him respectfully. "Padre, these are the unfortunate Jewish boys Don Giovanni brought from Varlungo." It was absolutely quiet in the room.

Monsignor Facibeni looked about sixty, had a small, intelligent face and vivacious eyes. The tip of a white handkerchief protruded from his chest between two buttons of his black cassock. The hand leaning on his desk had a slight tremor. He looked at us searchingly, yet kindly, for a long moment. "*Venite qui*," he said softly.

He motioned for us to come around to his side of the desk, asked each his name, and held our hands as we answered. Don

Giovanni briefed him on our personal backgrounds and how we had escaped. *"Poveri bambini,"* he sighed, still riveting his eyes on us. I'd been the last one in line, and he still hadn't let go of my hand. Silence set in once more.

I wanted to disengage my hand but sensed it was not the proper thing to do. I shifted a foot and several times let my eyes wander around the room, and then back to rest on Monsignor Facibeni after each trip, my hand still anchored to his. This suddenly struck me as funny, wondering what was expected of me. I caught Willy lifting his eyes to high heaven and felt giggles coming on. The more I tried to repress them, the more they wanted to erupt. Willy, that rascal, now put on his good-for-all-occasions sheepish smile. I started cackling nervously. Harry caught it from me, it spread to Willy, and we couldn't stop. It was utterly ridiculous and ugly. Here we were in a hushed, austere office, giggling in the face of a highly esteemed church dignitary who was putting his life in jeopardy to save ours. Monsignor Facibeni gave my hand a gentle shake and let go. "You'll be safe here. Don Nello will fix you up." We thanked him profusely and as we left, he said softly, *"Siate buoni."*

Outside, I felt a rush of shame and guilt. Our behavior had been disgraceful, and I couldn't offer Don Nello and Don Giovanni any excuse. They were charitable enough not to ask for any, perhaps ascribing it to all that we'd been through.

Don Nello and Don Giovanni debated what to tell the teachers, personnel, and the orphans. No one was to know we were Jewish. They finally settled on a story: we were Catholics, born in Bitonto in southern Italy, but had lived in Nice since early childhood. Bitonto was in Allied hands, and our story could no longer be verified. And living most of our lives in France explained why we had no recollection of Bitonto and spoke French but almost no Italian. Harry and I were brothers; Willy, our cousin. We hadn't heard from our fathers, who were serving in the Italian army. The last news was from the Russian front. Willy's mother was dead. Our own mother had gone south to settle a family farm matter. She was to have rejoined us in a few weeks, but had been cut off when the Allies landed in Salerno. Neighbors had looked after us; then we came to stay with Msgr. Facibeni, a dear friend of our parents.

Don Giovanni thought up new names for us: Willy became Mario—Harry, Francesco—and I, Nicola, which means Nicholas. We were all Capaldis. Don Giovanni then left, promising to be the liaison between us and Mother. He said we could pass letters through a cleaning woman who lived in his parish in Varlungo and worked at the Orfanotrofio. "Don't ever use the mail service," he warned.

Chapter Thirteen
WHAT I DIDN'T KNOW AT THE TIME

～

On the morning of November 6, Don Leto Casini had alerted Don Giovanni Simioni that Jews had just been seized in hideouts throughout Florence. Don Giovanni went to the hospital to break the news to a Mrs. Henny Tarnover that her husband, her six-year-old son Henry, and her seventy-year-old mother had also been apprehended. Mrs. Tarnover, who had a weak heart and was six months' pregnant, had been scheduled to join Mina Goldman and the other eleven women and girls in the Varlungo convent. After she had crossed the Alps from Saint-Martin-Vesubie, her condition had worsened, and she had to be hospitalized. She was an old friend of the Swiss consul in Florence, so Don Giovanni hoped the man eventually could use his influence to get her family released.

When Don Giovanni arrived at the hospital the director took him aside and, in a quavering voice, said that Mrs. Tarnover would have to leave. After the German raid, it was too dangerous for the hospital to keep her. Don Giovanni said he would find another place, but asked the director not to throw the pregnant woman out on the streets.

Don Giovanni feared a raid on the Varlungo convent and wanted to be there if the Germans arrived. He thought he might be able to dissuade them from breaking in, with a stern reminder that the convent was under **clausura papale**, *hinting there might be political consequences with the Vatican if they did. He made a phone call to the convent; everything was still normal there.*

He convinced a wealthy man living alone to take in Mrs. Tarnover. Before Don Giovanni left, he said he would see her in a few days, as soon as he returned from a promised visit to his parents in Ormelle, near Treviso. They were worried about his brother, whose army unit had been sent to the eastern front on the

River Don. They had not heard from him in the three months since the Russians launched their massive counteroffensive.

The next day Don Giovanni brought Louis and Harry Goldman from the Varlungo convent to hide in the Madonnina del Grappa Orphanage, where he hoped they would remain safe until the end of the war.

He went back to Varlungo to pack for his trip. There the nuns told him that some men who refused to identify themselves had asked for him.

"Jews in distress? Or secret police?" he asked.

The nuns could not say.

Don Giovanni went to Don Casini's brother, Tito, and asked to borrow some civilian clothes. Normally, a Catholic priest was forbidden to divest himself of his black cassock. A bishop had to grant permission, usually for special studies or voyages to countries where a cassock might prove to be an impediment or objectionable. However, in times of emergency, a priest could act on his own, conscience and common sense his judge.

When he reached the railroad station, he was startled to find Mrs. Tarnover waiting for him with her son Henry.

"Oh, Don Giovanni," she said, "the Swiss consul managed to get my boy and husband released, but not my mother. She's very old and my husband refused to abandon her, so they deported him with her. The Germans told my son if they caught him again, that would be the end. Please, Don Giovanni, I don't trust the man you left us with, only you."

The train was leaving in twenty minutes.

They traveled all night in the train's corridor, Mrs. Tarnover and her boy sitting on Don Giovanni's suitcase. As their train sped north, Don Giovanni thought of that other train carrying Jewish men, women, and children. He thought, too, of Mr. Tarnover, whom he had met shortly before his capture from the theater with Pinkus, Louis, and Harry Goldman. Seeing that Tarnover's shoes were torn and threadbare, Don Giovanni had given him a pair of his own. They were too small, but Don Giovanni had suggested that Mr. Tarnover wear them until he could find a larger size. He reproached himself for having added to the man's misery.

CHAPTER THIRTEEN

It was dark when they arrived in Treviso. Don Giovanni and the Tarnovers took a taxi to Ormelle, twenty-seven kilometers away, the village where Don Giovanni was born and his family still lived. His mother opened the door and stared, shocked, unable to find the words to greet her son, an ordained Catholic priest, tense, in civilian clothing, with a visibly pregnant woman and a child in tow. His sister, too, looked at them, agape. Then Mrs. Tarnover broke into tears.

"Mamma!" Don Giovanni pleaded, "what are you thinking, for goodness sake? I haven't lost my head, you know!"

The next day, claiming Mrs. Tarnover was French, Don Giovanni placed her in the hospital in Oderzo, a small town nearby. Her son remained on his parents' farm. He asked his sister to look in on Mrs. Tarnover until the baby was born. Two days later, Don Giovanni returned to Florence.

Chapter Fourteen

Monte Morello rose at the north end of Rifredi, dominating this populous workers' suburb of Florence. Below it, Orfanotrofio Madonnina del Grappa, a vast complex of buildings, stretched across most of the long expanse of Rifredi's Via delle Panche: There were school buildings, dormitories, dining halls, and a bakery. There were workshops for vocational training in metalwork, carpentry, shoe repair, and tailoring; as well as a printing plant that published the Catholic monthly *Il Focolare*. There was also an administration building with Monsignor Facibeni's office on the ground floor—his private quarters above—and the church, which could accommodate several hundred people and also served the local parish. All units were interconnected by archways, stairways, and a large playground with a nearby tree-lined alley.

Monsignor Facibeni had been an army chaplain in World War I in the northern Veneto region and took part in bloody combats on Monte Grappa, a mountain topped by a Madonna statue. He'd been awarded the Silver Medal for unstinting heroism under fire, caring for his wounded comrades. To those who lay dying in his arms he had promised he would look after their children. At the end of the war, he found himself with eighteen orphans. Returning with them to his Rifredi parish, he founded his orphanage, naming it after the Madonna under whose gaze he'd so often administered last rites. Since then, the Orfanotrofio had become home to two hundred boys, with other branches throughout Tuscany, all supported entirely by charitable donations.

CHAPTER FOURTEEN

Don Nello arranged for the three of us to stay in a little two-story house attached to the rear of the church. Willy had a room with a single bed, Harry and I another with two beds. Both rooms were on the upper floor with a connecting door; the rest of the house was unfurnished. We were its only occupants. It was an ideal arrangement; we could be together by ourselves, an impossibility if we'd had to sleep with the other boys, who were grouped by school classes, and aged ranging from thirteen to twenty-one. Not having to share dormitories and showers also meant much less risk of being discovered as Jews, less danger of exposure if boys questioned us about our Catholicism. Also, any curiosity about our special living arrangement could be explained away: we were Monsignor Facibeni's personal guests.

Our house had two entrances. The front door opened to a small, abandoned kitchen in which were stored wood planks and bricks from previous construction work. A stairway from the kitchen led directly up to Willy's room. The door in back of the house opened onto a large hall. There, another stairway led to a narrow archway, also to Willy's room. The only access to Harry's and mine was through his.

The windows in both our rooms looked out onto the courtyard. Our front entrance and the church wall took up two sides of the square, and the ground-floor offices the other two sides. A slanting red tile roof hugged the church wall just under our windowsill. Monsignor Facibeni's quarters were across the courtyard from ours.

The only furniture in Willy's room was a bed and a three-legged washstand with a removable porcelain basin, a matching water pitcher on the floor. Harry's and mine had a table with two chairs in front of the window, a dresser, and a wall cupboard with shelves. We had no need for them since we owned nothing but the clothes on our backs. On the dresser an infant

Jesus doll rested on velvet pillows atop a pedestal covered by a glass bubble.

There was a fascinating detail to our room. A square opening in the wall about three feet above the floor allowed us to look directly down into the church, midheight between the floor and apex, above the altar. Only a wooden grating separated us from the cavernous void in the church below. We could open and shut a hinged, double partition over the grating.

I wasn't interested in the house's neglected state, or our lack of belongings, clothes, even toothbrushes. Those could wait. *Were we safe?* That was my primary worry. If the Germans came, how would we avoid getting caught again? I was frightened to go to bed in the silent, empty house. Only two nights before we'd awakened to the rage of SS men. The details of our capture and escape still played havoc with my nerves. We must never again let ourselves get caught by surprise, helpless and paralyzed.

As the eldest, I felt responsible for our safety. I devised a defense strategy with Willy and Harry to afford us time to act in case of a raid on our house. I bolted the kitchen door and the rear entrance. Harry latched the inside door of the archway leading into Willy's room. We left the door between our two rooms open, but I fastened a sturdy rope over our inside lock. If we heard suspicious noises outside any of the three other doors, Willy could slip into our room. Then we would secure our door by knotting the rope between the handle and a nail in the wall.

Those measures were to gain time for an actual escape. Theoretically, we would be cornered in our room, but there was a way out onto the tiled roof beneath our window. In case the Germans were already on the roof, or in the courtyard watching the window, we could easily remove the wooden grating over the opening into the church. Willy tied a thick rope onto a metal hook already anchored to the wall and let it uncoil down behind the altar. Sliding down on it, we would have a ten-foot jump to the church floor. Then we could either hide inside the church or run out into the field behind the orphanage. Despite everything, we credited the Germans with having the decency not to invade a church.

I was puffed with pride over our escape-route, being one up on the Germans. So much for a raid by night! Of course, it could hit us anytime and anywhere on orphanage grounds, but at least in daylight we could see them coming and hide somewhere quickly. I had it all figured out.

Physical precautions weren't enough. As we prepared for bed, I insisted we rehearse the details of our fake identities so we could mingle confidently among orphans and staff. Before falling asleep, I thought of Papa. If only he could have the relative safety of a place like ours.

A few days after our arrival, Don Giovanni came to tell us Willy's father was safe. He, too, had escaped from the garrison over the wall, shortly after me. Sigi had boosted him up the first rung and was going to follow, but then Mr. Hartmayer slipped on the second rung and Sigi ran back to the toilet to distract an oncoming guard. Once over the wall, Mr. Hartmayer had hidden in a darkened building entrance until he saw two nuns passing by. He stopped them and pleaded, "I'm Jewish. Can you tell me where there's a synagogue?" They led him to Via Farini, but as they approached, saw that the synagogue was brightly lit. German soldiers were loading a truck with plunder, including Torah scrolls in silver casings. "Turn back! Run away!" the nuns whispered to Mr. Hartmayer.

Shivering in fear and from cold, he huddled among garbage cans. At dawn, he followed two people into a nearby church, sat in a corner, exhausted, and fell asleep. The sexton shook him awake. "Signore, this is a church, not a hotel." Mr. Hartmayer asked to see the padre.

When he told his story, weeping, the padre took him into his rectory and gave him coffee. "Don't worry," he said, "we'll help you," then sent a sister for food.

Later he brought Mr. Hartmayer to an old-age home. "But he's too young!" the nun in charge protested. The padre said, "You'll be proud of him. He'll make such a nice little old man."

As November 1943 drew to an end, our life took on a better look. We cleaned away the rubble in the kitchen to enable easy passage. We shared the chores of cleaning our rooms, making beds, sweeping and washing the floors. I tolerated no laziness. Little by little, the orphanage provided us with some warm clothing, towels, and other necessities. We ate our meals with the boys in the large refectory. It was pitiful fare. Meat was rare in the war-ravaged country, and I gnawed disconsolately at the *verdura*—unexciting chard and spinach—or halfheartedly slurped down the thick, tasteless polenta that appeared with exasperating frequency. Still, we were not complaining, aware that things could be much worse.

We didn't attend classes with the orphans, who had a full schedule of secular, vocational, and religious instruction. That was explained away by our ignorance of Italian. Don Nello was supposedly tutoring us, and we also studied on our own from French textbooks. Although we played with the boys at recess, making friends by helping them conjugate French verbs, I spent the greater part of my days reading and writing at the table by the window in our room. Since early childhood I'd developed a keen appreciation of the value of time. Now I was frustrated that my education had been interrupted while other boys my age were in classrooms, learning. I had no teacher, and it would be nearly impossible for me to catch up.

In desperation, I hoarded as many books as I could lay my hands on, even if their contents were beyond my reach or the language unfamiliar. I plunged headlong into *I Promessi Sposi (The*

Betrothed) by Alessandro Manzoni, in Italian, and the works of Pascal, Descartes, and Spinoza, fortunately in French. I copied down parts that impressed me in little notebooks, using whole pages to analyze them. When the stuff became too dry, I read adventure books and boys' magazines. I had only a rudimentary knowledge of English, yet started *Brave New World* by Aldous Huxley. It felt wonderful when I finally decoded a whole passage with my dictionary and could actually identify with Huxley's thoughts, as in his chapter condemning the shooting of birds to satisfy jaded palates!

Harry, Willy, and I also picked up some Italian through contacts with the boys and staff. We were soon able to get the gist of newspapers, their editorials printed in italics. Every morning we eagerly scanned military communiqués. We got only the German headquarters' version but read between the lines. A "tactical adjustment" on the Eastern front probably meant a good trouncing by the Russians. When the Germans bragged their U-boats had sunk eighteen Allied vessels in one day, I said, "Aren't they ashamed to print such lies?"

It was essential to our morale to interpret the news that way. The names of battles fought and cities bombed became part of our vocabulary, a course in geography: Vladivostok, Novorossiysk, Kiev, Solomon Islands, Dresden, Hamburg, Malta, Canterbury, Calais. I found a map of Europe in a pile of books on the landing by Willy's room and affixed it on the wall near my table for us to follow the sweeps and clashes of the giant armies. Every time a new name came up we stuck a pin in it and drew a pencil line connecting it to the others to get an idea of the front. We felt like top brass meeting at command headquarters, studying the pins and commenting on their advances or retreats. Our fate was directly connected to the movements of those pins. Could the seemingly invincible Germans, with their much-vaunted secret weapons, one day be smashed so one would not have to die anymore just for being Jewish? A pin moved half an inch eastward meant new depths of gloom, but to the left, ah, hope was allowed again. Lately, the pin in the operations nearest us seemed to be stuck forever at Monte Cassino, a point between Naples and Rome.

The orphanage sat between a railroad junction and the Galileo factory, which produced optical war instruments. These installations, as well as more-important ones beyond Florence, were obviously of great interest to Allied bombers. Alarms wailed daily, sending children and staff running into basement shelters until the sirens tore into the quiet, sounding the all clear.

But often, studying at the table, my trained ears detected, ever so faintly, ever so distantly, a muffled rumbling. Bombers approaching! I bolted out of the house, across the field, and into our *rifugio,* a covered hole in the field behind the orphanage that could hold eight people. Harry, Willy, and a few others were already hiding there. The rumbling became much louder. We craned our necks, trying to locate the planes in the bright blue sky.

There they were, high above—white specks moving in unison, invincible eagles. We watched them with mixed feelings. Surrounded as we were by the ubiquitous Germans and their formidable war machinery, those planes were the first visible evidence we had of the Allies. At the same time, we feared they might be heading our way. They were directly over us now, moving in a wave of deep, somber droning: several squadrons of silver-winged bombers in perfect formations. So beautiful, so precise, so deadly.

The lighter fighter planes dashed ahead and around them in graceful arabesques, protecting their elephantine brothers from a surprise attack. Suddenly, we heard the *ack-ack* of the antiaircraft batteries and saw little black clouds puff up next to the bombers. Unperturbed, inexorable, they proceeded on their course. Next we saw the clusters of bombs dropping. They sparkled as they caught the flash of the sun's brilliance, and in that brief instant seemed no more than a handful of harmless, silver-foiled suppositories. We ducked as the shrieking whistle of the bombs tearing through the air grew and pierced our ears, and we waited for the heavy thump of impact and explosion. It felt as though the bombs were zeroing in on our heads. Finally, the all-clear siren sounded. We looked around. Billowing black clouds of smoke and flames, amorphous remainders of the attack, sprouted from the ground a few kilometers away. Everyone ran around trying to find out if the orphanage had suffered damage. Monsignor Facibeni, in anguish over his orphans' well-being, shuffled feverishly from one area to the next in teetering little steps. Barely five-feet tall, his thin body was racked with a neurological ailment, which I had learned was Parkinson's disease. He leaned forward at a slightly precarious angle, supported by the helpful hands of two older orphans. Children rushed up to report that the orphanage had been spared.

"*E come state, ragazzi?*"* he asked when he saw us. He fiddled with his handkerchief, always protruding between two buttons of his cassock to make it easier to reach.

"*Bene, Padre, tutto in ordine.*"†

"*Grazie a Dio!*" He hugged Harry, then, releasing him, Monsignor Facibeni gave a sharp but affectionate smack on the back of Harry's head. "*Sii buono,*"‡ he said with a mischievous smile, delighting in that little prank of his.

---

*"And how are you, boys?"
†"Good, Father. All's in order."
‡"Be good."

Chapter Fifteen

WHAT I DIDN'T KNOW AT THE TIME

After the SS raid and roundup of Jews in early November 1943, the Jewish Committee met less frequently. It had become more dangerous to move about Florence. Joseph Ziegler never allowed the taxi to stop in front of the Seminario Minore, his family's refuge, when he came back from meetings or city errands.

One day Don Casini was alerted by a girl he knew at the telephone exchange. "Be careful, Padre. Your telephone is tapped. A red light comes on whenever you dial or someone rings you up."

Don Casini took the 400,000 lire he had and hid them behind some books in his brother Tito's apartment.

The Germans continued to break into Catholic institutions. Contessa Marucchi believed the Curia itself was under surveillance. At her suggestion, the Jewish Committee moved its meetings to a private office in Via dei Pucci, number 2.

Don Casini, Rabbi Cassuto, Kahlberg, Ziegler, and Marco Ischio attended a meeting on the evening of November 26. Kahlberg would have to leave early for his little girl's birthday.

By 7:00 p.m. the Committee members had reviewed most matters on the agenda. They were about to adjourn when eight SS men rushed up the stairs and burst into the room, pistols drawn. They ordered the men to remain with their hands up while they searched them. Among the various items on the table was a letter mistakenly addressed to "The Chief Rabbi of Florence, Leto Casini" by someone in need of help. Don Casini had assisted over a hundred Jewish families. He had also jotted down on the white endpaper of his breviary the names and addresses of many families he often visited in the institutions where they were hidden.

CHAPTER FIFTEEN

The SS put all the incriminating evidence in a briefcase. Two of them sin-gled out Marco and took him into an adjoining room. The Committee members heard muffled sounds of shouting and beatings through the closed door. Ten minutes later Marco was released. All the others were transported to an SS com-mand post on Via Bolognese in the Pietra suburb. The post was ominously known as Villa Triste, the "Sad Villa." There, they were searched again, lined up in the corridor, and ordered to face the wall with their hands up. An SS guard pointed a pistol at them.

They were called into a room one by one. When Don Casini's turn came, he saw his papers and personal belongings spread among other items on a table. "Which of this stuff is yours?" asked the interrogator, an SS captain. Don Casini pointed to his wallet, keys, and breviary. The captain reached for the breviary and, as he picked it up, two dozen passport pictures fell out. Don Casini had intended to send them to Bologna the following day to have forged ID cards made. The captain scooped up the photographs and threw them in the air. "Ahaaa! Now I understand where all those Sicilians are coming from. Polish Jews, French Jews, German Jews, nothing but lousy Jews! What do you have to say to that?"

"I belong to a committee which assists destitute war victims. Their religion is immaterial to me. Perhaps they're Jews, perhaps not. I didn't ask. The pictures were given to me as souvenirs, in gratitude by those I've been able to help."

"And all these tokens of gratitude, just by coincidence, are passport size? Come now, Don Casini!"

"They're the cheapest ones to make. I suppose that's all the poor souls could afford."

"We'll have plenty of time to look more closely into this at further interroga-tions," he said. He picked up the breviary along with Don Casini's other belongings, shoved them into a large manila envelope, wrote the priest's name on it, and filed it away. Don Casini and the other captives were then driven to Murate Prison, where they were kept isolated, each in a separate cell.

The young Committee member Matilde Cassin had been very late for the meeting that evening. As she entered the vestibule, the concierge came out and told her everything was closed upstairs. The following morning Padre Cipriano

Ricotti told her what had happened. He also had a message from Marco for her, for Raffaele Cantoni, and for the rabbi's wife, Anna Cassuto: their hiding places were no longer safe. Marco would wait for them at 11:30 a.m. in Piazza Signoria, the city's central square, to take them to new places.

Matilde did not go with them to be taken to a new place. She had scheduled appointments to distribute money to families. Only Cantoni, Mrs. Cassuto, and one of her relatives arrived in Piazza Signoria at the appointed time. They spotted Marco leaning against a car. As they approached him, Marco stepped aside. Two German plainclothesmen jumped out, hustled the trio into the car, and sped off. From Murate Prison, Cantoni managed to send Matilde a note through an Italian guard he knew. The message read, "Attenzione, Marco spia."*

Marco had delivered to the Germans the principals engaged in helping the Jewish community survive, and the addresses where he knew Jews were hidden. The SS paid him on a per-capita basis. Among those they caught were fourteen-year-old twin girls, the Laskers, who had been running errands for the Committee. The SS drugged them and threatened to ship them off to an army bordello unless they talked. When the girls maintained that all the Jews they knew had already been arrested, the SS allowed them to leave. Instead of returning to their apartment, they went to the home where their parents were hidden. The SS followed them and arrested the entire family.

Matilde again escaped arrest. She had placed a dozen toddlers in the Convento del Carmine, where she herself was staying. She was not in the convent when the Germans burst in at 9:00 p.m. and seized the babies. A nun, Suora Luisa, saved two by hiding them under her soutane.

In prison, Ziegler kept insisting that he was Italian, not Jewish. He showed his ID card. Bodo heard of his arrest and went to the SS to intercede for him. He stated that Ziegler was a personal acquaintance, Italian indeed, and not involved in any political activities. Bodo also guaranteed that his friend would not escape.

The SS released Ziegler the following evening. He hastily arranged a secret meeting with Don Giovanni, the chaplain at the Varlungo convent where Louis Goldman's mother was hidden. Ziegler gave Don Giovanni 150,000 lire and

---

*"Watch out! Marco is a spy."

said, "Who knows how long before they'll arrest me again! Use the money wherever help is needed. Keep no records. You have only to account to your own conscience."

At one o'clock in the morning a few days later, the Germans broke into the Seminario Minore. All the Jews hidden there, including Ziegler's wife, her mother, and the two children, were immediately deported to Auschwitz. The SS took Ziegler back to Murate Prison.

For weeks after their capture, additional Committee members and "political" prisoners were selected daily and transported to the SS villa in a big van. They were forbidden to talk among themselves.

While waiting in the corridor for his second interrogation, Don Casini heard loud shouts coming from the room, then the prisoner inside admitting that he was Jewish. Don Casini sighed, "At least it won't have been I who betrayed him."

He was called in next. The SS captain conducted the interrogation through a woman interpreter. "Well, you, at least, are not Jewish, but you will tell me what machinations they were hatching at those meetings. I want to know everything about Rabbi Cassuto, Cantoni, Kuhlberg, Ziegler, or anyone else connected with them. Let's start with this Ziegler. Why is he carrying a false card as an engineer in Italy's largest industrial complex?"

"I have no idea," Don Casini answered. "Actually, I don't know much about him. Only that he's a good man who's been very generous to the needy in my care. I don't ask a person his religion or background when he offers help."

"You're wasting my time, Don Casini. We know a lot about your Committee's activities through Marco. The shady characters you've been associating with are all enemies of the Reich. We think Ziegler's involved in more than helping other Jews. We suspect he's a British spy, and your whole group is plotting sabotage acts. Need I say, this looks very bad for you? Now, wouldn't it be to your advantage to tell the truth?"

Don Casini was dumbfounded that Marco was working for the SS. He shrugged his shoulders and said he had nothing more to tell. The interpreter handed him a pen and the SS captain told him to sign the transcript of his interrogation. Don Casini noticed his answers looked more persuasive than he thought they had actually been. He remained in custody at the Villa Triste.

Fluent in German, Ziegler did not need an interpreter at his interrogations, which were transcribed simultaneously and often lasted several hours. What did Ziegler know about Don Casini and Cardinal Dalla Costa? The questions revealed the Germans' conviction that they had stumbled upon an underground organization plotting against the Reich. They wanted to know if the priests were working with partisans or parachute-dropped foreign agents, and whether the money for Don Casini's social work came from Allied sources. They were looking for proof that Don Casini, the cardinal, perhaps the Vatican itself, were implicated in those activities.

Ziegler consistently replied that there was no political organization, that the money came mainly out of his own funds, and that it was used only to assist refugees in distress. "Everything we did was at my own initiative," he said. "Don Casini, who's been helping Italian war victims for years, was merely lending us a hand."

The Germans frequently rained blows on him and broke one of his ribs. When Ziegler still said nothing, the captain called for help. An SS man came in with a fistful of dangling telephone wires. They forced Ziegler to lie facedown over a chair, and while the captain held Ziegler's head between his knees, the SS man let go with a cascade of whippings over his sides, back, and buttocks. Still, Ziegler told them nothing new. He had nothing to reveal.

After another routine interrogation, the Germans led Ziegler to a room and told him to wait. There, he saw Marco for the first time since the raid on the Committee two weeks earlier. He had heard Marco had been released but not why. He asked him what he was doing there. Marco said he had been arrested again and had just gone through an interrogation. "I don't know what they want from me," he whined. "I did you a favor accompanying you to Florence and look at the trouble it's gotten me into! It's all the priest's fault, anyway. Of course, you know Don Casini is relaying messages between the Allies and the partisans."

"It's a lie! Have you actually seen him do that?"

"Not me, but everyone knows."

Ziegler shouted, "I don't believe a word, you scum!"

CHAPTER FIFTEEN

That evening Ziegler told the Italian guard at Murate Prison that he wanted to go to confession. The next morning, in the privacy of the confessional, he whispered to the prison chaplain, "Excuse me, Padre, I didn't come to confess. I'm Jewish."

"Then why are you here?"

"I have an urgent message for Don Casini. The Germans want to inculpate him on espionage. You must also advise Cardinal Dalla Costa. So listen carefully."

"Wait. I want to write this down."

"Padre! Have you lost your senses? Nothing written. You must memorize everything."

"Ah, yes, I understand. Go ahead."

"Tell Don Casini I've admitted to nothing but the truth. The money came from me. The Committee was helping refugees. That's all. If the Germans tell him I said otherwise or show him any signed statement that's different, he should know it's a trick. He should say Ziegler's a liar and insist on confronting me personally. Warn Don Casini not to let himself be trapped."

Ziegler made the padre repeat the message twice. The padre conveyed it to Don Casini when he made his own confession to the prison chaplain.

After Don Casini's arrest, Cardinal Dalla Costa sent an aide, Monsignor Tirapani, to inquire about getting him released. "Why are they holding him?" the cardinal said. "If they say he was helping Jews, tell them I'm the guilty one. He did it on my orders."

The SS captain told Monsignor Tirapani, "Don Casini? He headed an international ring of German enemies. He procured false documents and still tells lies. No, we don't release someone like that!"

The Germans pursued their probing regarding other "agents" on the loose, but Don Casini stuck to his story about Ziegler, the Jewish Committee, and his own activities. He was helping homeless people and their religion or nationality was no concern of his. At the end of his interrogation he signed another transcript. Again, he noticed that the answers he had given looked different and more convincing on paper.

The interpreter at Don Casini's questionings was from Yugoslavia, where she had worked for the Germans. They transferred her to Florence the same day the Committee members were arrested. She had a cousin in Florence, a university professor, and the next day they met by chance in the street. He inquired what she was doing in Italy. When she told him, he frowned, "A very dear friend of mine was arrested. A priest!"

"Don Casini?" she asked.

"Yes! How do you know?"

"I've been assigned to the SS. I saw his name on the list of people to be interrogated tomorrow."

"Please," her cousin implored, "do everything in your power to help him. You must do this for me, please!"

Ziegler was convinced that the Nazis would never let any Jewish captives out of their grip. On the slim chance that he or any of his family would survive, he sought the help of an Italian prison guard whom he deemed trustworthy. "You've been kind to me and Christmas is not far away," he said. "Tell the nuns at the Seminario Minore that I sent you and to please prepare a nice food package for you and your family. Then tell them I also need a personal favor. They should consign all my luggage at the railroad station and keep the receipt for me in a safe place."

However, a few days after the German raid on the Seminario Minore, Marco Ischio had shown up there, saying, "I've succeeded in freeing Ziegler and his family, but they must leave town immediately. He wants me to bring him his valises." Since the nuns knew Marco well, they handed them over to him.

When the guard gave Ziegler the news, he reported Marco's "spirit of initiative" to the Germans. The SS went to Marco's apartment, confiscated the four valises, plus the one he had reported lost on his return trip from Turin when his train had been "bombed." Then the SS threw Marco into a Murate cell, close to Ziegler's.

Chapter Sixteen

Mother and her group of eleven other Jewish women had settled into quiet routine in the Varlungo convent, though it had
not been easy for women of Judaic background to adjust to the
strange milieu. In the countries where they'd lived and from
which they'd fled, anti-Semitism had often been tolerated, even
encouraged, in Catholic circles. Now, ironically, they were hidden in one of the Church's most solemn institutions.

The women lived isolated from the nuns. Only the abbess
and four other nuns knew they were Jewish. Mother had
described their rooms on the first floor: two beds in each, separated by hanging white sheets. Pictures of Christ and crucifixes
hung on the walls. A gilded Virgin Mary, silver sprinklings on
the eyes, stood in the corridor. The asceticism and unearthly
quietude pervaded the convent, broken only by the echo of the
persistent coughing of nuns who had caught tuberculosis through
years of living in damp, cold rooms.

From their windows, Mother and the girls watched the older
nuns embroidering in the garden, and seventeen-year-old
novices, their vows of silence still not taken, laughing during
recess. Renée and Ruth, the two Jewish girls near their own age,
looked down at them wistfully. Though the young nuns were
cloistered, they still had more freedom than the girls did.

In the first weeks of their relationship with Don Giovanni,
the chaplain, Mother and the other women became very fond of
him. By his continuous devotion to their safety, he'd earned
their attachment and gratitude. And he was charming and witty,

not at all the grave ecclesiastic they'd first imagined a priest in a forbidding black cassock would be. Mother had said it was endearing to see him talk solemnly to a nun while surreptitiously handing out cigarettes to the smokers among the women. With his charges and religious duties at Varlungo, he had little time left to devote to his studies, a sacrifice he accepted. He said he would catch up later, when the dark cloud passed. Now, he had a more important task: saving the lives of other human beings, the Jews in his care.

On the afternoon of December 10, I ran out to hand a letter to the cleaning lady, our courier to Mother through Don Giovanni. As I approached the orphanage entrance, I was shocked to see Mother and Aunt Sonia standing before me. Behind them, holding their suitcases and looking ill at ease, stood a man of about fifty with a ruddy complexion—Giacinto, the convent's handyman.

I embraced Mother. "What are you doing here?"

"I have to leave the convent," Mother said anxiously. "I just found out. Where's Harry?"

I ran to fetch him and Willy. We sat in the parlor while Mother related what had happened. There were more arrests after the big raid of November 6, and Catholic institutions were no longer secure. Don Giovanni got the idea of hiding the women and children in an underground cave in back of the vegetable garden near the wall that surrounded the convent grounds, tool shacks, and greenhouses. It was a storage room for flowerpots and gardening tools, hidden behind a building with a water reservoir on its roof. To get to the storage room, they had to go down a few steps to a decrepit door, then down a few more into the vaulted cave lined with stone benches. Don Giovanni had straw laid across the benches, a screen of plants placed in front of the door. As additional camouflage, piles of straw and manure were heaped outside.

Mother said their group was crammed into a space of nine feet by nineteen feet, barely high enough for them to stand. They had no sun, water, heat, light, nor toilet, and little air. They urinated in a large flower pot. It created a reverberating sound, and even Mrs. Grunewald's five-year-old Diane winced every time she heard the trickle. She admonished them with her finger: "Shhhh, they will hear you!" When the pot was full, a nun removed it, always under cover of darkness. Their only light was a candle. They couldn't go out as they could have been seen from the windows of neighboring buildings. Day and night became indistinguishable, fused into a benumbing concept of time: interminable.

They sat all day on the straw-covered benches, nerves ravaged, talking in whispers. They slept either seated on the benches or stretched out on them, taking turns. A nun brought them food only at dark: soup, rolls, onions, a little coffee for the morning. With their prearranged signal, a raspy sound at the entrance, the women swung open the door and the nun shifted away the plants. For Ruth Glatt's birthday, Mother gave her ration of chestnut purée to Ruth as a gift.

Don Giovanni visited daily to reassure them and give whatever practical help he could. He brought them the latest reports from the BBC, and later the distressing news that Don Casini had been arrested.

One day in their third week underground, Don Giovanni failed to appear for his usual visit. It unnerved the women. Mother said her left palm was itching, a premonition that something unpleasant would happen. Also, she thought the nun had had a worried look on her face when she brought their food the night before, even though she had tried to mask it with, *"Poverini! Coraggio, ancora un po' di* *pazienza!*"* At the end of the week, much earlier than usual, they heard the nun's familiar signal. When they opened the door, Don Giovanni, looking anguished and pale, was standing there with the abbess.

"Don Giovanni, come in," Mother said.

"No," he answered. "I can't help you any longer; therefore I have no right to be with you."

"What happened? Please come in!"

Reluctantly, he came down with the two nuns. "Cardinal Dalla Costa sent for me. He said he was having difficulties getting Don Casini released. It's such a delicate task, he's not sure he'll succeed. If the Germans catch me, too, he won't be able to help. So he's ordered me to leave Florence for my own good. I've been walking around for three days trying to think of some way to stay, but the cardinal is adamant. I'm leaving for my hometown tonight. If they catch me, at least my family can visit me there in prison. The worst is that I must abandon you."

"My God, what will happen to us?" Aunt Sonia asked.

"I'll leave the money I've been given to provide for you. The nuns will care for you. They know the rules of this game by now, and the handyman, Giacinto, will be helpful, too. Maybe I won't have to be gone long." He stumbled with emotion over his words, looking annoyed at himself.

Mother said that two of the women, Mrs. Grunewald and Mrs. Schwartzwald, began to cry that they wouldn't have their guardian angel anymore. Don Giovanni looked stunned at the reaction to his announcement. Mother saw that he hadn't realized how much he meant to them. Moved, he turned his back to the group for a moment, in thought, and then suddenly faced it again with resolve. "No, I'm taking you all with me to

---

*"You poor things! Have courage, a little more patience!"

Treviso. We're leaving today. Whatever will become of you will become of me!"

"He's become a Jewish undercover agent," Mother said with a smile, finishing her story to us. She took Harry's hand. She said Don Giovanni had set his plan in motion immediately, disregarding only momentarily how perilous the trip could be. They would separate in twos and threes. Two of the women had decided to remain in the convent, disguised as nuns. Don Giovanni thought it less dangerous if Renée and Diane were transferred to the San Giuseppe Catholic Orphanage, which was willing to take them until he could return for them. The remaining women would follow Mother's group to Treviso the next night.

"Giacinto's taking me, Aunt Sonia, Mrs. Glatt, and her daughter Ruth to the station now." She hugged us. "I'm so glad I could say good-bye to you."

Harry began to sob. He'd never been able to accept the fact that he couldn't stay with Mother at the convent. But as long as she was in the same town and he had a way of communicating with her, he could live with the separation. The idea that Mother would now be so far away made his last bit of security crumble. I understood he was fearful of separation, but he was also headstrong, obstinate, and unpredictable, traits I found irritating. I wasn't able to be of great comfort to him now.

He continued to cry. "Be reasonable," Mother pleaded. "Treviso is Don Giovanni's home, and he'll be able to take better care of me there. The war will end soon, and we'll all be together again—Papa, too. Isn't that worth being patient a little longer?"

"No! I want to come!"

"Harry, you can't. It just isn't possible."

"But why?" Harry insisted.

"Because you're safe here. Be grateful for having such a nice hiding place. You can't ask Don Giovanni to take on an extra burden. Think of it, Harry. He has twelve people to hide and take care of! Can you understand that?"

My little brother just stared ahead, miserable, kicking the bench. It occurred to me that in our vast complex surely there was a place for Mother to do cleaning, laundry, or kitchen chores, and I said something to that effect. Harry's face lit up. "Yes!" he said eagerly.

I went to Monsignor Facibeni. I told him my mother had come to visit us before leaving for Treviso, and I would like her to meet him. "Of course, Nicola," he said kindly. "Bring her in."

We filed into his office, and he rose from his chair painfully to extend a shaky hand to Mother. She thanked him for what he was doing for us. "They're my *bambini,* too," he said. Eyes swollen with tears, Harry popped the question about Mother, adding that she would do any work to stay here. Monsignor Facibeni looked at all of us with compassion, then spoke gently to Harry. "Dear Francesco, it's more difficult for me to say no than for you to ask. You see, while it's been possible to pass you boys off as Catholics, an adult is much more conspicuous. You wouldn't be able to conceal for long that she's your mother. People would ask, 'So, how is it that she doesn't speak Italian? How could she cross the front line if she was stranded in the south? And why can't you all go back now to your home in Nice?' There are several outsiders working here, and who knows if they wouldn't compromise us all. So you see, keeping her here really helps nobody. Don't worry, Francesco, she's in good hands with Don Giovanni." It was all there. Harry couldn't argue with that.

As we came out of the office, Giacinto circled his hat in his hands nervously. "Don Giovanni may be at the station already. We must go now!"

Aunt Sonia still needed to say good-bye to Sylvia at the Catholic boarding school. We quickly kissed and embraced. Harry was crying again, and Mother, too. Giacinto picked up the valises. Harry, Willy, and I followed them into the street. Harry ran and held on to Mother's coat. I tried to restrain him, but he wouldn't let go. He was hysterical. "I want to come along, take me with you!" He was attracting unwelcome attention. People on the opposite sidewalk stopped, puzzled. Aunt Sonia and Giacinto kept walking. Mother tried to keep up with them, but Harry was still clinging to her coat. Finally, I grabbed him by the waist, pulled him away, and tried to soothe him. The distance between Mother and us increased. It was an awful moment. Before disappearing at the corner, she turned around once more, waved, and blew us a kiss through her tears.

Don Giovanni's ecclesiastical couriers let us know that Mother was safe in Treviso. I later learned from her that German soldiers had swarmed over Florence's railroad station while she was there. Swells of civilians spilled in and out of waiting rooms, bundles and *bambini* in tow, ears cocked for an announcement of a train's arrival or the scream of air-raid sirens. Mother, Aunt Sonia, and Giacinto found a dimly lit spot in the main hall from where they would be able to see Don Giovanni arrive. Mother's eyes were still swollen from the farewell ordeal with Harry. After more than three weeks of isolation underground, the sheer size and noise of the mass of humanity unnerved her. She was uncomfortable standing in one spot under such tension but preferred it to sitting in the waiting room, which could be a trap in case of an identification check. On her feet she could see police coming or detect any suspicious-looking plainclothesmen. The group made small talk, but the conversation always returned obsessively to Don

Giovanni's whereabouts. "Please don't worry, ladies," said Giacinto. "He'll be here shortly."

Giacinto wasn't much of a talker, but he was honest and trustworthy, a genuinely good soul. Devoted to Don Giovanni and the convent, he was ready to help with any task asked of him, even when it fell outside of his gardener and handyman expertise. Mother wasn't sure he really understood the surreptitious maneuverings and the dangers to him, but it was apparent that whatever was of importance to Don Giovanni mattered greatly to Giacinto.

When I had gone to visit Mother during the time I was still hidden in the theater, I couldn't suppress a giggle whenever I saw Giacinto, Don Giovanni, and his housekeeper, Ermida, walking together. Don Giovanni's pronounced limp came from his calcified knee. Ermida limped, too, but on the other leg, in a somewhat different rhythm. To complete the trio's crazy dance, Giacinto was also afflicted with a bad limp. Each was out of step with the other, collectively creating a chaotic to-and-fro, up-and-down choreography, as if caused by a puppeteer with hopelessly entangled wires.

By 8:00 p.m., Mother and the others had waited at the station an hour with no sign of Don Giovanni. Giacinto looked anxious. Finally, he said he had some important chores at the convent and could stay no longer. Mother and Aunt Sonia were petrified. Giacinto could at least answer for them in Italian if a stranger accosted them. He wished the two women good luck, his face further reddened by emotion, and limped away.

It was past midnight when Don Giovanni finally arrived with Mrs. Glatt and Ruth. "Sorry, so many things to do for everyone remaining behind. Now, on the train you mustn't talk to each other. If someone recognizes me, and I don't trust him, I won't talk to you, either. And in Treviso it might be better if we aren't seen together. Just watch me, get off where I do, and follow, but not closely. Let's go." He was brusque and businesslike. He said he was worried that a plainclothesman might have tailed him. As long as he was still in Florence, he didn't feel safe.

They boarded a coach and squeezed through the crowd jamming the corridor, pleading, *"Permesso? Permesso?"* All seats were taken. Even on benches that were meant for three passengers, four sat ramrod straight on the edges, knees pressed together, suitcases and packages on their laps, overhead, underneath, everywhere. Children wailed while couples traded seats to reunite families, angry voices raised in spirited flare-ups. It was a trainload of irascible, overtired people. Soon the clanking of wheels drowned out all the other noises as the train sped across Tuscany.

As a courtesy to a man of the cloth, a passenger offered Don Giovanni his seat, but he declined. It would be easier to anticipate trouble, standing in the corridor. He hovered not far from Mother, who pressed her forehead against the cold window to ease a throbbing headache. But the rattling of the pane only made it worse. She sat on her suitcase, a few feet from Mrs. Glatt's daughter. Ruth was seventeen and very pretty. A young Italian began talking to her. She ignored him, but soon his hand was caressing her knee. Ruth looked at Mother, mortified. Don Giovanni intervened sternly, "Don't you see the *signorina* doesn't want to be bothered?" The young man skulked away.

Don Giovanni came over and sat down next to Mother, trying to find room for his stiff leg. "You had a hard day, Signora, I know," he said soothingly. "The sudden departure, the separation from your sons. Giacinto told me everything. But don't worry, things will improve. Try to rest."

In the early morning they got off in Mestre, a city half an hour from Treviso, where Don Giovanni had a sister who was in a convent. There she took the women to a washroom with white basins, crisp towels, running water, soap! They were clean again after weeks of subterranean existence. Then she brought them to a lunch table covered with a beautiful hand-embroidered cloth and with food, which brought forth girlish oohs and ahs. A nun came to tell Don Giovanni that his lunch was ready in another room. "Thank you," he said, "but I'll eat here with my friends." When they were alone for a moment, Don Giovanni grabbed fruit and rolls from the baskets with both hands and passed them around. "Quick, hide them in your pockets. We may need them." The women hesitated, but he urged them on, "Hurry, don't be ashamed!"

They arrived in Treviso in late afternoon, after an eighteen-hour journey. Don Giovanni led the way to the Seminario Vescovile, a theological school and his alma mater. Once safe in the large waiting room he said, "*Grazie a Dio,* we've made it. Now wait for me here. I have to find my colleagues."

He was not gone long when a man in working clothes, per-haps a janitor, walked into the room. "Yes, are you waiting for someone?"

Mother haltingly answered, "Don Giovanni di Firenze." Any more would have betrayed her poor Italian. The man went upstairs.

A few moments later a black-cloaked priest came in. He politely asked the same question and got the same answer. He was about thirty, lanky, with a thin, intelligent face, high cheekbones, and a dignified presence. He smiled reassuringly—seemingly unconcerned by two rows of tobacco-stained teeth—then excused himself.

Don Giovanni returned, accompanied by a short, chubby priest. "This is Don Bortoluzzi," he beamed. "He's a professor at the Collegio Pio X where I used to be assistant rector. Now, I must ask you to be patient a little longer," he added. "I need one more accomplice." And off he went.

Don Giovanni came back to the waiting room with the same lanky priest Mother had seen earlier. He was slightly taller than Don Giovanni. He smiled knowingly at the women to show he'd already understood their predicament. "This," said Don Giovanni, "is my good friend Don Angelo Dalla Torre. We were classmates and were ordained together at the Seminario Vescovile. Now he's a professor of Italian, Latin, history, and geography at the Seminario."

"When Don Giovanni told me he had a group of persecuted people with him, I said, '*Senti,* I saw them downstairs.' Say no more. I'll give you any help you need." Don Angelo was soft-spoken, with a calmer disposition than his excitable friend's.

The three priests sat down to discuss which local people could be trusted and how to persuade them to incur the risks of hiding foreign Jews when their own nationals were looking for shelter, too. There were other problems as well. Food was strictly rationed through official identity cards, and Mother and the other women needed underwear. How would the priests go about acquiring brassieres and sanitary napkins? Finally, a priest caught hiding Jews could provoke the Germans into retaliating against his institution. Neither Don Angelo nor Don Bortoluzzi had had previous experience in clandestine operations. In their eyes, Don Giovanni was the expert, but he would have to be discreet. Treviso had only fifty thousand people, and everyone knew him. He was certain to have been noticed upon his return, especially with a bevy of strange women.

The priests prevailed upon the convent of Francescane Sisters to board Mother, Sonia, and the Glatts, who posed as unfortunate French refugees with Italian husbands at war. The chief inspectress for the province's Fascist organizations lived in the convent. Don Bortoluzzi was certain that the Germans wouldn't be looking for Jews there. But to allay suspicions, Mother and the others would have to attend church and comport themselves as born, practicing Catholics. Mother asked Don Giovanni what they were required to do at confession. "Simple," he said. "Kneel on the other side of the partition, tell me what you had for breakfast, and I'll tell you what I had for lunch."

As all rooms were occupied at the convent, they moved into a small, one-story house that stood adjacent to it, but there were no blankets or mattresses. Don Bortoluzzi said, *"Ci penso io,"** returned to his Collegio next door, "borrowed" some and, at a prearranged time, threw them over the wall. He also sent flying some wood for the stove. Mother had her first good night's sleep since before moving into the cave.

---

*"I'll take care of that."

Chapter Seventeen

After nearly seven weeks at the Orfanotrofio, boys and person-nel came to accept us as part of Monsignor Facibeni's "family." Our little, daily routine helped reinforce our sense of security. I spent most of my time reading, writing, and philosophizing about the human condition. Our Italian had improved enough to carry on simple conversations. I had even mastered the soft letter *c* in true Tuscan fashion. Willy and Harry didn't have the patience to stay indoors. They lent a hand at odd chores around the complex and played with the boys, especially enjoying weekly soccer matches after classes.

But Harry wasn't happy. He still hadn't resigned himself to the orphanage as the place for him, however safe or temporary. In every letter he pleaded with Mother, "I want to come, I want to be with you," and nagged me constantly about it, too.

I would have liked him to find protection in me, but didn't know how to give him the special cuddling he needed. I tried to reason with him, "What do you think I can do? Nothing. Be sensible, Harry, this is war, and even in peacetime nobody always gets his way. Let's be grateful that we have news from Mother and that all of us are safe." But when could he go to Treviso? he persisted.

Beppino, the simpleminded, roly-poly church sexton, pro-vided Harry with some moments of pleasure when he allowed him to take part in his bell-ringing ceremony in the *campanile*. As they swung the bells to and fro, Beppino's eyes glowing, Harry coaxed from them an ear-splitting *boommm...boommm*.

The daily air raids and bomber squadrons rumbling through the sky had also become routine. We'd grown carelessly used to them. However, every night before going to bed, we still faithfully reactivated our elaborate security system of locked doors and windows, rope from the nail to the door separating our two rooms, and, the ultimate weapon, the thicker rope that led down the wall into the church.

Safety no longer an obsession now, we talked incessantly of food. The meager meals the orphanage provided were far from adequate. The Italian orphans had an advantage: relatives brought them packages of salami, bread, cheese, fruit, even pocket money. We had nothing. We couldn't even buy a handful of sunflower seeds from the old vendor stationed in front of the church. I could have eaten bricks. During the day I often lay jackknifed on the bed to still my hunger pains. I had vivid dreams of Mother's *Shabbat* chicken noodle soup with sliced carrots floating around, *Pökelfleisch* with potato salad, bits of rollmops, or *matjes* herring on rye bread topped with chopped parsley.

We looked on with growling stomachs as the other boys bit into their delicious reserves. They never offered any, and we were ashamed to ask. Food ranked way above friendship. Willy once started a conversation with a boy who had half of his apple left. Right after his hello, Willy blurted, "May I have a bite, please?" The boy quickly choked down the rest and mumbled, *"Non c'è più."**

Concetta, a cross-eyed wisp of a woman, was the sister in charge of food distribution in the large refectory. Her voice had acquired a shrill varnish after years of yelling at hordes of hungry, undisciplined boys. At four each afternoon, she unlocked the kitchen cupboard where bread was stored and handed one slice through the serving window to each boy lined up. Morino,

---

*"There's nothing left."

a handsome and intelligent mulatto with a blinding white smile, the abandoned offspring of an Italian stationed in Cyrenaica in North Africa, often sneaked up behind Concetta and stole a whole loaf of bread, undetected. It was like seeing an artist at work. We thought of doing a similar trick, but the orphans accorded us special respect as the padre's personal guests. So we were trapped by our special status. Willy became an expert at shooting marbles, occasionally trading a handful of them for a bread roll. Up in our room we would divide it fairly in three pieces, a towel spread on our laps to catch any falling crumbs. It had the same pacifying effect as a banana on King Kong.

One day, however, Willy produced a whole, gorgeous loaf of bread from under his jacket. "Please tell me I'm not dreaming," I said.

"Ludi, I've never seen anything like it. It was beautiful. Concetta wasn't there. Morino broke the lock on the cupboard and he stood on a chair zipping the loaves to us like artillery shells. I grabbed one and cleared out. *Bon appétit!*"

On one cold December afternoon, I got up after a long stretch of text-chewing at my table. The room had no heat, and to restore circulation I went out for a short walk through the orphanage grounds. It was around five o'clock, already night-fall. As I passed the main building, the kitchen door opened and a shaft of light ripped the darkness before me. Concetta and a chubby nun were getting ready to carry out a heavy kettle of steaming soup.

Food! Of course, I stopped.

"Can I be of assistance?" I inquired politely.

"Oh, yes, please, if you're not too busy."

"But certainly, I'll be glad to help."

"In that case, stay here, Caterina," Concetta said. She gave me a large plate of fish to carry and took another plate of food herself. We lifted the soup kettle with our free hands and carried it between us. We passed the tree-lined main driveway, under the archway, the refectory, workshops, and classrooms, the playing field, all in near darkness. Classes were still in session, heavy curtains drawn in accordance with civil-defense blackout regulations. Light trickled through the cracks. At the far end of the playing field we stopped at a two-story house where twenty alumni lived.

Concetta and I brought the kettle and the plates into the dining room. She said, *"Grazie tanto,"* and I left, disappointed she hadn't offered me a morsel. The fellows living there got man-size meals. On the way back, the food's fragrance clung to my nostrils, and I began to dream up a plan.

Willy and Harry had the same reaction: "Too risky."

"But it's food. Let's liberate some!"

The next evening Willy circled the field of workshops to make sure all the curtains were closed. Then we showed up at the kitchen door. "Mario has come to help me," I said. "That kettle's a bit heavy for you, Sister." Willy nodded with his Stan Laurel grin. *"Ah, bene, bene,"* Concetta agreed. She was so severely cross-eyed that she was speaking to Willy while looking at me.

Each of us took a tray of food in one hand and carried the soup kettle between us. A large plate of food covered it. Concetta walked ahead, lighting the way with a flashlight. As we crossed the playing field, Harry came out from under the archway. Unnoticed, he walked slouched down behind us, grabbing small amounts of food from the trays and kettle plate and hiding them under his regulation cape. Just before we reached the house he disappeared. A few minutes later we were back in our rooms, sharing the booty.

Henceforth our appearance for voluntary kitchen duty became established procedure. With the little but regular additional supply of food, the war seemed less tragic, the daily siren blasts less irritating, a German defeat less unlikely, and hope for a life without persecution more permissible.

To spread the risks fairly, each took his turn as thief. There was variety in the morsels we daily pilfered from the trays, yet that unattainable hot soup was always tempting. I remembered a flower vase standing in a niche of a school building staircase. I'd never seen any flowers in it. Through long disuse, cobwebs and sediment had collected inside. I took it home, then washed and scrubbed it until the ceramic sparkled.

I sneaked up on the food convoy. Then, stooped à la Groucho Marx, I removed the plate resting on the kettle, balanced it like a waiter on the palm of one hand, while with the other dipped the flower vase into the soup. When I tried to lift it out again it slipped, and in horror I saw it disappear to the bottom of the hot kettle. Had it been thick minestrone or *fagioli*, it might have slowed its sinking. But in this thin vermicelli broth, it just went plop. I cursed to myself.

"What's the matter?" Willy hissed from the side of his mouth.

"I lost the vase in the kettle!"

"*Gewalt 'n Geschriggen!*"* he wailed.

Harry was seized with uncontrollable giggles.

"What's going on, boys?" Concetta inquired.

"I was just telling Francesco a funny story," Willy replied quickly.

I threw my cape back over my shoulders, rolled up my shirt sleeves, and once more plunged my arm into the steaming soup. We were nearing the house. The boys purposely dawdled, but I still couldn't get hold of the vase. It was like trying to catch a goldfish. I pulled my arm from the scorching heat. We were less than thirty feet from the house. Again I dived back into the

---

*A Yiddish cry of lamentation, untranslatable.

soup, still balancing the platter with my other hand. I splashed and fumbled furiously, got a precarious hold on the vase, then lost it again.

"*Nu?*" Willy asked anxiously.

"Nothing," I grumbled.

Ten feet away I made one last desperate attempt but failed again. Just before the door opened I put the plate back on top of the kettle and hid. Hot steam rose from my arm dripping with noodles. Aghast, I looked on as the boys carried in the kettle, convinced that within the hour the whole orphanage would be buzzing over the phenomenon of the emerging flower vase. Unbelievably, nothing happened.

The next time it was my turn to play thief, I spotted herring among the other goodies heaped on the plate covering the soup kettle. The plate had an upended dish over it to keep the food clean. Herring! I couldn't wait and helped myself to one. I took a false step, and the porcelain dish snapped back on the plate with a sharp plink. Concetta veered around abruptly and the beam of her flashlight hit me full face, the herring's tail sticking out of my mouth. I prayed a hole would open in the ground and cover me. I stood paralyzed in the glaring light, the stupid herring pointing at the nun. Stuck halfway down my throat, I couldn't swallow it. It would have been disrespectful. Willy's jaw dropped and Harry nearly lost his grip on the kettle. I yanked the herring out of my mouth, said, "*Scusi, Sorella,*" and disappeared into the night.

Our kitchen duty came to an end by mutual, though unvoiced, agreement.

Chapter Eighteen

WHAT I DIDN'T KNOW AT THE TIME

Following the Nazis' mass raids of November and early December 1943 in Florence, thousands of Jews were deported to concentration camps, but the Jewish Committee members were still being held at Murate Prison. Despite several interventions, even Cardinal Elia Dalla Costa had been unable to obtain Don Casini's release. To alleviate their plight somewhat, the cardinal sent the prisoners food parcels regularly, and the Italian warden allowed his Jewish inmates to eat theirs in his office.

Three weeks of intensive interrogation and brutality did not bring the Germans any closer to their fancied spy-network, but they did not give up. Around the middle of December they played their trump card. Before dawn Joseph Ziegler was jolted out of his sleep and brought to the warden's office. Two armed Carabinieri were waiting. They got papers signed for the prisoner's transfer and took him away in a car. The ride, during which not a word was spoken, ended a short time later in an open field. The Carabinieri ordered Ziegler out.

An officer and two SS men from the Villa Triste unit came up to him. "Ziegler, good morning," the officer said. "You realize where you are, of course. Those men over there are going to be shot before the first ray of daylight. Perhaps you'll tell the truth now. If not, you'll join them. This is your last chance."

In the blackness Ziegler could make out a group of German soldiers and, squatting on the ground some distance away, a small knot of civilians. "All right," he said. "Lost is lost. I'll talk."

The SS took Ziegler back to the Villa Triste. In the interrogation room, one of the soldiers inserted a sheet of paper in a typewriter. The SS officer crossed his arms and enjoined, "Go ahead, Ziegler, I'm listening."

"What exactly do you want from my life?" Ziegler blurted out. "I've told you the truth all along, and it doesn't satisfy you. So, please tell me what you want to hear, and I'll give it to you, custom-made."

The SS officer dragged Ziegler into an adjoining bathroom. He filled the tub with near-freezing water and forced Ziegler to sit in it. Then he regulated the shower to drip at a slow but steady rhythm on Ziegler's head. He was kept in the tub until late at night. The SS sent his food parcel back to the cardinal with the notation fucilato.*

On December 21, Ziegler and Don Casini were brought once more from their cells to the Villa Triste. They were the only prisoners in the small Volkswagen. It was the second time they had seen each other. Haggard, Ziegler dropped his handkerchief and, bending down, mumbled between coughs, "Please, help me." The guard sharply ordered him to shut up.

They were separated at the Villa. While Don Casini waited in the corridor, a passing guard winked at him. Perplexed, Don Casini wondered what that meant. A few minutes later he faced the SS captain, and the woman interpreter relayed, "You could be free tonight if you answer right."

"In that case, I hope the questions will be easy."

It turned out the questions were the same ones the captain had been pursuing all along. He was fixated on Ziegler and his espionage system.

"There's really nothing I can add," Don Casini said. "I just know him to be a generous donor. In fact, I find his unselfish involvement with other refugees admirable. With his wealth, he could easily have sat out the war. What more did I need to know about a man like that? Besides, I can't even talk to him. He doesn't speak Italian."

The captain remained silent for a moment, and then dropped the ruler he was toying with. "All right, we'll let you go."

The release had been decided beforehand, the last interrogation merely pro forma. Either the Germans had decided that Don Casini was not an "agent" after all or else the Vatican's intercession had been effective. After Cardinal Dalla Costa's plea, the Vatican had told the Germans, "If you have a case

---

*Shot (executed).

against Don Casini, put him in front of a military tribunal. If not, set him free. It is nearly Christmas, and his congregation demands its priest."

The captain signed some papers and left the room with them. Don Casini spotted his envelope lying among some dossiers on the filing cabinet. The interpreter smiled, "Well, how does it feel to know you won't see the Murate again?"

"Wonderful, of course. But excuse me, don't I get my things back?"

"Why, yes." She took the envelope and handed it back to him. He put it in his cassock. Then, with one hand tucked inside, he tore from his breviary the endpaper containing the compromising addresses and slipped it under his shirt.

In late afternoon Don Casini was released. He had been in German hands for almost four weeks without revealing anything.

The Jewish Committee members remained incarcerated in Florence another month, were then sent to San Vittore Prison in Milan, and from there to Auschwitz on January 30, 1944. Cantoni succeeded in jumping off the train in Bolzano, Italy. During her two-month imprisonment in Florence, Anna Cassuto steadfastly denied that she was the rabbi's wife; her four children and parents were still safely hidden in town. When she heard that the men were about to be deported, she admitted her true identity. She was deported with her husband in the same sealed wagon. The official German transportation order, however, still listed her as Ledig ("single").

Chapter Nineteen

The day before Christmas 1943, Don Giovanni came to see us at the Orfanotrofio. He said everyone at the Francescane convent was well. He'd been rehearsing with the women how to say the Rosary, Pater Noster, and Ave Maria prayers, and how to make the Sign of the Cross so they could blend into the crowds at the upcoming midnight Christmas Mass. Mother had become quite adept at tipping her fingers into holy water along with other worshippers.

The priest put his arm around Harry. "I went to see the bishop. Because you're still young, he's allowing me to take you along with Mrs. Grunewald's little daughter Diane, to stay in the convent with your mother. Harry jumped in the air, almost knocking Don Giovanni to the ground.

We arranged for me to bring Harry to the train station at seven o'clock in the evening the Monday after Christmas. Don Giovanni gave Willy and me money to have passport pictures taken and told me to bring them along. "What for?" I asked.

"If I can get you forged papers, I want to be ready."

Christmas night we listened with the priests and orphans to Pope Pius XII's radio broadcast from Rome. It was the first time I'd heard a pope speak. He bemoaned the tragedy of war, the destruction, the bloodletting. He appealed for reason, peace, justice. I wished that his message would have some impact, but felt nothing would change. I envied those around me their belief that the world would heed the pope's plea.

Don Nello had coached us for the midnight Christmas Mass, but orphans were so spread out among the overflow crowd that no one could tell whether we'd received the Eucharist.

When I arrived with Harry at the train station on Monday, December 27, I hardly recognized Don Giovanni. He was wearing a suit and tie. "Easier to melt in the crowd," he explained. Three times in the past few weeks he'd been seen coming and going from the Treviso station with strangers in tow. A priest in nearby Ormelle had even remarked about Mrs. Tarnover, "You know, that pregnant woman you put up at the Oderzo Hospital? People are talking about you."

Don Giovanni had chuckled, "Let them talk." He said he was glad to have diverted him from the truth but worried he was still in danger of being apprehended in Florence. There were guards riding on trains, positioned at platforms and ticket checkpoints at the central station and in Rifredi's. "Your mother showed me how to fix my tie properly," he added, self-consciously touching the unfamiliar knot at his throat.

Little Diane and another girl were with him. He introduced us to Renée Czopp. She was about thirteen, small in stature, with enormous, gleaming, charcoal eyes in an intelligent face, and given to blushing easily. Don Giovanni said the mother superior at the orphanage had tried to convert Renée to Catholicism. He'd gone to speak to her.

"Converting Jews caught in the Nazi horror should not be your reward for saving their lives," he'd said. "God has placed them at our mercy, and we must do our duty. Our own war victims can eat tree roots, if necessary. They're free to move about and to fend for themselves. These children are not. Are you willing to help them or not?" But defiantly the mother superior only stared back at him in silence.

Angry, Don Giovanni had returned to Renée and said, "Pack your valise! You're leaving with me today." He was taking her to the Francescane convent, too.

I continued to talk to him in the time remaining. I sensed Renée was piqued that I was ignoring her. Well, after all, she was much too young for me. I was grown up! With Don Giovanni I could be all business and discuss important matters. But in truth, I was uncomfortable around girls. They made me stutter. I had no idea what to say to them and, afraid to sound foolish, felt the safest strategy was to remain remote. I was fifteen when our family had fled Paris, and in the three years since of running, hiding, and trembling daily for my life, young girls had rarely crossed my path.

When the time came to take leave, I embraced Harry and said, "I'm sad to see you go, Gingel, but at the same time I'm happy for you and Mother. Just one thing: Don't make a nuisance of yourself. Don Giovanni already has enough on his mind, and when you're unreasonable it upsets Mother very much. Take good care of her, you hear?" I hugged him tightly. Who knew when and if there would be a reunion? I was sad at the prospect of remaining alone with Willy. As amusing a fellow as he was, he was not my brother. As they boarded the train, I called good-bye to the others, and then left. There was no point in waiting until it pulled out and exposing myself to additional danger, for I was alone, without the protective presence of Don Giovanni.

A railroad station was the last place in which a Jew in hiding wanted to find himself. That's where one was most likely to get cornered. Nazi and Fascist uniforms were everywhere, and God only knew how many Secret Service trench coats. Most evident were the German military police. They were tall devils, walking in pairs in impeccably fitted and pressed gray uniforms, gloved hands joined behind their backs, and simonized boots clicking in slow, synchronized rhythm. A polished metal plate with the engraved word *Feldgendarmerie* hung from their necks by a chain like a wine steward's emblem, and it swung on their chests as they watchfully zigzagged through the crowd.

It was dark. As I hurried to catch the tramway back to Rifredi, a feeling of fear took hold of me. I realized it was my first time out in town by myself since I'd jumped the garrison wall. The Orfanotrofio cape was the only identification I had. I reached my destination without incident, and it felt wonderful to be back. I realized the Orfanotrofio had become my home.

A couple of weeks later, one of Don Giovanni's trusted messengers brought news from Treviso. Relief! Harry and the girls had arrived safely. The scheduled transfer of those from Florence was now completed. Don Giovanni would later tell me there was one scary moment aboard the train. He'd warned the children to keep their voices and chatter down to a minimum. They had found a compartment with four empty seats, only a dim blue night bulb above the sliding door. He took one side, and Harry, Renée, and Diane the other. Renée and Harry giggled when they felt Don Giovanni's rigid leg probing and poking in the dark until it came to rest on the bench between them. Suddenly, the door slid open and a flashlight shone on them. Two Italian militiamen with rifles over their shoulders demanded, *"Documenti!"* Don Giovanni straightened up and warned the children with his eyes to stay quiet. He was worried because his ID showed him in clerical dress. One of the soldiers went ahead to the next compartment while the remaining one examined Don Giovanni's card, taking a long time comparing facial features. Don Giovanni had told the children that if he were arrested, they were to proceed to Treviso on their own and ask for Don Angelo at the Seminario Vescovile. Earlier, Renée had proudly shown Harry her bulging coat lapel, where Don Giovanni had sewn in extra money for an emergency.

When the militiaman looked at the children, even five-year-old Diane shrank up so much, she practically disappeared into her seat. He asked Don Giovanni, "Are these children traveling with you?"

"Yes."

"And this young lady?" pointing to Renée.

"My sister."

"Va bene." The militiaman handed the card back, closed the door, and went on. Would he have been so lenient if his partner had still been there? Had he sensed the group's distress?

When the group reached Treviso, Mother related an incident that occurred at Christmas Mass. She, Aunt Sonia, the Glatts, and the others had arrived near midnight. Before long a crowd of over fifty people filled the convent chapel. The Mass was being celebrated by Don De Zotti, Don Giovanni's friend from the Collegio next door. Don Giovanni had told Mother, "Don't worry, he knows about you. You're already familiar with the rituals, so just watch the others and copy them. I understand how difficult this will be for you. But concentrate on your families and how one day you'll be reunited."

At Mass, the women moved up front to be near Don De Zotti, feeling safer there. Mother was impressed with the grandeur of the occasion: the festively adorned altar, the solemnity of the Latin service, the fervor of the worshippers and singing of hymns. She followed the ritual, genuflected at the right times, everything going well. She watched with interest as Don De Zotti held up what looked like a piece of round *matzo*, solemnly showing it to the congregation and giving a blessing. He then turned to the altar, ate the *"matzo,"* and drank from the chalice. At that moment a crowd of communicants surged toward the altar rail. Since she was at the front, Mother said she was swept forward, too.

CHAPTER NINETEEN

Don De Zotti held the chalice and, accompanied by an altar boy, came down the steps toward the rail. Mother watched the first row of worshippers each kneel down with rapture to swallow a small wafer offered by Don De Zotti. Mother felt uneasy, not knowing what was going on. If this was holy communion, Don Giovanni had not explained it. The crowd pressed on. She followed. When it was her turn, she knelt, closed her eyes, and put on an expression that she felt sure was a good simulation of what she'd seen among the others. With eyes closed, hands clasped, and mouth open, she waited. She felt Don De Zotti hesitate before her. She opened her eyes. The altar boy, holding the communion plate under her chin, glanced up at Don De Zotti. The priest's voice broke as he pronounced, "May the body of our Lord Jesus Christ keep your soul for eternal life." He gave her the host, reluctantly, then to the other Jewish women as well. When she swallowed it, Mother thought it actually tasted good, and was rather pleased that she'd acquitted herself so well in this unfamiliar situation.

Don De Zotti pronounced the end of the Mass, *"Dominus Vobiscum. Ite Missa Est."*

The women returned to their rooms. An hour later, Mother was taken aback when Don Angelo and Don De Zotti came to see them. "Ladies, ladies," Don Angelo wailed. "It's a terrible thing that happened. No one would have noticed if you hadn't taken the host from Don De Zotti. It's a sacred ritual, the giving of Christ's body. We're forbidden to give it to non-Christians."

Mother apologized, saying they meant no disrespect, that they thought they were expected to take part in the entire ritual. The priests understood that the women didn't realize they'd created an imbroglio. They all finally agreed that it was a Christmas to remember. Mother decided that next time she would behave less like a devout Catholic.

Louis Goldman with Don Giovanni in later years

Louis Goldman at the former garrison; Florence, 1994

Commemoration of Florence's liberation from Nazis;
Palazzo Vecchio, Florence, 1994

Sigi Hartmayer,
Louis Goldman, and
Willy Hartmayer at the
former garrison; Florence,
Italy, during 1994 com-
memoration of the
liberation of Florence
(fiftieth anniversary)

(Left to right)
Louis Goldman,
Don Facebeni
(seated), and
Don Nello, 1953

A young Louis
Goldman, 1954

The family portrait, of Pinkus Goldman, Mina Goldman,
Louis Goldman, and Harry Goldman

(Left to right) Don Giovanni, Mina Goldman (Louis
Goldman's mother), Aunt Sonia, Renée (fellow refugee),
front row; Harry, cousin Sylvia; Florence, 1945

Don Angelo Dalla Torre (left) and Don Giovanni Simioni at the grave of Harry Goldman (Louis Goldman's brother); the Nachlat Yitzchak Military Cemetery, Tel Aviv, Israel

Willy Hartmayer, Louis Goldman, Sigi Hartmayer;
1994 commemoration of the liberation of Florence

Louis Goldman
in later years
(1986)

Louis Goldman, the photographer (1967)

Chapter Twenty
WHAT I DIDN'T KNOW AT THE TIME

Don Giovanni realized that the Francescane convent's lenient policy of unchecked comings and goings opened the Jewish group hidden there to too much scrutiny. He decided to go to Venice to ask Cardinal Piazza for permission to hide Jewish women in Treviso's other Catholic institutions. Don Angelo ran his secret operation in the Seminario Vescovile complex across the street from the Patronato San Nicolo, the boardinghouse for students, teachers, and priests, where Don Giovanni also lived. He and Don Bortoluzzi cautiously checked around for permanent hiding places and were able to make new arrangements throughout Treviso and in nearby towns in the Veneto region.

Renée Czopp was assigned to an orphanage, but she had become so deeply attached to my mother that she was disconsolate at the prospect of being separated from her. Don Giovanni did not insist. They were moved together to the Figlie della Chiesa, a convent school for nuns, and were quartered in a large, empty dormitory lined with twenty-five beds. The nuns knew they were Jewish, so they no longer had to act out a spurious Catholicism. Don Giovanni often came to play the organ at services in the adjoining San Stefano Church. Mother and Renée sat and listened in a corner of the tribune.

Harry had been placed in an orphanage a few kilometers from the convent. He immediately started haggling for a location nearer to Mother. Six days later he was brought to the Patronato di San Nicolo to room with Don Giovanni, who passed him off as a relative.

Mrs. Schwartzwald and Miss Sabine Adler were transferred to a convalescent home maintained by Catholic nuns in Crocetta del Montello, twenty-seven miles from Treviso. Mrs. Wolf went to Ormelle, Don Giovanni's hometown, to lodge in a nursery school run by Elisabettine nuns. Don De Zotti took Ruth Glatt and her mother to Mestre, outside of Venice, and introduced them to his family. "These ladies are Jewish, and we're going to hide them here. Don't ask questions and don't talk." Mrs. Grunewald and Diane were put up with a reliable farmer at the nearby village of Pezzan di Carbonera. To the neighbors, she was an Alsatian woman whose Italian husband had disappeared in the war.

In early January, Don Giovanni traveled to Florence to transfer fourteen-year-old Sylvia Rosenstrauch from the Catholic school there to be with her mother Sonia in the Francescane convent in Treviso. Don Giovanni had to cajole the protective nuns into calling the cardinal's secretary at the Curia for corrob-oration, before they would agree to release the girl from the school.

To avoid bombings, trains traveling north from Florence could no longer enter Bologna's central railroad station. The passengers had to get off at San Rufillo, just south of the city, and walk eight kilometers in the middle of the night to Corticella, a small train junction north of Bologna. Don Giovanni's knee hurt from the long walk. He suggested they take hotel rooms, but Sylvia, afraid of him, refused. She had met the young priest only once before and, having recently finished reading an extensive volume on the life of the lascivious Russian priest Rasputin, was filled with apprehension about being in Don Giovanni's care. Don Giovanni finally rented a railroad worker's tool shack and Sylvia, her exhaustion overcoming her vigilance, fell asleep on a cot. Don Giovanni covered her with his overcoat and tried to catch some sleep himself. Once on the train again, however, Sylvia never left her compartment, even to use the bathroom. The customary five-hour trip took two and a half days. When they reached Treviso, Don Giovanni took Sonia aside and whispered, "Quick, take her to a toilet. I think she's about to burst."

By mid-January 1944, all the women and children were settled in their new hideouts. By not having more than two at any one place, the priest felt they had reduced their risks of capture. Don Giovanni felt it would be safe for Sylvia and her mother to be the only two remaining at the Francescane convent.

Clasping a closed umbrella and gripping the broad flat rim of his black hat to keep it from flying off, Don Giovanni Simioni leaned into the wind, limping hurriedly down the Cal Maggiore in Treviso on a January afternoon. Pedestrian traffic was sparse and he stopped only for a moment to exchange a greeting with an acquaintance. After crossing Piazza dei Signori he turned into the arcaded Corso del Popolo and entered a religious bookstore. Chimes over the door still echoed after he closed it. The proprietor looked up from his customer. "Ah! Don Giovanni, excuse me! I'll be with you shortly."

"No rush," said Don Giovanni, nodding to the customer. "I'll just browse around a little."

Books sprawled across shelves and were piled on tables: catechisms, breviaries, missals, and bibles, also crucifixes, statues, rosaries, and holy pictures. Two young theology students were absorbed in the text of a heavy leather-bound volume. The chimes sounded again. Don Giovanni turned; the customer had left. He approached the proprietor. "Well, Signor Marton, the book I ordered?"

"Yes, it finally arrived." Mr. Marton took a book from a shelf behind his cash register. He wrapped it meticulously, and Don Giovanni slipped it inside a pocket of his cassock.

"Many thanks. How much do I owe you?"

"There's time," answered Signor Marton. "You can pay me at the end of the month."

"Most kind of you. **Arrivederci**."

When he returned to the Patronato di San Nicolo, Don Giovanni went directly to his room. "Draw the curtains," he told Harry Goldman, hurrying out of his overcoat. He sat down at his desk with the book. "Lock the door."

Don Giovanni unwrapped the book and leafed through it, removing seven loose pieces of folded double-weight paper with some printed lines on them. "Tessere! Italian identification cards. All I have to do is fill them in and then someone from the underground will apply a fake official seal. Now I can make you safe and legal."

Don Giovanni had feared for his refugees if they were caught in a raid. Spread all over the area, they were no longer under his direct supervision as they had been in Florence, and he would be able to do little for them. With an "official" document to substantiate their claim that they were French but naturalized

Italians through their husbands, and that the children were Italian but raised in France, the women could then withstand interrogation.

In the large urban centers there were professional fixers who, for a hefty fee, could supply fake documents, but not in Treviso. Don Angelo argued against false papers. He believed that humane assistance should not be tarnished by an unsavory partnership with forgery. Don Giovanni had no such qualms. To save lives, even illegal means were permissible. As a priest raised in Treviso, Don Giovanni knew a large number of families. Some of the young men he had grown up with had vanished to join the partisans. Their families did not openly acknowledge it in the community, but among trusted friends who were known to despise the Germans, they talked about their sons with great pride. Don Giovanni got in touch with those families. Word was sent along the underground channels. After weeks of silence, Don Giovanni was told to contact Don Ferdinando Pasini, priest to the local clandestine Liberation Committee. Pasini had sent Don Giovanni to see Mr. Marton, whose bookstore was a vital relay point for coordinating resistance operations.

Don Giovanni intended to make two cards for Willy and me at the Madonnina del Grappa Orphanage in Florence. The remaining five were for Harry and the women and girls hidden in Treviso, who were exposed there to a higher concentration of Germans and Italian Fascists. The other refugees were in smaller, relatively safer villages. The farmer sheltering Mrs. Grunewald in Pezzan di Carbonera had managed to get a genuine card for her from the municipality without questions asked. On it, her name was Odette Fiorentino.

Don Giovanni took everyone to a portrait studio in town for passport photographs. Then he composed a detailed list of the fictional data he would use for each. He also fabricated complete family histories for them to sound more convincing in case of an interrogation. When the photographs were ready, he borrowed a typewriter, and then waited for evening. During the day, there was always the chance someone might come knocking on his door. He would have to make the caller wait while he hid the incriminating evidence. The caller, once admitted, might then reach the wrong conclusion about why Don Giovanni had locked himself in with young Harry.

As the Patronato's priests and boarders began to retire for the night, Don Giovanni listened for receding steps in the corridor. "Now it's all right," he said. Harry checked the door, and then sat near the desk.

Don Giovanni first did some random typing to familiarize himself with the machine. A mistake could mean the loss of a card. Corrections were not possible. There were no erasures on genuine cards. After much practice, he inserted the first card in the typewriter, then carefully pecked out one letter at a time.

Slowly, Mina Goldman emerged as Ida Capaldi. Then, separately for each subsequent card, he filled in fake data opposite the lines for **father, mother, born at, nationality, profession, place of residence, street,** and **date of issue.** The room's silence amplified the clicking of the keys. Don Giovanni cringed at the noise he was making. Aunt Sonia Rosenstrauch and cousin Sylvia were renamed Maria and Silvia Borelli. Willy Hartmayer and Harry and Louis Goldman officially became Mario, Francesco, and Nicola Capaldi, cousins born in Bitonto, a small, southern town near Bari.

Several days earlier Don Giovanni had asked Mother, "How old is Ludi?"

"Eighteen. He'll be nineteen in June."

"I'll give him seventeen."

"But why?"

"You never know. It's better to be younger."

Don Giovanni also made Willy younger by a year.

His work proceeded late into the night. When he had finished typing he started pasting on the photos. The last step required a personal touch: the signature of the municipality official—Per il Sindaco, il Delegato. He signed the same false name at the bottom of each card.

Don Giovanni leaned back and examined the finished results. There, in front of him, were the means that could guarantee the survival of his Jews.

Dawn was only an hour away. And so, Don Giovanni Simioni, ordained diocesan priest of the Catholic Church and amateur forger, having violated the laws of the state to protect Jewish refugees and risking thereby the severest penalties, finally went to bed, exhausted but happy.

He returned the "book" to Mr. Marton and picked it up a few days later. Neatly embossed over the lower part of each card's photograph and the adjoining area was the circular seal: *Comune di Bari*. When Don Giovanni handed the cards to the women, he emphasized that unless they thoroughly memorized all the data in them, the cards would be worthless. Accordingly, even as they lay in bed awaiting sleep, Mother and Aunt Sonia cross-examined each other to gain the deep-rooted familiarity they needed to answer any question without hesitation.

When Mrs. Tarnover had arrived with Don Giovanni in November, she was in her eighth month of pregnancy. The baby still hadn't arrived as January slipped into its second half, and hospital bills were accumulating. Mrs. Tarnover had miscalculated by a month, blaming slovenly arithmetic on her bewildered state of mind and the terrifying events following her escape from Saint-Martin-Vesubie. She was also afraid her health would fail her and that she would die in labor.

"Nonsense," said Don Giovanni. "Everything will be all right. We just have to wait a little longer."

The baby arrived the first week of February. It was a boy and, according to Jewish ritual, he had to be circumcised on the eighth day after his birth. The **Brit Milah** is a hallowed religious tradition and mandatory for every male Jew, symbolically marking his solemn covenant with God. The ritual dates back four thousand years to Abraham, and even Jews whose Judaism had thinned almost out of existence would not, for hygienic reasons alone, leave their sons uncircumcised. The **bris** is performed by a **mohel**, an orthodox Jew who has received specific medical training.

"We can't have a circumcision now, Signora," said Don Giovanni when he arrived at the hospital. "You would be endangering your baby and everybody else, too."

"But it must be done, Don Giovanni!"

"Signora, please, it's impossible. This is war and there are Germans all around us. Besides, where would I find a circumciser in these times?"

"It doesn't have to be a **mohel**. Let the hospital surgeon do it. I'll do the praying."

Don Giovanni frowned. "We can't do that. Once the surgeon finds out you're Jewish, who knows to whom he'll blab? There are Fascists everywhere who wouldn't hesitate for a minute to denounce you and all of us to the Germans. Will you feel better going to a concentration camp with your boy circumcised?"

Wiping away tears, Mrs. Tarnover shook her head. "But, my God, if my poor husband knew his son hasn't had a bris!"

"In these times one has to make sacrifices. You can have it done later when this nightmare's over."

Mrs. Tarnover calmed down. Don Giovanni smiled, "Now, what name shall we give the boy?"

"Schloime."

"Schloime! Jesus!" Don Giovanni braced himself on the arm of a chair. "Signora Tarnover, you can't call him that!"

"Why not? Solomon, after his grandfather."

"Out of the question. You can't give him that name now any more than you can have him circumcised now. Our lives are hanging by a thread and you must camouflage anything Jewish." In a gentler tone he said, "Look, why don't we call him Silvio for the time being? Later on you can change it officially back to Schloime, all right?"

"If you knew how painful it is to renounce traditions that mean so much!"

He nodded, "Unfortunately, there's no other way."

"Wait a minute," Mrs. Tarnover said, panicking. "If my baby's not Jewish, then there has to be a baptism. Isn't that so? I don't want him to be baptized Catholic."

"Heavens no, of course not."

"Well, then how can we...?"

"Don't worry. When you leave the hospital you'll go live with Don Angelo's mother in Ponte di Piave. So, here we say that Silvio will be baptized there. And there we'll say he was baptized here. D'accordo?"

Chapter Twenty-One
WHAT I DIDN'T KNOW AT THE TIME

When the Germans had caught Don Casini, there had been over a hundred foreign Jews still out in the open, awaiting shelter. Padre Cipriano Ricotti, Contessa Marucchi, and Matilde Cassin had carried on the work in Florence. Most refugees had exhausted their resources while Don Casini was in prison.

The news spread rapidly when Don Casini was set free in December. His phone began ringing, but each time he cut the conversation short before anything incriminating could slip into it. There was also a rumor that among the refugees there were two who worked for the Germans, pretending to be Jews. After the experience with Marco Ischio, Don Casini was not sure whom to trust anymore. His first concern was to distribute the 400,000 lire still stowed away in his brother Tito's apartment. Through a few reliable acquaintances he informed the refugees that for the next several days he would be on the Ponte Vecchio from ten o'clock to noon, and in the Church of San Stefano in Via Porta Rossa, from four o'clock to six in the afternoon.

Florence's Ponte Vecchio, the city's oldest, most picturesque bridge, was lined on both sides with arcades in which jewelry craftsmen, since the sixteenth century, had displayed their wares. In the mornings, Don Casini mingled in the lively crowd, idly strolling near the bust of Cellini. Refugees sidled up to him and surreptitiously he slipped them allocations in proportion to the size of their families. He handed prepared envelopes of 12,000 lire to those who preferred to leave for Rome, either to hide or in the hope of proceeding farther south and perhaps even of crossing the German lines.

In the afternoons, Don Casini meditated inside the Chapel of the Madonna at San Stefano Church. Refugees wandered in, took turns kneeling next to him, and lire passed from under his cassock into their coats—a money changer in a different temple, AD 1943.

At the beginning of January, Don Casini received a plea from the bishop of Spoleto. He urgently needed funds for a small group of Jews he was hiding. Don Casini went to Spoleto with the 85,000 lire he had left. The bishop needed only 15,000. Don Casini then went back to Florence and doled out the remainder of the lire, including his own scant personal money.

On a tramway one evening, Don Casini and a friend discussed an assassination attempt that had occurred the night before at a political rally in town. A woman had tried to throw a grenade at a speaker, a prominent Fascist leader. How ironic, Don Casini commented, that the grenade exploded in the woman's hand, killing her, while the intended victim walked away, free.

As soon as Don Casini and his friend got off the tram, they were seized by two plainclothesmen who had overheard their conversation. It was February 2, 1944, barely six weeks after the SS had released him. They were whisked off to party headquarters and handed over to the Banda Carità, a group of fanatical Fascists named after Mario Carità, Florence's most militant collaborator with the Germans. While the Fascists beat Don Casini's friend, the priest kept tearing off and swallowing small bits from a list of Jewish names he had in his pocket.

The Fascists hauled Don Casini in front of Mario Carità. One of the plain-clothesmen who had made the arrest claimed that Don Casini was a known Jew-sympathizer.

"Splendid!" exclaimed Carità. "I know just the right people for him," and he phoned the SS.

"Don Casini?" the SS said. "We've already investigated him. For the time being we don't want him."

"Never mind," grumbled Carità. "We'll deal with him."

The Banda Carità held Don Casini several days while they searched for damaging evidence. They found none. Still, they brought him to trial. The district prefect sentenced him to fifteen days in prison for inciting unrest against a public official.

After Don Casini's release, Cardinal Dalla Costa ordered him to move to the countryside for a well-deserved rest, and to stay away from notoriety for a while.

One of the nuns at the Figlie della Chiesa, the convent in Treviso where Mother and Renée were hidden, remarked to the parish priest Monsignor Scattolo that the priests' personal attention to the women was unnecessary. Advised by the monsignor, Don Angelo's reaction was that whatever the implications of the remark, it did not warrant action. But he would stay alert.

The vicar-general summoned Don Angelo to his office, reporting that there was talk at police headquarters about a priest from Treviso who, dressed as a civilian, frequently went away and brought back groups of Jews. They didn't know the priest's identity but Treviso was not such a large place that they could not find out if they really wanted. The vicar said the bishop was giving Don Giovanni forty-eight hours to return to Florence. Don Angelo insisted that his friend's actions had been necessary. The supporting operation was equally vital. Was it to be discontinued? No, the vicar replied, but Don Angelo would have to take charge of it. Don Giovanni was too compromised. Therefore everyone else was in danger.

When Don Angelo gave him the news, Don Giovanni said he felt like an outcast. First he had been banished from Florence, now from Treviso, both times by the highest ecclesiastic authority. He finally consoled himself that at least some of his charges had false papers, and that he would be able to watch over the others again from his post at the Varlungo convent while he continued his university studies.

Aunt Sonia and Sylvia were visiting Mother and Renée when Don Angelo arrived. "Don Giovanni will be going back to Florence," he said, ill at ease, fumbling with his hat.

"But he promised he'd stay with us," Sonia protested.

In the four months since they had come down from the mountain, they had never been separated from Don Giovanni.

"I'm sorry, too," Don Angelo said, "but I'll take good care of you."

Before leaving for Florence, Don Giovanni gave Don Angelo the bulk of the remaining money, about 90,000 lire. Then he made a hurried round of goodbyes to the women, promising to visit them when it was safe again.

Chapter Twenty-Two

Willy and I looked at the map of Europe on our wall. My eyes panned easily over the cluster of western and central countries, and then inevitably got lost in the vastness of Russia. Its disproportionate size never ceased to awe me. Even when scaled down to a piece of paper, Russia remained a colossus I couldn't take in all at once. In January and February of 1944, we moved the pins on the Russian front progressively westward. Leningrad had finally been freed, and the Germans had been forced to evacuate Novgorod. Gigantic battles swirled between the Baltic and Black seas, a constant shifting of armies. The Germans were launching massive counteroffensives in an attempt to regain the initiative. The daily Wehrmacht communiqués, printed in the Italian newspapers, told of the annihilation of whole Russian regiments during the consolidation of the German lines. We read stupendous claims of 2,500 tanks smashed...20,000 dead...40,000 prisoners...2,000 planes downed...6,000 guns captured...20,000 vehicles destroyed. And yet, every time we found the locality on the map where those engagements were taking place, it was just a little to the left of the last battle pin.

Willy shook his head knowingly. "They can call it 'elastic defense' all they want. I, Generalissimo Wilhelm Von Hartmayer, am telling you that they're on the run! And that Berlin is getting bombed."

"Let's not be too optimistic. The Russians' winter advantage will wear off soon. Who knows if the Germans won't dig in at another Stalingrad and not be budged for another year."

136

CHAPTER TWENTY-TWO

In Italy, there was no progress. Tremendous Armageddon-like battles were being waged at Monte Cassino, but it was still in German hands. British, American, French, Polish, free Italian, Australian, Canadian, and colonial Indian troops were hurling themselves in vain at the monastery-turned-fortress. I couldn't help but admire the tenacity of the entrenched Germans. And the Allies seemed unable to push out from their Anzio beachhead. It looked as though it would take another year before Florence could entertain any hopes of being liberated.

My greatest thrill, however, was that such thoughts were now possible. It was no longer absurd to conceive that the seemingly invincible Nazi monster might indeed be beaten. Timidly, I dared to visualize a day when we would be free to go about the sweet business of life, unoppressed, unmolested, even as Jews. Weren't the people of Salerno, Naples, and Taranto—until very recently still under the Nazi yoke—at that very moment dancing in the streets and breathing freely again? I tried to imagine how it would actually be to have the terror in my heart suddenly lifted after being deprived of liberty for so long and horrible a time. What feelings would fill the vacuum? Intoxication, delirium—perhaps insanity?

I wondered how Papa was doing. No word from him, assuming he was allowed to write. He didn't know where we were, and I doubted whether he memorized the name of the convent where we'd last seen Mother. At the garrison they had said a train would be leaving for Auschwitz. I had never heard of anyone returning from that place. The guard at La Zecca had told us that Jews were being sent to labor camps to help the war effort, and that they would be well provided for; but because that favorable account came from the Germans, I was convinced of the opposite.

And yet, I couldn't accept the fact that Papa might not be alive. He was a hard worker and could adapt to difficult situations. I remembered how, in the south of France in 1942, we'd done maintenance work together along the railroad tracks, a grueling job shoveling gravel and replacing worn-out transverse beams to strengthen the track bed. He'd acquitted himself handily although he wasn't used to that kind of work, nor endowed with great physical strength. And carrying heavy loads of grapes during harvest—was that any easier? No matter what work the Germans would put him to, he would do it well. However, when they took him, his wound was still open. I assumed a doctor would change his bandages and let him regain his strength before sending him off to hard labor. Sigi must have been in the same transport. He'd stick by Papa and help him. Did the Germans permit them to stay together? I was afraid of the answers. How wretched he must feel, alone, sick, far away, terrified, and worried about us, too! Yet, I convinced myself that he would manage to survive each hardship and someday our family would be reunited.

Willy and I were not sufficiently protected against the winter's bitter cold. There was no heat in the Orfanotrofio, and our rooms had bare slate floors. After going through the whole routine of sealing the doors and laying out our escape rope, it became an act of bravery to undress and slip into the glacial bedsheets. After Harry's departure, Willy had moved into my room. For warmth, we pushed the twin beds together, lay in our underwear, back to back, rubbing our limbs, teeth clattering away, until our body heat slowly spread under our two thin blankets. Then we dozed off. Now and then I worked up enough courage to ask Maria, Monsignor Facibeni's maid and cook, for the bed warmer for the monsignor. We propped up our bedding around it to trap the warmth of its remaining embers. Our tent resembled a shrine to some glowing divinity.

Willy was even more miserable than I. In extreme cold the scars on his throat from an earlier glandular operation swelled up and became bright red, pus forming underneath. He said it was very painful, and always kept a scarf wrapped around his neck, even at night. His tonsils also gave him trouble. At the beginning of March they became so inflamed he slept in the dispensary to get proper care and to avoid infecting others. The nurse urged him to have them removed, but he was scared. We finally convinced him to have the surgery, and one morning Willy, unenthusiastically, was taken to a nearby hospital. The nurse gave him an injection in preparation for the tonsillectomy. While he waited for the surgeon, an air-raid alarm sounded, followed by explosions and machine-gun strafings. Twenty minutes later, ambulances unloaded stretchers with German soldiers, injured and dead, casualties of an attack on a troop transport. Willy took one look at the blond heads partially visible under bloodstained sheets and panicked. Doctors and nurses were too busy to pay attention to him, and in the ensuing confusion he ran away. The inflammation eventually receded, but Willy felt something had to be done to survive the cold.

I don't know where or how he pilfered them, but in a short time we had eight blankets. They gave more weight than warmth and, if we wanted to change positions, we had to lift them together and roll over at the same time. But it was an improvement. Twice a month we aired out the blankets in the courtyard, delighting in snapping them with a thunderous boom. We knew we'd achieved perfect pitch if Maria came out onto the kitchen terrace, wiping her hands on her black apron, worriedly scanning the sky for the little black puffs of antiaircraft guns. But all she heard was Beppino singing at the top of his voice as he went about his chores.

In the morning, only the thought of coffee in the refectory could propel me out of bed. I kept my socks tucked under the blankets all night for warmth. My trousers were within arm's reach, my shoes in such a position that my feet didn't have to touch the freezing stone floor. It was impossible to wash, shave, or brush our teeth. The water in the pitcher was almost frozen solid. Instead, taking turns each morning, one of us enjoyed the luxury of staying under the covers while the other, fully dressed, splashed a few drops on his eyes and ran to the kitchen to fetch a pitcher of steaming water. I cringed at the liquid ice on my face, yet felt guilty at the same time. If only I knew Papa were in a secure place, too.

One day we made the startling discovery that we weren't the only Jews in the orphanage. We'd never paid much attention to the two Italian janitors, a father and son, who kept the grounds tidy and swept the halls, courtyards, and staircases. They were always in the same tatters, mumbling in an unintelligible dialect. The old man seemed besotted or in a stupor, shoulders rounded over his broom, unseeing, unhearing. But his son must have reached the conclusion that we were Jews, for he started a conversation with us and confided, "I'm from Fiume...and Jewish."

Willy and I said nothing, too cautious to unmask ourselves to any stranger.

There was also Sandro, a short, curly haired boy of fourteen who lived, worked, and studied with the orphans. Although he betrayed his identity and curiosity no more than we did, we felt certain that Sandro was Jewish. We were always friendly with each other, but none of us ever asked questions or dropped hints.

"I really pity the poor fellow," Willy said. "Up at 6:00 a.m. and in church every morning with the boys."

Monsignor Facibeni never mentioned other Jews and we didn't probe, a mute understanding to keep secrets secret.

Chapter Twenty-Three

The first week of February 1944, Don Giovanni gave fake ID cards to Willy and me. We noticed he'd made our ages younger. He said it was safer to keep us under eighteen. At the beginning of March he returned for good. We were delighted. He gave us some pocket money and each a pair of slacks, a gift from Don Angelo.

One day in early spring, the Orfanotrofio's accountant, Signor Luigi, took me aside. He was an intelligent man of about forty-five, with a wide face that broke into a broad smile every time he saw me and Willy. He was the only person besides Monsignor Facibeni and Don Nello who knew we were Jews. His usual attire was a floppy brown overcoat and gray hat. Although not a priest, after seventeen years he belonged to the triumvirate of decision makers.

He greeted me with his enormous, toothy grin, reminding me of the French comedian Fernandel, and inquired about our well-being. Then he went on to say, somewhat apologetically, that he and the other two priests felt that since we'd already been at the orphanage for several months, with no end to the war in sight, it would be wise for us to take on some kind of occupation. Other boys were either attending school or learning a trade in the workshops, and we were doing neither. Our privilege of unsupervised idleness might come to be resented, he feared, and it would be best to prevent suspicion.

He left the choice of workshop to us. Willy and I instantly felt our professional talents would achieve their fullest potential at the *mulino,* which supplied the bread for the whole orphanage.

To our great sorrow, the master baker needed no extra help. The orphans there behaved like angels knowing how coveted their jobs were. We considered other crafts: tailoring, no, too tedious...printing, too smudgy.

Willy opted for the cobbler's shop because he already had "experience" in Saint-Martin-Vesubie, where he'd resoled his own shoes with patches of old tires. I selected the metal shop because I liked the precision it demanded. The workshop was airy and well equipped with modern lathes and machinery. In addition to serving the orphanage, it handled outside customers' orders for anything from industrial boilers to gate hinges. The foreman who came from town each day to oversee the workshop constantly despaired of the other boys' lack of serious application in shaving another fraction of a millimeter off a metal cylinder. But I enjoyed working, glad to make myself useful. Unlike Willy, I put in half-days only because I was intent on pursuing my studies.

I helped the foreman install a foolproof lock on the donations box outside the main gate and reflected on the irony of an institution devoted entirely to helping others needing to take steps against thievery. The lock seemed a sad admission of man's real nature.

In the afternoons, I returned to my cherished books or sometimes dropped in on Willy, who sat with a mouthful of nails, hammering away. He'd learned the trick of bringing up one nail at a time from the cavity of his lower jaw and was very pleased with his professional shoemaker's touch. Knowing he'd just "reloaded," I brought him a glass of water and teased, "Here, you hardworking little shoemaker, you must be thirsty." He blew a volley of nails at me.

Every orphan had a "good" uniform for special occasions: Sundays, outings, church services. Willy and I finally received ours, too, custom-made at the orphanage's own tailor shop:

medium gray pants, a straight-cut jacket, a three-quarter cape fastened at the neck with a small chain, and a cap. The metal Madonnina del Grappa emblems were pinned on both points of our jacket collars. The outfit gave us the look of military cadets rather than schoolboys in an orphanage, and we thought them splendid.

Monsignor Facibeni and Don Nello thought it would be safe for us, now dressed like the other boys, to join them for an occasional movie at the local theater. The smart uniform and prospect of seeing a movie cheered us. Every other Thursday afternoon, Willy and I eagerly lined up with about forty boys in rows of two. Don Felicino, a bony, young priest with a long, thin, pimply face magnified by an undersized pince-nez, led the column of cadets out of the orphanage. He pounced on any who strayed from their lines during the brisk, ten-minute walk to the Cinema Flora in Piazza Dalmazia.

Streets, people, cars, trolleys, shops! Being outside the confines of the orphanage was exhilarating. My eyes avidly took in the animation in the streets. Now and then, German or Italian soldiers stepped off the sidewalk to let our column through. I felt ambivalent: secure in my disguise in the midst of the orphans, yet fearful someone, somehow, would uncover us.

Halfway to Cinema Flora, the column broke ranks at the *castagnaccio* stand where a family made the popular brown, farinaceous sweet from the pulp of chestnuts. It had the look and consistency of steamed rubber, especially when hot, but it didn't taste too bad to our starved stomachs. Willy and I gorged ourselves on as much *castagnaccio* as Don Giovanni's pocket money would allow.

A little farther and we arrived at the theater. Willy and I made note of the exit locations. Lights dimmed, excited whispers died down, and the picture started weaving its magic. It was wonderful to let myself become wrapped in the unfolding story, forgetting the war, my fears, our persecution! The films were mostly Italian, some recent, some of scratchy vintage: sword epics, comedies, romances, songs, and adventures in fabled Arabian lands.

On the way back we rehashed the highlights. Later, I analyzed the films in my notes, commenting at great length on holes in the plot, development of characters, quality of editing, and especially camera shots that had impressed me.

Air raids continued with maddening regularity, even at night. We waited with other hastily dressed Rifredi residents in the darkness of the open field, ready to dive into the *rifugio*. In the silence that followed the wailing of sirens, we could see swarms of bombers and Spitfires crisscrossing, unstopped, to missions of destruction beyond Florence. We never saw German planes responding to their attackers. Perhaps the big air battles were being fought elsewhere. Occasionally, German soldiers wandered in from the street. They stood small-talking among themselves, smoking with cupped hands to shield the glow of their cigarettes.

My annoyance at having to get up from a sound sleep was often compensated by a spectacular sight: flares dropping from invisible planes suddenly illuminating the landscape as if a hundred spotlights had been switched on in the sky all at once. Hanging from almost motionless parachutes, flares helped bombers pinpoint their targets. In the garish, inundating light I felt naked and singled out. The flares burned for a long time, then slowly drifted, faded, and gave us back the night.

During day raids, instead of running to the *rifugio,* I preferred the *campanile,* the bell tower accessible only through the church. A ladder led to the first landing and from there steps at a sharp incline continued to the top. The summit's open arches afforded me a good view of passing planes, plenty of fresh air, and the advantage of standing up instead of crouching in the crowded hole. Although the *campanile* was solid rock, its engineered flexibility would make it sway instead of crumble, except on a direct hit. It had an added psychological benefit as an easily recognizable religious symbol that no God-fearing, Anglo-Saxon pilot would want to destroy.

Often, however, I was barely back in my room after an all clear when sirens started up again, as often as four or five times during the day and two or three at night. After several months of this I didn't bother to run out of the house anymore, thinking I could always make a dash to the *campanile* in time.

A generous March sun warmed my hands and flooded the room with light. It was around three in the afternoon when I perceived the first faint rumblings of bomber squadrons. I opened the window to scan the patch of blue sky visible between the buildings. A few seconds later sirens blasted. I could see no planes and went back to Huxley's *Brave New World.*

The rumblings persisted, but I'd grown accustomed to a certain pattern. They would soon reach their peak, decrease, and fade away as the bombers proceeded north on their missions to Pistoia, Livorno, La Spezia, or other cities. But these rumblings became louder and seemed to be nearing as seconds ticked away. My God, I realized, they're coming in lower!

I still couldn't see anything in my limited sky view, though I saw orphans and grown-ups running for shelter. The air reverberated with the heavy roll of engines, like a blanket of sound waves suspended overhead: *vroom...vroom...vroom.* The hypnotic droning throbbed and saturated every cubic inch of air. I deliberated whether it would be wise to run out and risk being caught in the open. No, too late! I heard the deadly, shrill whistle of bombs drilling holes through the air, the high-pitched, ear-splitting sound as they got nearer. I dived under the table. In the next instant there was a tremendous explosion. The house shook under its impact. Window panes flew across the room, breaking into a thousand tinkling shards, and a dark cloud of smoke drifted in with the stinging stench of sulfur. A rivulet of plaster, sand, and chips trickled down from the ceiling beam.

I uncovered my ears and looked around. The house was still standing. Immediately there were more explosions. Deafening thuds and whistles succeeded each other at intervals of a few seconds, mixed with the unrelenting droning of the bombers into a horrifying cacophony. "This is it," I said to myself. "They're after the Galileo factory, and a stray bomb is going to pulverize us all any second!" I trembled, realizing I'd never been so close to death. No flashes of significant memories of my life passed through my mind. Only one stubborn thought: I must survive, I must survive!

The bombardment continued for twenty minutes, then moved away. At last, the all clear sounded. I ran outside. A curtain of dense smoke was slowly drifting across the orphanage grounds, making it seem like night, although somewhere behind it the sun was still shining. Everyone was gathered there, talking excitedly, and I soon found Willy—disheveled and covered with dust and dirt—but unharmed. Monsignor Facibeni appeared shortly, looking drained. Sustained by a boy under each arm, he wandered through the debris, trying to ascertain the damage to his beloved orphans and their home. To each boy who came running up to him he murmured, *"Grazie a Dio, Grazie a Dio!"*

There was great commotion in the streets: ambulances racing by to evacuate the wounded, people running and shouting or just standing in a daze. Flames and black smoky billows spurted out of buildings. Lingering over the whole desolate spectacle was the nauseating smell of sulfur.

A neighbor came up and said the first bomb had fallen less than two blocks away. The Rifredi railroad junction was destroyed but the massive Galileo factory was still standing. It was such an easy target that I could only speculate it had been spared because the Allies would need its installation if they were ever to occupy Florence.

We found a ten-inch jagged bomb fragment among the debris in our room. "Well, Herr Professor," Willy sneered, "at the next alarm I'll throw your books out the window. Then you'll have to come down."

Don Giovanni phoned immediately to find out if we were all right. The following day he came in person. He was visibly shaken when he realized how close we'd come to being killed. "Never would I have had enough courage to write your mother," he said, "and even less to face her." We agreed not to mention the bombardment in my letters. Instead, I wished Harry a belated happy birthday.

Harry had turned thirteen on March 10. In ordinary times he would have had his *Bar Mitzvah,* as I'd had, a solemn yet joyous occasion in a synagogue filled with proud family and friends. But who even knew where Papa was and what had befallen him? I was sure Mother was saddened by all the changes brought by war. Harry, on the other hand, was unencumbered by recollections of normal family life and would have no regrets for a *Bar Mitzvah* that should have been.

Willy and I took our weekly walk with Don Giovanni. We looked forward to his visits. It was like seeing a beloved family member, one with whom we could discuss freely our private problems. I hoped that strolling arm in arm and talking with him projected to the other boys a close relationship that made our Catholicism look kosher. At the end of his visit, he handed me a special present from his own library: two volumes of the *Storia d'Israele* by Giuseppe Ricciotti.

Then he gave us some pocket money, which we duly set aside for the next *castagnaccio* orgy.

Chapter Twenty-Four
WHAT I DIDN'T KNOW AT THE TIME

⌒

Both after his classes at the Seminario Vescovile, and on Sundays, Don Angelo hopped on his motorcycle and covered long distances to look in on the women scattered around Treviso.

Mrs. Tarnover and her two sons were living in his mother's home in the village of Ponte di Piave, sixteen miles away. They were pretending to be French, the husband and father Italian but absent. Mrs. Tarnover's older son, Henry, had turned seven but was not sent to school. The priests explained that he still had language difficulties. However, a few curious neighbors cornered the boy. "Say, Enrico," one of them asked, "are you French?"

"Yes."

"Where were you born?"

"In bed."

After that they left him alone.

Don Angelo had asked a trusted friend to take Mrs. Tarnover and the children out of his mother's home at the slightest sign of trouble and hide them elsewhere. Don Angelo's father had been killed in World War I. Then, within a few days, Don Angelo's brother and three sisters, between four and eight years old, died from the Spanish flu. Only Don Angelo had survived. His mother was saved from going insane only because she herself had been in a coma with the flu when her children died.

When Don Angelo visited his mother, she told him, "The woman sitting next to us in church remarked that Mrs. Tarnover seemed remote and was not praying much. I told her she was concentrating on keeping the baby quiet. I hope she got the message to mind her own business."

CHAPTER TWENTY-FOUR

The Benedizione della Puerpera, the blessing for a mother and new child, was coming up for Mrs. Tarnover's baby. The ceremony takes place forty days after the baby's birth. "Some busybodies around here are sure to put their noses into that, too," his mother said worriedly. "What then?"

"We'll just have to cheat," Don Angelo replied. "When the day comes, have Mrs. Tarnover dress up and make sure people see her go to church with the baby. Hang around a little, but don't let the priest see her. Then come back. I don't think anyone will double-check. And don't worry about Easter communion. I'll be here to take care of it."

After Mina Goldman and Renée Czopp had been at the Figlie della Chiesa for two and a half months, the mother superior told Don Angelo that she wanted a letter from the cardinal of Venice authorizing her to continue keeping them.

"We're all soldiers in this battle," he told her, "and if we fall, we fall. But our cardinal mustn't. You know very well we work with his tacit approval. That should be enough. So don't expect him to put anything like that in writing. The situation makes its own laws."

But the mother superior gave him an ultimatum. Without the letter, she would not keep the women any longer.

"In that case," replied Don Angelo, "please give me a few days to find another place."

Two days later he succeeded in transferring Mina and Renée to the Patronato Carolina Polacco, a boardinghouse for women run by Catholic nuns.

Soon after, the Seminario's rector, Monsignor Vittorio D'Alessi, called Don Angelo to his office. "Be careful what you do," he told him. "I should really order you to stop. You understand that if you get caught, the repercussions would be terrible for us."

"Monsignore," Don Angelo answered, "these people cannot be abandoned. Our Christian teaching tells us to pay even with our lives to save our brethren."

The rector sighed. "Yes, yes, I knew you would give some answer like that, but my conscience dictated I warn you. Very well then, continue with your work."

On Friday, April 7, 1944, Don Angelo made his daily visit to Harry, who was now living alone in the room Don Giovanni had shared with him at the

Patronato San Nicolo. Harry had a swollen throat and was running a high fever. "Be good and stay in bed all day," Don Angelo urged him, "but if there's an alarm, make sure you wrap yourself in a blanket when you go down. Otherwise, that fever might develop into something nasty."

Then Don Angelo went over to the Patronato Carolina Polacco to look in on Mother and Renée. He said it was a lovely day and suggested they take a walk to see Harry. Don Angelo then excused himself. It was Good Friday, and he still had a lot to do for Easter.

As the two women were about to leave, they heard the low, ominous rumble of bombers. The alarm sounded. Mother blanched when she looked out the window. The sky was so thick with planes it looked like a thundercloud moving toward the city. They ran down the four stories to the ground floor. The building had no underground shelter. They ducked into a large, recessed area under the first flight of stairs. It was already crowded to capacity with boarders, outsiders, nuns, and their seventy-year-old mother superior.

Then the Angel of Death went to work. Announcing their arrival with shrieking whistles, bombs ripped open the earth with tremendous blasts, even heaving up the ground of areas not directly hit. The Patronato's walls trembled and cracked. Clouds of choking dust and smoke swirled in. Explosions followed explosions, the bombs appearing to fall on top of each other, ever louder, ever closer to the building. One slammed into an outer wall: the steel girder at the far end of a corridor bent as though made of putty, and doors flew off their hinges. The nuns knelt, holding their rosaries, intoning fervent Ave Marias and Pater Nosters. Mother cradled her head in her hands and moaned. The mother superior tried to calm her. Everyone was black with soot and covered with debris. There was such hysteria under the staircase that no one was sure whether they had been hit or not. And the bombs continued unabated.

Over at Patronato San Nicolo, the mother superior there burst into Harry's room as the alarm sounded and got him out of bed. He dressed and begged her to come down with him. "In a moment," she said, "I still have to take care of a couple of things. Run along now, hurry!" Holding his shoes, Harry ran downstairs and then across the street into the Seminario's **campanile**. A few priests and students were already there, but Don Angelo was not among them. The campanile *was a massive, eighty-meter-high, solid-rock, centuries-old bell tower. The bombs started raining all around. The* campanile *shook and swayed under the blows. With each blast Harry felt death coming closer. Sweating and quivering with fever, he cried out, "Mamma!" At that moment the ground under him suddenly convulsed and belched, as if trying to shake him off. The Patronato San Nicolo across the street had just taken a direct hit. Though shaken to its foundation, the* campanile *remained intact. For ten more minutes, waves upon waves of Flying Fortresses systematically let loose carpets of bombs over the city. The fury finally subsided. In shock, people crawled out of their holes and wandered about aimlessly.*

Almost the entire city was destroyed, a modern Dante's Inferno. The streets were littered with dismembered bodies sprawled in grotesque positions. Buildings were disintegrating in pyres of soaring flames, and wails of agony filtered through thick layers of rubble up to the street level. Hanging ghostlike over the desolation, the heavy, foul stench of death mingled with the lingering, acrid fumes of destruction. Twelve hundred people had been slaughtered in a half hour. At the Patronato San Nicolo, the mother superior was buried under the rubble along with everyone else. Weeks later, broken bodies would still be dug from caved-in buildings and shelters.

There was nothing about Treviso that justified such a raid. The city was relatively insignificant in size, location, and military importance. Subsequently, British Prime Minister Winston Churchill was called by Parliament to account for the savagery of the attack. Later, there was a widespread rumor in Treviso that it had all been a ghastly mistake. The squadrons were supposed to bomb Tarvisio, an important alpine pass, or Treviglio, a city near Milan, but the pilots had mixed up the names. Other later rumors claimed that the bombing was unleashed to coincide with a secret Hitler–Mussolini encounter, or a war council of top German commanders.

But that was afterward. Immediately after the raid, Harry ran wildly through the streets in his socks toward Mother's place. He climbed over heaps of bodies and debris. Where obstacles proved to be too difficult for him, rescue workers lifted him and passed him on, hand to hand. A mass exodus of dazed survivors, fearful of follow-up raids, had started streaming out of the city.

Mother and Renée, trapped at Patronato Polacco, stopped some people passing by and asked whether they knew anything about Patronato San Nicolo. A man answered, "Così!" moving his hand flat over the ground.

Harry continued to zigzag his way to Mother's, but it was a slow process. Whole streets had been razed flat. He was black from head to toe, his eyes burning from fever and smoke. Exhausted, he finally reached the building. He yelled and pounded on the door. Someone came out to see what the noise was about and brought Harry inside. He and Mother fell into each other's arms. The abbess advised them to leave the city and head toward Santa Bona, a village four kilometers away. As they started out, the alarm sounded again, and they dashed back for cover. New waves of bombers came but passed on. When the engines' rumblings faded away, they ran toward Santa Bona.

The roads were congested with a steadily swelling flow of refugees. As they reached the open fields, they saw Aunt Sonia and Sylvia in a group ahead, powdered by thick layers of dust. Aunt Sonia's hair shot straight up as though sprayed with cement. Their shelter had caved in when a bomb exploded nearby. One pillar sustaining it collapsed. The other, near which they were standing, held. That, and a steel door, had saved their lives. No one had information about Don Angelo.

After another twenty minutes the group reached Santa Bona. With no goal, they wandered around with other refugees, still stunned. A priest came running toward them. He was dragging a bicycle, its handlebar twisted out of shape. His cassock was ripped at the shoulder and half the front buttons were missing. It was Don Angelo. He clasped both hands together over his head.

"My God, how happy I am! I promised Don Giovanni I would look after you."

At the all clear in Treviso, Don Angelo's heart had sunk when he saw the Patronato razed to the ground. But someone told him Harry had been seen running away. On his way to Santa Bona Don Angelo saw two wailing mothers with haunted looks, each carrying an infant in her arms. The faces had fresh rosy coloring and the mothers, benumbed, could not comprehend why their babies kept their eyes closed. Don Angelo had tried artificial respiration, but his efforts were in vain.

"Don't return to Treviso," Don Angelo insisted. "I'll try to find you accommodations here."

They followed him to a parochial school adjoining a church and waited outside while he went in to talk to the village priest, Don Bruno Franceschini. Don Angelo spoke of the sfollati* without mentioning that they were Jewish. The school was not in operation, as it was already sheltering several families. Don Bruno agreed to turn one more small classroom upstairs into living quarters.

While Mother and Aunt Sonia stayed in their new room, Don Angelo took Harry, Renée, and Sylvia back to Treviso. They borrowed a handcart and, picking amid the ruins of Patronato San Nicolo, loaded it with mattresses, blankets, and bed frames, and wheeled them all back to Santa Bona. That evening they replaced the classroom's school benches with the new furniture. Don Angelo also gave them an electric heating plate for cooking, and his own electrical immersion heater to brew tea.

"I think you'll be all right here," Don Angelo said. "I'll look in on you frequently. I can give you three thousand lire a month to live on. I hope that's enough for the five of you. Let Harry or the girls come to Treviso every day. I can arrange to buy a regular supply of milk and bread from the Seminario. That way you won't be at the mercy of unreliable deliveries. Ration cards will be a problem, but I'll think of something. In the meantime, with so much confusion, grocers won't be too strict."

The "Five French," as they came to be known in Santa Bona, were no longer Jews in hiding, but living out in the open as war evacuees among hundreds of similar victims that the bombardment had created.

---

*Refugees.

Chapter Twenty-Five

On one of his visits, Don Giovanni surprised Willy and me with a small crystal radio set. It was a strange-looking device called a *galena*. No dial, no loudspeaker, no tubes, no buttons. It consisted merely of a pair of earphones and a short wire which, by tickling a quartz a few inches away at just the right spot, could pick up just one channel. It happened to be the German armed forces' radio station! I listened spellbound for hours to Hitler's speeches, reports from the battlefronts, greetings from soldiers to their folks in the *Vaterland,* humorous sketches, romantic stories about a soldier on leave and the girl he'd left behind, requested German tunes—"Unter der Laterne" was the big hit— and a lot of peppy military marches that set my feet tapping. I thought it ironic that the Germans were providing the main diversion I had while hiding from them.

There were also German programs in English intended to persuade the GIs and Tommies that they were fighting for evil warmongers against an invincible and righteous Third Reich. To seduce the listener, propaganda was mixed with popular English and American tunes. For the first time in my life I heard Bing Crosby, Frank Sinatra, Glenn Miller, and Tommy Dorsey. In France I'd been exposed mainly to Charles Trenet, Tino Rossi, Maurice Chevalier, Rina Ketty, Lucienne Boyer, and Ray Ventura, although big American numbers like Duke Ellington's "Caravan" were also played often. But my biggest thrill in listening to the English broadcasts was that it established, if ever so shadowy, that Englishmen and Americans were out there—real people!—the saviors who would someday put an end to the Nazi tyranny. The bombings had proved their presence, but tunes in English brought a whiff of free and peaceful living on the other side. The broadcasts also confirmed that, despite all the reading, translating, and studying, my English was still inapt.

Before we got our regulation uniforms, Don Nello had instructed us to lean conspicuously against the wooden grating in our room and thus, to everyone who saw us, we'd attended Mass. It must have seemed strange to the boys when they looked up during services and saw our two heads poking out from an opening in the church wall, way up there. However, once we had our uniforms, Don Nello expected us to attend services in the church itself.

We were extremely self-conscious the Sunday of our first, full-fledged appearance in the packed church. In perfect unison with the worshippers, we crossed ourselves, knelt, prayed, sat down, got up, and genuflected faultlessly. Still, I was afraid we might betray ourselves by a mistake and frequently exchanged glances with Willy.

For the Benediction, Monsignor Facibeni took the thurible from the altar boy, incensed the paten and chalice, then slowly circled the altar. The altar boy took the thurible, incensed Don Nello, then came down to the rail and incensed the congregation.

We were standing a few rows away and a wisp of gray smoke drifted toward us. Willy swayed on his heels and pretended to swoon, as though he'd just been sprayed with the most enticing perfume. In the surrounding solemnity, Willy's mild prank was elevated to undeserved proportions. I felt giggles coming on. I tried to stifle them by lowering my head in prayer. Of course, my eyes were irresistibly drawn back to Willy. Pleasure was smeared over his face like a baby's first ice cream.

The soaring liturgical Sanctus, a congregation in fervent prayer—yet there was Willy, nostrils fluttering in a gallant fight against an irrepressible sneeze. My giggles shot up like bubbles in a freshly shaken soda bottle. Willy's eyes flashed anguished pleas: "What can I do? Here it comes. Watch out!" The sneeze announced itself with a momentum that could have swept away three rows of people. I pressed my lips together, but squirts of laughter hissed out. People turned around. My God, I thought, what disgraceful behavior. How pained Monsignor Facibeni would be when he heard it was us, the Jewish boys, who'd so scandalously desecrated his Mass. How could we do this to him? Willy looked shocked at my comportment. I buried my face deeper into my chest, my shoulders shaking with barely suppressed laughter. Just before irreparable disaster, Willy put an arm around me, patted me gently and, his face a painting of angelic compassion, turned to the puzzled worshippers and whispered, *"Il povero, e' commosso, piange!"**

Fortunately, the padre didn't hear about the incident, or else he chose to say nothing. The last thing I wanted was to hurt him or seem lacking in respect. Willy and I knew the dangers to him and his institution for hiding us. Never for a moment did we forget that except for him we would probably have been recaptured.

Initially I was guarded with the monsignor, my reserve probably due to the throes of having to adapt to yet another new milieu. I'd never lived in one place long enough or openly enough to consider it home. The only people I knew were my immediate family and our few friends. I was also indiscriminately distrustful. Since the age of seven I'd suffered for being a foreigner and doubly for being a Jew. I had first experienced anti-Semitism in first grade when gangs of German boys followed me all the way home with a barrage of insults. I didn't understand why they attacked me. Then, in France, I saw how the Prefecture de Police clerks enjoyed humiliating my father

---

*"Poor boy, he's so moved, he's crying."

when we needed a sojourn extension. Our experiences got worse after France fell under German boots. We were *Juifs etrangers,** the kind to stay away from if you knew what was good for you. The few people I could be at ease with, trust, and be accepted by were *us*. Anyone else was *them*.

I'd never had much contact with Catholics. I knew theirs to be a powerful religion that grew out of ours, remote and mysterious to me, but I respected all faiths as I'd been taught. At the same time I was aware that it had no reputation of brotherly feelings toward Jews. Then fate caused me to live among Catholics, in a Catholic institution. Although I'd begun to witness instances of Catholics helping Jews in distress, at the time I entered the orphanage, Monsignor Facibeni was still definitely a *them*.

I became aware that the monsignor's fame for good deeds had spread throughout Florence, where he was honored as a true priest of the people, and addressed simply as Padre or Don. For nearly thirty years he'd gone into the community to alleviate the miseries of the poor and the sick, and the tormented individuals and families who'd come to the orphanage for help. I saw grown men drop to their knees in the streets when they encountered his stooped figure and try to kiss his hand, which he struggled to withdraw. An expression of profound reverence came over their faces, as though they were in the presence of a living saint. He was indifferent to honors, and it was impossible not to be touched by his humility and unshakable faith that Divine Providence was watching over his boys.

The monsignor had a kind word for each of his orphans, a chiding look for hair that was too pomaded, or a playfully startled reaction to the first shadow of a mustache. Many older boys who'd gone on to the university came back as teachers or counselors. Others visited often, their bond with Monsignor Facibeni

---

*Foreign Jews.

unsevered. He'd given them the comfort, love, and support of a family. Perhaps it was no coincidence that Facibeni means "do us good."

However, two hundred teenage boys could not be ruled by love alone, and those misbehaving or with failing grades feared Don Nello's wrath. With a mien of ominous severity, head tilted back and dark eyes narrowed to slits, he was a tower of reprobation. Clasping a breviary, he would extend a hand toward the culprit as if in blessing, then snap it back: *"Vieni qui!"*

One day Don Facibeni stopped me in a corridor. "Ah, Nicola, are you busy now? No? Very well then, accompany me a little," and he leaned his frail body on my arm. Although I felt too much reverence for him to be at ease in his presence, I also felt flattered. It became a habit thereafter to walk with him on his rounds, and he often invited me to chat. The attention added considerably to my stature in the boys' eyes. I didn't know what I'd done to deserve it. My elementary Italian and shyness made me less than a sparkling conversationalist. I thought perhaps he wanted to express his compassion for the lot of a persecuted boy.

I sometimes sat by his desk, observing him as he finished a letter, his hand crawling agonizingly across the page. What impressed me most was his serenity. Bent over and absorbed in his writing, he was not always aware that a drop was forming at the end of his nose. It monopolized my attention as it grew, and I tried to project whether it would land on the letter or his cassock. Then, just before splashdown, I boldly took his handkerchief and wiped off the drop. *"Grazie, figliolo,"* he'd say.

We talked about the war, always the war. Would it never end? He shrugged. *"Pazienza,* we're in God's hands." We also talked about human nature, philosophy, and religion. I observed that no one could seriously believe man had evolved from a fish or monkey without some higher force orchestrating such a miracle. "Yes, that's faith," he answered. "It's sheer folly to think there could be any meaning to human destiny without faith in God!" I listened attentively as he spoke in a thin thread of a voice. I ventured other opinions untested by experience, but he never belittled them.

He held that every heart, no matter how hardened, contained a fiber which, when found and touched delicately, would give forth goodness. But he got very agitated about the Nazis and the immeasurable misery and cruelty they'd brought to Europe. Monstrous beasts he called them, with more anger than I thought him capable of showing. *"Dio, Dio!"*—then a long silence.

The ticking of the clock tiptoed through the room, its corners pockets of darkness which the declining daylight no longer reached. From his window I looked out across the courtyard. "Poveri ragazzi," I heard him sigh. I turned and realized he'd been looking at me. Then he smiled and said, *"Corraggio, su, corraggio!"*—Have courage!

The padre never made the slightest effort to lure me from Judaism, even though the circumstances couldn't have been more favorable. Confused, afraid, grateful I was a natural prospect. And I was certainly no intellectual match against this priest so well versed in both religions. Yet Monsignor Facibeni did everything he could to strengthen me in mine.

One day he said excitedly, "I have something I want to give you," and went looking for it on his bookshelves. He handed it to me with obvious pleasure. It was a small volume on Hebrew grammar. I was touched by his gesture and the sight of the familiar characters. His generosity moved me.

"You must hold on to your beliefs and traditions, Nicola, even if you're going through a difficult period in your life now. Never give up your faith."

He gave me an affectionate squeeze. I waited patiently for the releasing knock on the back of my head.

Chapter Twenty-Six

Willy was always rummaging around, or playing with the boys in the hope that they would share some of their extra goodies with him. On rare occasions he came back with a slice of bread or salami, which we forced ourselves to chew very, very slowly.

As the war went on, the Germans pilfered everything they could in Italy, and the Orfanotrofio found it increasingly difficult to maintain even the substandard meals it had been serving. No longer did the orphans leave unfinished portions on their plates that Willy and I could polish off when no one was watching.

Hunger brings on meanness. Once, at lunch, one of the boys kept looking dejectedly at his soup. A ray of hope must have shown in my eyes. "You want the *minestra*?" he asked, pushing his plate toward me.

"Yes," I instantly replied.

As I leaned forward he calmly pulled the plate back to him and said, "Me, too." There was a good laugh around the table at his clever trick.

If hunger made me miserable, there was at least encouraging military news. Would that also prove false? Since the beginning of the year the German armies had been in bad shape the entire length of the Russian front. Initially, their communiqués justified the pullbacks and evacuations of cities as moves not only to consolidate their lines but ultimately to bring about Russia's collapse. I believed them. In four years of warfare, despite the Germans' setbacks in North Africa, their armies' invincibility had become legendary. Any day the Russians would discover they'd fallen into a trap. My reasoning was a protective device against the temptation of building the Nazis' reversals into omens of defeat. That delicious vision, my private reserve of hope, was not to be indulged in frivolously. It was too precious, too fragile, and allowing it to take wings could risk its ruin.

However, after several months of tremendous battles the German armies seemed unable to regain the initiative in their counteroffensives. It was April 1944, and Willy and I moved the front-line pins on our map progressively west. The Russians had retaken Tarnopol near the former Polish border, then ten days later, Odessa on the Black Sea. And fighting continued in the Crimea.

In their communiqués, the Germans mentioned cities and rivers we couldn't find on the map, so, regrettably, we had to leave some pins behind. Nevertheless, the general trend seemed to be that the Germans were being driven back relentlessly toward Poland, Romania, and Hungary. And, ever more frequently, there were reports of German cities being heavily bombed: Cologne, Essen, Berlin. Were the Germans actually allowing all that to happen with impunity? What did they have up their sleeves? There were increasing reports in the newspapers about a devastating secret weapon.

But in Italy, still nothing. The Allies had rained enough bombs on Monte Cassino to turn every square foot bottoms up, but the Germans held, seemingly determined to outdo the Russians at Stalingrad. The Allies were blocked.

Air raids continued. Since the attack when the orphanage had barely escaped obliteration, everyone now ran for shelter the instant an alarm was sounded. But a mind fixated on something, in my case, food, will compulsively assess any new possible solution: The kitchen personnel also ran for cover. Did they take the time to lock the doors first?

At the next alarm I ran to the school building instead of the *campanile* and hid behind a door. As soon as the footsteps and voices faded away, I came out and tiptoed down the corridor to the kitchen. The door was ajar! Easy now, Louis, careful. Just in case someone was guarding the fort, I shouted, but not loudly enough to be heard outside. "Anyone in there?"

Silence.

I pushed the door open.

Nobody.

In the center of the kitchen, on the big, square, black oven, an assortment of partly uncovered sizzling pots yielded the most delicious aromas. Heaps of vegetables, fruit and bread, plus a lot of cooking paraphernalia, covered the tables, all of it hurriedly abandoned. I stepped into a dream and started stuffing myself with wild abandon: a ladle of piping hot soup, a chunk of celery, a crusty bread end, an apple, a slice of meat, a handful of macaroni. I gulped the food down as fast as my mouth could haul it in. I went about it so frantically and with such excitement that it was a while before the bombers' rumblings sank in. A flash of sanity returned, and I got scared as I realized I was foolishly risking my life for a bit of food. Or, perhaps reason could prevail only after the belly had been filled.

I ran to the *campanile,* wiping my mouth on the way. How stupid of me. To have been privileged to elude the Germans for so long and then to endanger my life in such a reckless way. And what about the irony of dying in the end, not at the hands of Nazis, but under an American bomb through my own fault! As if the prospect of death itself wasn't enough, I was also distressed at the ignominy of being the only corpse discovered later under kitchen rubble. I pictured myself being dug out with macaroni still clutched in my hand. They would all point an accusing finger and sneer, "Despicable! God's punishment for being a glutton and a thief!"

CHAPTER TWENTY-SIX

I couldn't bear the thought of leaving such a last impression on Monsignor Facibeni and the people who'd shown me nothing but kindness, so on subsequent alarms I headed straight for the *campanile*.

The padre's health was worsening. His arms and hands became increasingly rigid. When I asked if there wasn't some cure, he smiled, "No, they tried. It's God's will, Nicola." I assisted him in any way I could. Even getting up from the fauteuil was a task he could no longer manage by himself. His mind, however, was bright and alert. He was pleased to hear that Mother and Harry were safe. Together we speculated about Papa's fate. "So much wickedness in this world!" he said, shaking his fist. "Don't those Nazi barbarians understand that the only hope on this earth is faith in God and love of fellow man?"

Amore, amore. That word in its humanitarian context was always on the monsignor's lips. I pointed out that, at least in his immediate domain, he had reason to be gratified. He'd built a magnificent institution dedicated to that noble principle. The boys loved him and would be influenced by his spirit forever. "I hope so," he said pensively, "but they grow up and go out into the world, and who knows what really becomes of them on the inside?"

"From what I've seen, they come back to visit you even after they've been away for several years." In fact, there were more young men in their early twenties than ever before, living in the house at the far end of the playing field.

"They'll stay here until they can organize their lives again, Nicola. But don't talk to them. You must always be careful. And especially stay away when you see boys in army uniforms with black shirts. They've been recruited to new Fascist units fighting alongside the Germans. They, too, are my boys, but I don't know where their real sympathies lie. Beware!" I'd noticed a few such boys visiting on Sunday afternoons, and instinctively made a big detour around them.

One day Monsignor Facibeni told me that the boy who used to shave him had left the orphanage. "I'll gladly do it," I said. I'm sure any one of the boys would have given away his last slice of bread for the privilege. To be the Monsignor's barber! *Te Deum!* I'd never shaved anyone but myself and approached the new task with apprehension.

The padre reclined in his armchair and I stuck a napkin in the collar of his cassock. I tried to work up a thick lather on his face with the brush and wartime soap, but all I achieved was a transparent, milky coating. The blade, too, could have been sharper. I was worried. He tried to chat while I worked, but I was much too engrossed. I was also conscious of the unusual circumstances: a Jewish refugee boy shaving an eminent dignitary of the Catholic Church. I was shaken by the "power" conferred upon me. He raised his chin obediently, but the folds of skin around his thin throat didn't offer enough resistance for a close shave. I apologized when I had to pinch his nose for better access to the area over his upper lip and the blade had a tough fight against his stubborn, gray stubble. I had to go over each area several times, but he endured it with good humor and seemed to have utter confidence in me.

After much resoaping and rescraping, the job was done. I washed his face and brought him a mirror. "Bravo, Nicola, bravo!" he said, smiling. I felt very proud of myself. His face had a new sparkle, and he looked ten years younger. Every other day thereafter I worked my magic on him.

I'd just finished soaping his face one afternoon when Maria burst into the room. "Padre, there are Germans inside the Orfanotrofio." I remained with the razor poised in midair. Germans on the premises!

"Go and hide, Nicola, quick!" the padre ordered. I put the razor down and started to wash the soap off his face, but he pushed me away. "Never mind, just go." As I dashed out of the room I heard him ask Maria, "Did you alert the others?"

I ran downstairs, along the corridor, through the archway leading to the church, my eyes darting left and right. I reached the *campanile* in less than two minutes. I shut the door and climbed the ladder to the first landing, then pulled up the ladder and bell ropes, closed the trapdoor, and sat down, out of breath, my ears straining for the clumping of heavy boots.

It occurred to me too late that if the Germans came looking into the bell tower, using the simpleminded Beppino for a guide, he would probably wonder out loud, "Gee, there's usually a ladder here up to the trapdoor. And the ropes—who pulled up my ropes?"

I hoped Willy had gotten wind of the Germans in time. And what had the padre meant by, "Did you alert the others?" Did he mean Willy, or were there *other* others?

After half an hour I ventured a peek out. Everything seemed calm. Three boys were looking at some postage stamps that a fourth was pulling out of his pockets. I waited a little longer, then came down. Life seemed to be going on in normal fashion, so I went back to Monsignor Facibeni.

"Nothing," he laughed. "Some German soldiers just wandered in out of curiosity. They weren't looking for anything in particular. I would have sent for you, but I had no idea where you were hiding. Come, let's get rid of this beard."

Chapter Twenty-Seven

I was reading in our room when Willy came in. He stood by the table and looked at me with raised eyebrows and his all-purpose grin. *"Nu?"* I asked.

He pulled a white sheet of paper out of his pocket. It was about eight inches by ten inches, with many little rectangles printed on it. "A whole month of bread coupons!"

"But what good is it? It has *annullato** stamped all over."

"We can still use it if we scratch it out."

"Scratch out rubber-stamped impressions? Any more bright ideas?"

"If Morino can, so can we," Willy said impatiently. "I surprised him and a few other boys scratching away at a pile of sheets in an empty classroom. He found them across the street in the grocery store's garbage can. They hid them from me, but when I promised not to squeal they let me have one."

Italian citizens were issued a separate ration sheet once a month for major food items. Each had daily-dated coupons for bread printed on it, or periodic ones for meat, fats, and sugar. To discourage black-marketing, the whole sheet had to be presented to the grocer. Although most complied, the rule wasn't strictly enforced. Store owners had known their customers for so many years they overlooked annoying bureaucratic regulations. Some people cut out individual coupons and left the sheets at home.

We split a razor blade and started scratching. I'd learned the craft of eliminating wrinkles and skin blemishes on negatives at

---

* Canceled (expired).

166

the photographer's studio in Montpellier. However, even with the light touch I'd acquired, the papers' fibers bristled up and the coupons looked flagrantly tampered with.

"Actually, it's better than what Morino did," Willy commented.

"It stinks," I said. "We have to be ten times more careful than the others. All they would get is a reprimand. We would be risking our necks."

We gave up the idea. Better to stay hungry but safe. That night after we locked the doors according to our security ritual, Willy said, "Hey, remember how you copied that official seal for my father just before we were captured in the theater? A darn good job you did with that."

"A good job?" I repeated with irritation. "It turned out unusable. Don't you remember how fake the signature I made looked?"

"How about making a copy of a new coupon?"

"You want me to forge an official government bread coupon? You can't wait to get us arrested, can you?"

"It's no more illegal than recirculating an *annullato*."

"Some logic! Why not forge money, too?"

Willy got up and handed me the sheet. "Take another look. It's not such a crazy idea."

A coupon was a three-quarter-inch square, divided in two vertical halves by a black line. Each half bore the same information in black type: the word *Pane* in capital letters on top, the day on the next line, the month below, and at the bottom, *Firenze*.

"Willy, you're *meschugge*. There are seventeen characters plus two numerals. And that's only on one side! Then I would have to repeat the whole *megillah* in the second rectangle. They're the size of thumbnails!"

"Three hundred grams of delicious bread! I'm drooling already."

"Very funny. How convincing do you think I can make printed type look by hand? *PANE* isn't too bad with its bold letters. But *Aprile* and *Firenze* are too tiny. I don't want to do it. It's too risky."

"Ludi, I'm sure you could do a superb job," Willy pleaded. "There's so much talent in your hands!"

"A true patron of the arts! I'm flattered."

"If it turns out unusable, we haven't lost anything."

"Tell you what," I said, "I'll make a test and I alone will be the judge of whether it can pass or not."

"Yes, maestro."

Three hundred grams of bread had been whispering their siren song all during our discussion. "Who'll face the grocer with it if it turns out presentable?"

"I will," said Willy, undaunted.

I found a sheet of paper with a thickness and shade of white very close to the coupon's and cut off a piece. I lined it up against the typeface, made pencil marks of the border, thickness, height, spacing, and placement of the letters in each line. Next, I drew the letters lightly in pencil from the marks I'd made.

Willy sat next to me. He was very quiet, seemingly overwhelmed by the painstaking process.

I wiped my glistening pen against the rim of the inkpot and began to trace the letters. On the diagonal of the N in *PANE* the pen ran dry. I filled the letter with new ink, but two different shades of black resulted.

My palms were sweating and I stopped frequently to wipe them dry and review my technique. It took nearly three hours, well into the night. I felt cramps in my arms and down my back. Finally, I cut the superfluous paper from around my coupon while Willy cut one from the original sheet. He cleared an area on the table and laid them side by side.

"Beautiful!" he decreed.

I tried to rub focus back into my eyes. It didn't look too bad, but I was painfully aware of several flaws. Not all the letters were smooth, and some of them were either too tall or too short.

"Only *you* see that," Willy argued, "because you're too finicky. No one else would notice."

"I suppose it'll improve when I erase the pencil marks after the ink's really dry."

"Don't worry so much. It'll be fine. We'll look at it again in the morning."

"That's what I'm afraid of. This thing can pass only in complete darkness."

I went to bed with visions of impending disaster tossing around me. My conscience printed colossal headlines: *Two Jewish Boys Caught Forging Bread Coupons inside Catholic Orphanage! Our Beloved Monsignor Facibeni in Shock at Dastardly Behavior.*

I was already awake as the morning gray drifted in. I shook Willy.

"Hey, listen!"

He shot up, alarmed. "Germans?"

"No, I made a big mistake. I put on yesterday's date!"

Willy lay back. "Damn it. Real stupid of us to have overlooked that." Then, after a moment he said, "I still think we should go ahead. If the grocer discovers it's a fake or grumbles about the date, I'll play dumb and say I got the coupon from another kid."

Before even washing or dressing, I carefully erased the pencil marks and we examined the forgery again. I wished I could make corrections, but it was too late. *"Of'n ganev brennt's hittel,"** Willy said.

My hesitations faded. Maybe my coupon wasn't a failure after all. We washed, had a quick breakfast in the refectory, and

---

*"A thief feels as though his hat is on fire."

rushed back to our room. Willy slipped the coupon inside his jacket and, as he left, I said *"Mit Mazel."* I had an impulse to shake his hand or slap his back, but felt it would be melodramatic. I waited by the window, praying and hoping like a mother who has a son on the front line.

It seemed much longer, but in less than ten minutes he was back. He spread open a newspaper with three golden brown bread loaves inside. His face beamed with a gamut of emotions: the delight of success, pride of the hero, and smugness of having been proven right. "Nothing to it. I waited my turn, then handed him the coupon. He just glanced at it and threw it into a glass jar full of coupons. I paid, said, *'Arrivederci,'* and took a detour back here, just in case."

I stared at the loaves, amazed. "That easy?"

"Let's eat, huh? We deserve it."

The loaves, called *filoncini,* were about seven inches long. A raised crust curved into a nipple at each end. I crunched into mine, releasing the delicious, intoxicating aroma. A gust of boldness swept through me. "You know, I could do another one tonight!"

Every day I made a coupon. We took turns at the grocer's. He or his plump and pretty wife always weighed the *filoncini* carefully and cut off or added a little piece to match the allotted ration.

I was able to streamline the complex markings since the lettering remained the same for a whole month. Only the digits changed from day to day and I copied the set from 0 to 9, as well as the other months from canceled sheets. Still, there were setbacks. Often, the graceful swanlike neck of a 2 would come out too angular, or the small e would fill up with ink and I had to start over again. But with practice, I could make a coupon in little more than an hour. The quality improved, too. I even added finishing touches, creasing or aging them with floor dust. Also, since grocers often used the backs of ration sheets to add prices of goods, the backs of my coupons sported random, truncated digits. Luckily, our type of bread coupon had the highest value: 300 grams. On plain white paper, it was the easiest to forge. The others had designs on colored paper.

Our biggest problem was getting the right paper. It had to be the precise shade of off-white, feel neither too thick nor too thin to the experienced touch of the grocer's fingers, and absorb ink without bleeding. There wasn't much paper around that qualified. On safaris throughout the orphanage we fingered every piece of paper we came across with the intensity of textile experts assessing fine English wool. Nothing was safe from our inspection: magazines, typewriter sheets, drawing pads, and especially books with a white page inside the cover. Many a boy who left his exercise book unattended while Willy was on the prowl never knew what contribution a missing page meant to our cause. In one of the classrooms I found a small map of Italy with a lovely margin all around it. I snipped it off and it kept us in bread for two weeks.

We didn't tell Don Giovanni how we were spending the pocket money he gave us. We were fearful of embarrassing him or, worse, that he would tell us to stop. At any rate, my conscience felt much lighter than when I had stolen food from the kitchen, and seeing other boys eat no longer induced bulging eyes and salivating. But the main benefit reaped from our daily *filoncini* was that it somehow made the future seem less dismal.

Chapter Twenty-Eight

Don Giovanni had told us about the bombing of Treviso and my family's subsequent move to Santa Bona, so I was anxious to hear how they were getting on there. It wasn't until the middle of May, when Don Giovanni handed it to me personally, that I finally received a letter from Mother. I ran up to my room to read it in private. She said that the five of them were managing to live, sleep, and eat in the same room and that they were relatively content running their own independent household. Except Harry.

His bitter cup was the daily trip to Don Angelo for milk and bread. It was not the two and a half miles each way that bothered him, but the indignity of having to walk them in Mother's shoes, "with those stupid, little heels." His own shoes had fallen apart and, since he was the only male in the group, there was nothing else for him to wear. Mother said he put on her shoes with all the enthusiasm of someone facing exploratory surgery. He danced around in them mockingly and, having thus girded himself against the greater humiliations he expected in the city, he left on his *Via Dolorosa*.

He was having difficulties with the girls, too. Complaining that they didn't "feel well," they refused to help with his errands. Harry thought they were just lazy. Friction also rose with Aunt Sonia, whose asthma had gotten worse in Santa Bona's humid climate. She cleared her bronchi somewhat by inhaling the smoke from special medicinal herbs she burned on a plate. Harry found the stench sickening. He wanted the room aired;

Aunt Sonia wanted it closed. She wanted darkness; he wanted light. Mother said she was constantly mediating to maintain peace. Even when air raids sounded, Aunt Sonia chose to remain inside rather than aggravate her asthma in the damp shelter. In addition, Harry often had to run to Don Angelo, who already knew which medication to get for her at the pharmacy. Against more acute attacks she needed injections. She was quite good at administering them herself, but everyone's stomach felt queasy every time she laid out the needle, vial, and alcohol.

Don Giovanni expanded on Mother's guarded letter. There was another problem. Santa Bona's priest, Don Bruno, was not part of Don Angelo's network, and the parochial school where they lived was situated between his house and the church. There were barely seven thousand people in the village, and Don Bruno knew nearly everyone's record of church attendance.

The group couldn't skip services without antagonizing him or making him suspicious. He'd already noticed a certain awkwardness in their comportment in church, a somewhat different way of going about it, different enough to make him ask, "Is that how they do it in France?" Mother, Aunt Sonia, and Harry attended fairly regularly, but Sylvia and Renée were definitely not good Catholics in his eyes. After they'd failed to show up several times in a row, Don Bruno took them to task. "Why didn't you come? Look here, there are three Masses every Sunday. Those who can't sleep come to the first, those who pray come to the second, and to the third, girls looking for dates. *Allora,* at least come to the third!" The girls promised they would. Then he asked, "Isn't it about time you also came to confession?"

On Don Angelo's next visit, they asked him what they should do. "Tell him you prefer a French-speaking priest, so you come to me," he said. "Leave for Treviso early in the morning. Go sit somewhere in a café and return a few hours later. When Don

Bruno sees you again, tell him you've been to confession—and look blissful for having obtained forgiveness for your sins."

However, there were new complications for the Glatts who were living with Don De Zotti's family in Mestre. Don De Zotti's brother had fallen in love with Ruth. Embarrassed, Ruth talked to Don Bortoluzzi, but he and Don Angelo couldn't find a face-saving pretext to transfer her somewhere else.

Mrs. Glatt unwittingly provided the solution. In May she suffered a spine ailment from a dislodged bone in her neck. The priests put her in Treviso's state hospital, which, after the bombardment, had been evacuated to Casier, a small locality in the city's outskirts. The priests told the De Zottis that Mrs. Glatt wanted her daughter to be near her, and moved Ruth to a room in Casier.

Mother and Renée visited Mrs. Glatt occasionally. She was a pathetic sight, ensconced in plaster from her chin to her hips. She couldn't open her mouth and had to suck crushed food through clenched teeth. After several weeks in the hospital she still hadn't improved.

Don Giovanni reassured me that, despite the problems in Santa Bona, my family's spirits had survived the bombing in Treviso.

Chapter Twenty-Nine

On May 18, 1944, stupefying news set the Orfanotrofio buzzing. The Allies had driven the Germans out of Monte Cassino! Having smashed the formidable Gustav line that had held them in check during eight months of fierce fighting, the Allies could start battling the Germans in less-defensible terrain. Nine days later the Allies on Monte Cassino joined forces with those on the Anzio beachhead and pushed north.

The news from the Russian front was equally heartening. The Germans had abandoned the Crimea and were retreating.

For the first time, I had the unequivocal feeling that the Nazi nightmare would indeed come to an end. There was a contagious excitement in the air, with everybody speculating about what would happen next and when Florence might be liberated. But no one expected it to be quick and easy. At dinner, some orphans said the Germans would fight hard for every inch of Italy; others thought the Nazis would spare Florence a bloody street-by-street fight out of consideration for its art treasures.

Until the breakthrough in Monte Cassino, Willy and I only suspected that most of the orphans harbored no sympathy for the Germans. Although they rarely engaged in political discussions, it was unrealistic of us to expect them to look forward to an Allied victory with our same burning hope and impatience. Now some boys started venturing their pro-Allied feelings. Willy and I remained cautious, afraid enthusiasm from us might offend any hard-core Fascists.

We tuned in to the German military station on our *galena* with increased interest. Unfailingly, whenever the German High Command had ordered a "consolidation" of the front line, the announcers reported that "crippling" losses had been inflicted on the enemy. And the German, English, and American music continued.

An American jazz number kept replaying itself in my mind. One day I was whistling it absentmindedly on my way to the metal workshop when one of the alumni that Monsignor Facibeni had referred to as having to "reorganize" his life stopped me. *"Scusi,"* he said. "I hear you're listening to that station, too." Caught off guard, I pretended not to know what he was talking about. He smiled and said, "Great tune, huh?"

"I love it," I said, realizing that listening to a German station wasn't *verboten*. The fellow was about twenty-five, shabbily dressed, and with an unshaven black beard. He must have left the orphanage at least ten years earlier, yet he'd returned to his padre, to his home.

Marshal Albert Kesselring, the German commander in Italy, fought hard to slow the Fifth and Eighth Armies. But the towns of Vellitri and Valmontone fell, and then, on June 4, Rome itself. Our elation at the announcement had hardly subsided when it was topped by another: On June 6, British and American troops landed in Normandy! We quickly stuck pins on a part of the map we'd seldom ever looked at before: Bayeux, Isigny, Caen, Saint-Malo, Cherbourg.

Yet, on my nineteenth birthday, two days later, instead of being grateful to be alive and for the happy turn of events, I felt deeply depressed. Time! Time! That priceless commodity was being squandered away by the war. It was the period of my life in which to learn, improve, achieve—to make something of myself. I'd read George Bernard Shaw's comment that youth was wasted on the young, but it didn't apply to me. I was keenly aware of its once-in-a-lifetime, never-to-be-repeated opportunities. I saw life as a stack of calendar sheets, one for each of my days, a sheet torn off every day whether I'd made the most of it or not. No glue in the world could paste them back on. There I was, with infinite possibilities theoretically open to me, but instead, I'd been forced into hiding, wasting my life. I hadn't even been able to find out where my aptitudes lay, what profession to pursue: engineer, teacher, lawyer, doctor, architect, or my dream, cinematographer. I felt I could be anything if I applied myself, and whatever it was going to be, I wanted to excel.

Time had mockingly marched on while I was forced to stand still, compounding daily the irreparable damage. To reduce it, I'd disciplined myself to read and learn and think as much as possible at the orphanage. A pitiful effort at best. If only time could be stopped, at least until I, too, could have a fair chance in the running! I was so obsessed that I found some consolation when my beard grew and I could still let several days pass without shaving.

Assuming I would one day be free again, how could I ever hope to make up for lost time? Whether in school or learning a trade, I would have to be in classes with boys ten years younger than I. No chief comptroller of the "Ministry of Time Allotment" would later check my claim on a master list and say, "Louis Goldman? Let's see. Ah, yes, here's your certificate: 'Good for One Normal Youth Retrospective to Age Seven, Nontransferable.'"

So I faced my birthday in wretched self-pity. Nineteen was such an important milestone. The last of the young years! The threshold to the decade of the twenties!

Dramatically, I wrote in my diary, "Alas, a day of mourning, but instead of condolences, I was offered congratulations." Then I separated those words from the rest of the text with a black, boxed line, like an obituary in a newspaper.

It soon became apparent that the Allies couldn't progress easily in Normandy. That they'd succeeded in landing at all was astonishing. Had not the Nazi propaganda machinery proclaimed for years that Europe was such an impregnable fortress that no Allied soldier would ever set foot on it? And always there was the hint of a secret German weapon so powerful it would bring the Reich's enemies to their knees. Sensational rumors were spread constantly by hawkers who basked in the attention. Although Willy and I considered them propaganda as well, to keep alive the myth of Germany's invincibility, in the back of our minds crept the thought that maybe the Germans did have such a weapon, after all.

Barely a week after D-day we were in for a shock. V-1 bombs were raining on London and southern England. The German communiqué jubilantly predicted the Allies' imminent defeat. I didn't fully understand why the new weapon was so lethal until I read the gory details in a newspaper: "These self-propelled bombs launched from the continent need neither pilot nor airplane to zero in on their targets. They arrive unheralded, catching the enemy population by surprise, and cause thousands of casualties. There is no defense against them." The editorial added, "We do not rejoice when we hear of the victims in England, but at a time when the Allies are savagely bombarding Berlin and scores of other European cities, this is fair retaliation. We, too, have a right to victory."

Was that the end of our hopes? Back to the darkest days of 1941, when nothing could stop the Germans? On its weekly cover with action-packed drawings, the *Domenica Del Corriere* depicted Londoners running and screaming in terror as black birds of death struck without warning. In the background whole sections of the city were in flames.

To our relief, the new German weapon didn't seem to deter the Allies from continuing their offensives. They pressed north of Rome, and in France, although they hadn't achieved a decisive breakthrough in Normandy, they consolidated their strongholds and took Cherbourg on June 26. The German radio station reported that the harbor had been completely destroyed and would be of no use to the Allies. The radio station had a chipper new program entitled *"Und Es Wird Weiter Gerommelt,"* meaning "And the Rommeling goes on!" Between bursts of catchy regimental marches, the program blazoned the exploits of Field Marshal Rommel, the "Desert Fox," who now commanded the German forces in Normandy. In rah-rah-rah style the announcer told how Rommel, dashing about in skillful countermaneuvers, was trapping and decimating the Allied units. With its sunken ships, destroyed armor, and dead invaders littering the shore by the thousands, Normandy would become the graveyard of Roosevelt and Churchill's foolish dreams. "And the Rommeling goes on! Music!" Willy and I listened, transfixed. Could they be right, God forbid?

The regular *filoncini* kept our spirits up. For two months our forgery had continued without a hitch. There were days when I prepared several consecutive coupons in advance, or cockily gave the grocer two at the same time: one for that day, one for the previous when I couldn't come, which, of course, had been Willy's turn with his two coupons. At times we experienced an *embarras de richesses* and could scarcely close the drawer where we kept our bread.

Banking on protection from his Orfanotrofio uniform, Willy ventured into the city about once a week to visit his father at the old-age home. We were in a position even to send along bread for him and Mr. Haberman, his companion from Saint-Martin-Vesubie. Both men were in their mid-forties, but by letting their beards grow, and walking with a little stoop, they fit right in. Willy's father even added a touch of deafness and was in charge of chasing the sly old-timers from the toilets where they hid during prayer service.

One day Willy came back very agitated. He said he'd been riding on the tram's open rear platform next to three German soldiers. They were in a lighthearted mood, regular Wehrmacht personnel, and he wasn't worried about them. But through the sliding door he suddenly saw two plainclothesmen checking passengers' identification papers. He didn't have his fake ID with him. He wanted to jump off the platform but realized he would be giving himself away. In the Orfanotrofio uniform he stood no chance of escaping and, if he tried, might even be shot. Just before the men opened the sliding door, Willy turned to the soldiers and, in German, asked what time it was. They were pleasantly surprised, "*Oh, ein Landsmann!* Where are you from?" Seeing a blond, young fellow in a vague sort of uniform, cheerfully engaged in conversation with soldiers who seemed to be his friends, the plainclothesmen left Willy alone and got off the tram. Willy dropped off the *filoncini* for his father, and then raced back to the safety of the Orfanotrofio.

At the old-age home, Willy frequently encountered Mr. Haberman's fourteen-year-old daughter, Lya. She was hiding in a private room not far from us, near Piazza Dalmazia. Emboldened by our uniforms, Willy and I occasionally left the orphanage and furtively met her in the Cinema Flora, not just to see the movie, but to talk about old times, the iffy future, a craving for a heart-to-heart chat with someone of our own; Jews are the original soul brothers. In the darkness we slipped her my forged bread coupons. Lya's baker also accepted them as genuine.

The success of my fraud didn't mean I was at peace. I wished I knew if the grocer and his wife accepted the coupons because they thought them real, or whether they'd known all along but kept quiet out of sympathy. Were we stretching our luck? What if they took the coupon with wet hands? The ink would smudge and we'd be doomed!

On most days we returned so quickly, we were able to gobble the bread down right away, still warm. I was returning from the grocer early one morning when I ran into Don Nello. He'd been away for over a week, so I couldn't greet him with a mere *"Buon giorno."* I held the *filoncini* under my cape and little wisps of trapped steam rose from my collar, past my chin and nose. Don Nello stared, entranced. Looking straight at him, I smiled sheepishly. "Hot bread, you know." He said nothing, which left me uneasy.

Our regular diet of illegal *filoncini* began to show. Even the normally taciturn Maria was moved to comment on my resplendent mien. "Your cheeks look like you're playing a tuba." I shrugged it off, attributing my looks to all the polenta we were being fed. However, her remark rekindled my apprehensions. Was it not time to stop, while we were ahead? By all odds, yes, but the memory of the lean days was too painful. As July came around, we were still at it.

After Rome's liberation, the Allied armies had continued to push north over a mountainous terrain, which made decisive gains difficult. Nevertheless, they'd taken Civitavecchia, Terni, and Viterbo, and were pressing on to Perugia. The retreating Germans exacted a high price for the territory they yielded. To our keyed-up anxiousness, the Allied advance seemed agonizingly slow. We eagerly shifted the pins on our map every day, but Perugia was still 170 kilometers away. In the darkest days of the past four years, when we'd been losing our hopes one by one, like a tree its autumn leaves, we would have been overjoyed to know that deliverance was as close as a mere 170 kilometers. But as the distance between the Allies and us shrank, each remaining kilometer became increasingly important. The Germans might well dig in again somewhere almost invulnerable, as they did in Monte Cassino or, worse, retake the offensive.

It occurred to me that instead of waiting for a liberation that might never come or still take many months, we should move south and hide as close as possible to the front. But there were no more civilian trains to Perugia. Also, a stranger wouldn't be able to get past the German security net along the way in the front-zone towns of Arezzo or Siena, not to mention the diehard Fascists. We needed friends, a secure hiding place, and some money, none of which we had. Finally, moving about the countryside in a battle zone could well mean never living to see liberation day at all. No, all things considered, there was nothing to do but wait in the Orfanotrofio.

Chapter Thirty

The summer was hot and we kept the window in our room open all day. On the afternoon of July 2, I was reading as usual at my table overlooking the courtyard when I heard Willy's hurried footsteps on the staircase. He rushed into the room, gasping, "Ludi, Germans are all over the place!"

"Again? But what's the panic? Last time they just walked around a little and left."

"There are lots of them and they're all carrying weapons. They've rounded up some boys from the alumni house. What should we do? Run out in the street?"

We heard hobnailed boots. I took a peek. Three German soldiers were positioned in the courtyard, arms ready. I quickly pulled back and felt that familiar knot in my throat. "We can't run anymore. It's probably a house-to-house search, and the bastards are going to do it systematically. Ours looks deserted from downstairs. Maybe they'll skip it, but let's get ready anyway. Stay away from the window and be absolutely quiet."

Willy went to lock the door leading from the empty room in front of ours to the back stairway. It was too late to go down and lock the two house entrances. The Germans would see us through the kitchen door's window, and surely others were stationed near the rear entrance. We didn't lock the door to our room. We didn't want it to look like we'd thrown up a barricade. I pulled down the map and pins and hid them with the coupons and *galena* under the Jesus doll's pillow inside the glass bubble. Willy wrapped a woolen scarf around his neck, making sure his red scar protruded. He undressed, jumped into bed, and pulled the covers up to his chin. He managed to look really sick.

I sat down at the table with a book and writing paper in case Germans came up through the front entrance or front door. I tried to act natural, but I was trembling. We didn't grab the rope and swing down into the church because we had Italian papers and didn't even know what or who the Germans were looking for. So why give ourselves away by escaping? If they intended to comb the orphanage, they would get to the church, too. I saw myself arriving at the bottom of the rope with a German waiting for us at the end of our clever escape-route.

As the minutes ticked away, my tension mounted. I became aware of the blood pulsing in my temples. Down in the courtyard I heard soldiers walking back and forth, some shouting orders. After a quarter of an hour of agonizing suspense, I heard a loud thud very close to us; then another, even louder. They were banging against the door that Willy had locked in the adjoining room. I was terrified. If they broke down the door, it would mean we'd put up resistance and it could be the end of us. On the other hand, if we remained quiet they might decide there was no one in and move on. Willy and I looked at each other, trying to reach a decision. The pounding continued another three, four times, and then I heard the sound of cracking wood. One more second and we would be hopelessly compromised. "I'm going to open up," I said. I ran into the other room.

The upper part of the door had been split but was still solidly secured at the latch. Through the gaping hole a snarling German was hacking furiously away with the butt of his submachine gun, trying to make the opening large enough for him to reach the latch. His face was beet-red from physical exertion, the heat, and his rage. Rivulets of sweat were streaming down and soaking the collar of his uniform. Behind him, another German was cursing, his submachine gun hanging from his neck. His fingers gripped the wooden handle of a hand grenade.

Conspicuously holding the book and the pen I'd grabbed before running out, I approached the door rapidly, acting nonplussed by what I saw, a harmless scholar indignant at being interrupted in his deep studies by all the uproar.

"Un momento," I exclaimed. *"Che succede qui?"**

The first German stopped midstrike and screamed at me, *"Mach die Tür auf, Du Schwein!"*†

"Ma sicuro, subito."

Wedging the book between my legs, I tried to slide the latch out of its groove, but, because the door had been bent, it took me longer than I judged favorable to good public relations. As soon as I got it open, the two Germans swept me along with them into our room, their weapons ready to fire. I didn't know what they expected to find after having had such trouble getting in but, when all they saw was a sick boy in bed, they calmed down somewhat and began searching the room. They were *Fallschirmjäger,* paratroop commandos with short-rimmed helmets. They looked under the beds, in the cupboard, in the dresser, everywhere but under the infant Jesus.

The German holding the grenade pulled the covers off Willy and asked him why he was in bed. Willy pretended not to understand German. He showed his scar and replied in Italian that it hurt him very much. The German gestured impatiently for him to get up. Willy swung out of bed as fast as was compatible with his declared condition. The German put the grenade back in his belt and asked both of us to show our identification papers. While he studied them, the other German who'd been breaking down the door examined the things lying on my table. He picked up the fountain pen, looked at it closely, and put it in his

---

*"Just a moment. What's going on here?"
†"Open the door, you swine!"

pocket. It was the one I used to make all my notebook entries. I wanted to say that I needed the pen very much but, fearing to hear I wouldn't be needing it anymore, I kept quiet.

"This one here is seventeen," said the German with our papers, showing them to his comrade. "The other one's fifteen."

"Leave him here. Just take the big one."

He handed us back our cards. I took mine and showed it to the German with the submachine gun, pointing at my birth year. *"Komm komm,"* he snapped, and pushed me out of the room with the butt of his gun, through the broken door, and down the back staircase. Willy followed timidly to see where they were taking me.

From the bottom a voice yelled up, *"Alle achtzehn und über, an der Wand stellen."** Terror shot through me. I shouted up to Willy, *"Vai dal padre!"* The German behind me snarled, *"Nix padre, nix,"* and kept pushing me downstairs.

As we came out in the open, I saw a dozen of the older fellows lined up against a wall. Three German soldiers faced them about twenty feet away. One motioned for me to stand against the wall, too.

I stood on the extreme left of the line, dazed and scared. No one talked. We stared straight ahead at the Germans. They stared back at us, guns in hand. Beppino was in the line, too. The unshaven boy who'd talked to me about the jazz piano number was on my right. Suddenly, he and some of the other young men no longer looked like alumni. Were they in hiding, too?

A thorough combing of the Orfanotrofio was going on. I could see and hear more Germans around us. A flash of hope suddenly popped up and I thought, It isn't possible we're going to be shot! Here, in the orphanage? No. We all seem to be eighteen or older, so they're checking us out because they think

---

*"All those eighteen and over, against the wall."

there might be escaped Allied prisoners or partisans among us. Are there any? Or, we've been selected to work for the hard-pressed German army: load trucks and dig trenches, just for a few days maybe? Never mind, as long as they don't know I'm Jewish. Should I make an issue of my age again? After all, if I'm not eighteen, what am I doing here? Better not. They might start wondering how I know that age is a factor in the selection. So what! I learned a little German, and I can count to twenty. But what if they get vicious because I'm making a fuss? To speak up or not?

I decided to wait. Just as I had when we were captured at the theater. A way out would surely reveal itself.

I'd been standing in the line about five minutes when a young officer came around the corner, accompanied by a soldier carrying a submachine gun. They joined the soldiers guarding us. I couldn't hear a thing the officer said to them. The soldier with the submachine gun took a step forward, pointed it at us, and pulled the trigger. It was so sudden, so outrageous, so fantastic that my mind couldn't make the connection. I didn't scream, try to run, or cover my face. I was simply transfixed. Where was that touch of decency, the pro forma ceremony: "Gentlemen, we would like to notify you that we're now going to shoot you. *C'est la guerre!*" Or the blindfold? Or I don't know what. I mean, *anything*. But just like that?

I realized I'd heard no *trattattattat*. No bullets. The machine gun was jammed. Another soldier took the gun from his comrade, examined it, took out a metal part, reinserted it, and, pointing the gun at the ground, pulled the trigger. Nothing. The officer and soldiers huddled over the gun. One of them pushed and pulled the bolt back and forth rapidly several times, then looked at the officer, perplexed. The officer said something to his men and, while listening, they looked back at us now and then, studying us with cold stares.

A moment later they broke up and walked over to our line with a corporal. He pointed at me and the fellow on my right and ordered, *"Ihr beide, mitkommen."**

As we started walking away, I glanced back and saw that the other boys were also split up in small groups. We crossed the courtyard and exited the orphanage. Soldiers stood guard along the sidewalk, too. It would have been futile to run out earlier.

The two soldiers led us up the street.

I was still shaking.

Obviously, it was a big raid, thoroughly planned and carried out like the one the previous November. But what were they after this time? Certainly not just two Jewish boys hiding in an orphanage! Besides, if it was us they were looking for, whoever alerted them would have pointed us out. If not Jews, then for who or what was all the display of brute force? Partisans, German deserters, escaped prisoners? Arms? Did they find any?

It must have been something big and important to justify bulldozing in like that and passing the entire Orfanotrofio through such a fine-tooth comb. Had they really expected armed resistance? And what about the padre? Had the Germans arrested him, too?

The two Germans continued to walk up the street, rifles pointed ahead. They kept me and the other boy between them while they surveyed the houses on both sides. I wondered why we were being taken and where. To be lined up against some other wall? The brutal episode constantly replayed in my mind. I still couldn't grasp that we'd been about to be shot and yet were still alive, thanks to some mechanical defect! Why hadn't they just used another gun to mow us down? Another imponderable! Even taking into consideration the known bestiality of the Nazis, I couldn't find any explanation for the execution order in the first

---

*"You two, come along."

place. A reprisal for a German who'd been shot in the neighborhood? And why were *we* selected to line up against a wall?

Some hundred yards ahead, a German soldier carrying a burlap sack came out of a house just as we were passing. He must have been one of the corporal's men. The corporal called him by name and asked what was in the sack. "A live hare. From the garden. The house is abandoned."

"Good. Give it to this fellow and come along."

I slung the sack over my shoulder, and we walked on. The hare's paws clawed and pedaled frantically as the animal tried to escape, jabbing me sharply all over my back. I had to grasp the sack firmly with both hands. Just what I needed, I sighed to myself. But despite the pain inflicted, I felt a certain kinship with the creature: we were both trapped. I didn't talk to the boy next to me, sensing our guards might get angry, thinking we were plotting an escape. We proceeded along the road at the same unhurried pace. Soon the houses, with most of their shutters closed, became sparse, giving way on the right to stone walls and fields beyond. Now and then the Germans stopped at a house. Two of them went in while we waited outside with the third. I assumed the Germans were looking for items to pilfer, for food supplies, or for specific people. After each foray they returned empty-handed. The whole area seemed deserted.

I tried to find out from their conversations what they had planned for us, but to no avail. The road was taking us north, away from the city. So far, we hadn't encountered another human being. The sun was scorching. Absolute stillness lay over the landscape. An ideal setting to shoot us and leave us where we fell. I thought of making a dash over the walls, but the open fields beyond thwarted any hope of success.

Nothing in the three Germans' attitude hinted that they had orders to kill us. They were casual, almost lazy. I had no idea how someone would comport himself when having to carry out such orders, and although I knew well enough that they could do it in cold blood, somehow my fears ebbed a little. One of the soldiers even cracked a faint smile when he saw the sack jump wildly on my back. It means nothing, Louis. Be on the alert, I warned myself. While we waited at the next house I heard a droning in the sky. At first, I saw nothing in the vast, simmering blue expanse, but soon made out the silver wings of a plane circling leisurely above us. An Allied spotter plane, I thought. He'll see the German uniforms and dive for us. There's my chance! The German squinted up for a moment, too, then relaxed. Did he think the plane was too high or wouldn't bother with us? Was it a German plane? His indifference doused my hopes.

The other two Germans came out of the house laughing, holding an enormous pair of women's woolen underwear. One of them said he would send one half to each of his two girlfriends. I thought the moment was right and spoke up, making deliberate mistakes: "Excuse me, I studied only a little of German. You could please tell me where you're taking us?"

"To headquarters," he reacted with faint surprise.

"Ah, thank you. And then?"

"To Germany. Armament factory, construction, I'm not sure."

"Thank you."

We walked on. At least we weren't going to be shot. Then, my momentary relief sank at the prospect of being sent to Germany. No, not Germany! Not after having gone through so much and arrived at this late stage when liberty was almost palpable! Looking back, I could still see the orphanage's bell tower. No more than a ten-minute fast run to the haven that had become my home and where, until an hour earlier, I had the sweet hope of freedom. Instead, every step was taking me closer to Germany. I knew the farther away we got, the more difficult it would become. Now I was dealing with only three Germans; later, there would be sentries, hierarchy, a regimented organization. Then a whole system of entrapment—typed reports, registration, lists, groups, roll-calls. Transports, like the one that took Papa away.

After what I felt was a decent interval, I addressed the German near me. "Excuse me, but do you think I might be here by mistake? I'm a theology student and have only seventeen years."

A few seconds went by. He called over to the corporal ahead of us, "Hey, listen, this one here says he's a theology student, not eighteen yet."

"So?"

"Suppose it's true?"

"Not my concern. Let him tell it to the Kommandant."

Chapter Thirty-One

About a mile farther we turned onto a dirt road and arrived at a massive farmhouse. It was SS headquarters. The corporal took the sack from me and ordered us to join the rest of the civilians. There were nearly forty men corralled in the front yard, including the orphanage boys who'd been lined up against the wall with me. Obviously they'd been brought by a shorter route. Right away I started pumping them for information, but they knew no more than I. Off to Germany! We were allowed to move around freely in the yard, but armed guards were positioned at strategic spots. I could see no way out.

Ten minutes later, we were all ordered into the farmhouse. We entered a large, empty room with small windows and heavy beams on a low ceiling. The guards moved aside to let an officer come into the room. An aide stepped up to him, saluted, and reported that they'd gathered thirty-seven civilians. "Good," he answered. "It won't do them any harm to do some work for a change." A tall, powerful-looking man, he stood examining us with a sullen expression, his thumbs hooked inside his belt.

The wheels of the robot machinery would soon spin faster, perhaps sucking us in ever-deeper, making our escape or extrication more difficult with each turn. Yet, there might be one fleeting opportunity to get away, some ladder to climb, some wall to scale. The question was how to recognize it.

Experience had taught me that the main thing to avoid was a list of names. That factual record, no sooner completed, achieves the status of divine law—a revered document by which those who compile and inherit it are guided blindly, a mystic power that has to be obeyed. To take a single name off it was nearly impossible. No one would dare. It required the permission of superiors, with explanations, written statements, carbon copies, signatures, countersignatures, rubber stamps. A list became the means by which a person could be checked on, accounted for, discovered missing, traced, tracked—transported.

I stepped in front of the officer. "Excuse me, Herr Offizier," I said in fractured German. "I'm a theology student at the Rifredi orphanage. I don't know, but I think perhaps by mistake I'm here. I have seventeen years." I showed him Don Giovanni's card. To my surprise, he didn't shout at me for my impudence. He took the card and studied it. I waited. The soldiers were looking at me. Still holding the card, the officer slowly inspected me from head to toe.

"That's a good pair of boots you're wearing. Military?"

They were heavy shoes that laced to above the ankles, with thick soles. "Military! Heavens no! They're from the orphanage. A charity donation."

He lingered on the boots for a while, then looked back at my card. I wondered whether I should offer him the boots, but was afraid he would take offense at the clumsy bribery attempt. Besides, it would reveal how eager I was to get away. For the moment, my motivation was factual. I was merely inquiring about the possibility of an administrative error, very dispassionate, a technical matter. But why was he taking so long to study the card? Had he smelled a forgery?

"You're only seventeen, you say?"

I shrugged my shoulders, puzzled he should doubt that. "Yes."

"A big, strong fellow like you?"

"I'm sorry, it's not my fault. You should have seen my mother!" I spread my arms for emphasis and even risked a little

193

smile. I wasn't sure I hadn't overstepped the limits with my bit of clowning, but I saw mild amusement in his eyes.

He gave me back the card, and I put it in my pocket, wondering what was on his mind.

"Stand there," he ordered, pointing at a spot about three feet from the open doorway. I went to it and stood facing him. "Now turn around." I made a half-turn and faced the doorway. All I could see was the blinding, sunny landscape outside. "Very good, very good," I heard him say. I stood waiting in anguish. Was I going to be shot in the back, an example to the others for having lied? "Now stand still." At that, I heard feet come running toward me and, as they reached full momentum, felt a kick in the behind with such force that I went shooting over the threshold. I braced myself for the fall and rolled over in the dust, dazed and aching. The officer was standing at the door. "Good luck. Don't let me see you again," he shouted, and went back inside.

I got up, quickly sent two emphatic *"Danke schöns"* after him, and dusted myself off as I started walking away. *Free, Free,* unbelievably F-R-E-E! Out of the clutches of the Germans once more. Easy now, Louis, don't show happiness. Wait until you're far away from here. Then you can run and scream and jump and fly. Yes, I know I can fly. For now, contain yourself, walk normally, and just concentrate on getting the dust off.

The guards at the farmhouse entrance had probably witnessed the scene with the Kommandant, for they let me leave without hindrance. I took the shorter side road, uneasy about going back along the main one we'd taken earlier. I didn't dare believe in my good fortune until the farmhouse was well out of sight. Then I quickened my pace and let the whole swell of happiness flood all through me unchecked. Oh God, never was your world so beautiful! That sky, those fields and trees! I could move among them at will. I wasn't dreaming, was I? Not fifteen

194

minutes before I was a prisoner destined to be dragged deep into Germany, and here I was walking back to the orphanage, my heart singing deliriously.

"Don Giovanni, Don Giovanni! You beautiful rascal," I thought, "you've saved my life again! The card you forged did it. A piece of paper I was fortunate to have on me at the right moment, and your ingenious idea to reduce my age. On how little a person's fate hinged. May every blessing of the Universe be bestowed upon you!"

While I pressed onward along the narrow, winding road, my thoughts went back to the others at the farmhouse. Would they be transported? Would they find a chance to escape on the way? They would have to succeed while they were still in Italy, because once across the border...And at the orphanage, had anyone been hurt or shot? Had the Germans left? I'd better make sure of that before walking in.

I was still some distance from the orphanage when, rounding a curve, I saw at about two hundred feet ahead of me a small figure dressed in black walking with a little boy. They were coming my way. I stopped and studied them. A priest, obviously. Another few steps and by the shuffling walk and white handkerchief, I recognized Monsignor Facibeni. What was he doing there?

He hadn't seen me, carefully watching his steps around the potholes and loose stones on the road. When I was sure he and the boy were alone, I ran as fast as I could to meet them. He looked up, and a smile lit up his face as he opened his arms wide. Out of breath, I lay my head on his shoulder, holding my arms around him while he hugged me with all the strength his frail little body could muster. "Nicola, Nicola, how happy I am to see you again!"

"Me, too, Padre, believe me. The Germans took me, but they let me go. It's a miracle!"

"How fortunate! I'm even more surprised than you. I heard you'd been caught with my other boys. Maria came to tell me. Some partisans were hiding with them."

I realized that's who the padre was referring to when he asked Maria if she'd alerted "the others" the last time the Germans came inside the orphanage. He'd also given refuge to anti-Fascists.

"There was talk you older boys would be shot, that arms had been found. A boy who'd hidden in the *campanile* told me he saw you carrying a sack. If the Germans had got it into their heads that the arms belonged to you, they were surely going to execute you. So, I was on my way to offer myself in exchange for your freedom and that of all my other boys."

"But, Padre, there were no arms."

"*Sì*, Nicola, the partisans hid some grenades in a flour bag at the *mulino*. Wasn't that your sack?"

"No, Padre, no! That was a hare the Germans stole and made me carry."

"A hare? Not grenades?"

"No."

"*Grazie a Dio!* Do you know if they found any arms?"

"No, all they said at the farmhouse was that we were going to be sent to work in Germany."

"*Meno male, meno male*. Run along to the Orfanotrofio. The Germans are gone. I'm going to the farmhouse with Luciano to see if I can accomplish something."

"*Buona fortuna*," I said, and watched for a while as the courageous old man made his way painfully down the road, leaning on the little boy. I was moved to the depth of my heart that Monsignor Facibeni had been willing to put his life on the line for me.

At the orphanage I was greeted like a returning hero. I had to tell my story over and over again. Willy kept hugging me. At our window he'd seen me at the wall and watched in horror as the gun was raised against us.

Toward evening the padre returned, unsuccessful, from his rescue mission. The boys were strong and healthy and were needed for work, the Germans had told him. No reason to worry because they would be well-fed and cared for. We all pretended to believe that.

That night, sleep was elusive. The horror of the day replayed itself in my mind endlessly. The following day Willy and I boarded up the door and fixed the lock. Next time, at the slightest sign of trouble, wherever we were, we would make a mad dash to our room and slide down the rope into the church, without hesitation.

Chapter Thirty-Two

On July 3, Siena was liberated. It lay only ninety kilometers directly south of Florence, and obviously we were the next large population target. Fearful of more German raids, and that Rifredi might become involved in heavy fighting for the city, Monsignor Facibeni ordered the boys to be evacuated to two other orphanages at Montecatini Terme and La Quiete, both north of us. He left Willy and me free to join them, but we weren't inclined to increase the distance that separated us from the Allies.

After the evacuation an uneasy stillness settled on the Orfanotrofio. Only the padre, a few boys, teachers, and some of the staff remained. Gone was the boisterous shouting, the playing at recess. The playground was deserted. Empty classrooms still had bits of Latin or math equations on their blackboards. In the evening, darkened corridors echoed the steps of some lone person regaining his room.

We huddled together at meals, in a doleful mood, unaccustomed to the new quiet and, in turn, hushed by it. The orphanage seemed much too large suddenly—too desolate and ghostly. It functioned, but as a skeleton of its former self. At night, the silence in the streets surrounding us seemed deeper, too. Their work done, the people of Rifredi, like everyone in Florence, scurried back early to the relative safety of their homes. The Germans had dictated a strict dusk-to-dawn curfew for the entire city.

I lay awake, my mind spinning furiously. Florence's liberation seemed assured. Would the weight of fear be lifted and vanish, or would some of it linger on unshakably? Oh, to be free again, I dreamed. I'd forgotten the taste of it. I could only fantasize what it might be like.

And how would that colossal event come about? I felt Florence would be declared an open city in deference to its magnificent buildings and art treasures. One day, perhaps, would we simply notice the Germans had pulled out?

I tried to visualize that delicious moment when I would first see a member of the Allied forces. He would be an officer, and I rehearsed what I would say to him with my little English. "Sir, you don't know how much happy I am to see you. I am Jew." There was so much more I wanted to tell him, but even in rehearsal I was so overcome by emotion I found it difficult to go on. The officer would understand, of course, and smile warmly, placing his hand on my shoulder. I knew I wouldn't care at that moment whether it was proper or not, but I would kiss him.

The fierce squealing of a pig pierced the night and jolted me from my reveries. Willy woke up. We heard a group of men talking loudly in German outside the Orfanotrofio. Soldiers probably, but we couldn't see them. In a matter of seconds we locked the doors, got dressed, and uncoiled the rope. We waited. The Germans were cursing roundly at the noisy animal for refusing to come along peacefully. After moments of deliberation and sarcastic comments on the wisdom of having requisitioned the creature in the first place, squeals and voices faded into the darkness.

Willy and I scanned the news daily in anticipation of new developments. But that was no reason for me to waste time. If I were privileged to live to see the miracle of liberation, I would immediately be confronted with the problems of starting a new life: reuniting with Mother, Harry, and Papa, learning a trade, earning money, deciding where to go, what to do—all weighty preoccupations. I must go on using my time to the fullest, I thought, as though nothing were happening. So I doggedly continued to read, write, and study. I enjoyed committing to paper everything that passed through my head, although I felt arrogant for bestowing such importance upon my mental meanderings. In orderly handwriting, never skipping a line in my notebook, I filled page after page with comments on religion, faith, truth, integrity, wisdom, cupidity, decency, and selfishness. The list went on and on.

I was fascinated by the elements that shaped the sum total of a human being: personality, opinions, feelings, strengths, and weaknesses. Were some or most predetermined and inherited at birth, or could circumstances and influences form human character? I devoured books on the philosophy of Pascal and Descartes and wrote down the passages I considered brilliant and the ones that so eloquently expressed ideas I agreed with. Why? Because, I finally decided, they were in step with values I'd cherished, acquired at home from parents, teachers, friends, enemies, and each of my life's experiences.

I took a critical look at myself. I knew I was excessively stubborn, pedantic, and meticulous. The definition of a perfectionist—one who takes great pains (and gives them to others)—fit me perfectly. I envied other people their ability to command respect, or for their engaging personalities, or ease with strangers. My utter lack of contact with the other sex disturbed me. That my inexperience might later make me only more miserable and increase my awkwardness, filled me with anxiety. All in all, I concluded, there was ample room for self-improvement. I worried a lot.

I wrote down all those thoughts, with the date. However, I was careful to avoid Jewish topics in case the notebooks fell into the wrong hands.

Though an underlying tone of despondency ran through my notebooks, I was still grateful just to be alive.

Chapter Thirty-Three

Toward the middle of July a series of momentous events gave us fresh hope. On the seventeenth, General Erwin Rommel was badly wounded in an air raid while driving back to Germany. Three days later, there was an attempt on Hitler's life. On the radio Hitler said it was God's hand that had protected him, proof that his mission to lead Germany was sacred. However disappointing the news, there might be other efforts to do away with him, and better luck next time!

On the twenty-fifth, the Americans broke out of Saint-Lô, and the Russians, who had already recaptured Vitebsk and Minsk, entered Brest-Litovsk on the twenty-eighth.

A sluggish, smoldering July dissolved into August. Life at the Orfanotrofio had ground nearly to a standstill. Monsignor Facibeni thought it best that he, too, join his evacuated orphans in La Quiete. Again, he offered to take us along, but didn't insist. Liberation was by no means a certainty, and staying closer to the front wouldn't make it happen sooner. In fact, Montecatini or La Quiete probably would have been safer than Rifredi. But only sheer force could have moved us from the orphanage. No more running.

Besides us, only Maria, Don Felicino, two nuns, Morino, and a few other boys in charge of maintenance were still living at the orphanage. The silent emptiness created a feeling of life suspended, the air pregnant with imminent and drastic change. Waves of cannon thunder rolled in from various points on the horizon, sometimes muffled, then nearer, a dialogue of angry, giant lions that continued throughout the night, as bolts of man-made lightning rent the sky and outlined distant hills.

Rifredi was almost deserted. The few now left at the Orfanotrofio bunched together, feeding on rumors from drifting strangers. One said that British and colonial-Indian troops had taken San Gimigniano and were advancing on San Casciano. A mere twenty kilometers south! Nonsense, came another eyewitness report. The Germans had stopped them. Another passerby assured us he'd seen the American flag at Incisa, twenty-seven kilometers southeast. The German radio station was still broadcasting, but day by day, albeit couched in euphemisms, the news was unmistakably of retreat. When there were reports on the fighting in Italy, it was about our area now, confirmed by ever-louder artillery-shell bursts.

As the Allies progressed closer, shells zipped over us, slamming into German-held hills farther north. Battle lines shifted, and ensuing silences were disheartening after the ear-rending explosions. A day or so later, with the German cannons repositioned behind us, shells crisscrossed and shrieked over our heads from both sides, crashing within sight of the orphanage. Willy and I sat for long hours tucked deep inside the *rifugio* out on the field, often joined by tenants from neighboring buildings. It was a new, terrifying experience. I preferred air raids by far. Their warnings allowed us to gauge the planes' course, followed by sirens announcing the all clear. Cannon shells, on the other hand, struck unexpectedly at any time, from anywhere. Flares, seemingly nailed into the sky by their parachutes, guided the artillery pointers. After an interminable lapse, they would burn themselves out. It would be dark again, silent again. Back to bed. An hour later the duel would resume, and we would dash to the field once more. Clearly, we were in the thick of the front-line zone.

CHAPTER THIRTY-THREE

There was nothing to do but wait, and waiting was an inducement to do nothing else but drift through the day, tuned to the latest reports. It worked like a unique opiate: mind alert, body torpid.

Willy and I wondered why Don Giovanni hadn't been to see us in nearly ten days. Varlungo, at the southern end of Florence, had probably gone through similar shellings. Was he all right? It was dangerous to move about, and the Germans had no doubt restricted the comings and goings of civilians.

With surprise, I noticed that my longing for the day of liberation, encouraged to fever pitch, was tinged with unease. The future, no matter how bright, would also mean change—abandoning people I'd grown fond of and things to which I'd become accustomed. The thought of losing them distressed me, and I couldn't understand why.

On August 3, I made an entry: "I'm reading 'To the 20-year-olds' by Georges Hoarnaert. He writes, 'Force yourself to take notes on your moral state daily, or once a week. But do it briefly, without the slightest literary vanity as you do not write for posterity but for yourself. You will find it useful and interesting later to read the history of your soul. You will then understand that providential plan that you could not discern at the time.'" My entry went on: "I'm happy to see a writer dealing with young people's education recommend what I already started on my own a year and a half ago and intend to continue."

That same night a series of loud and frequent explosions kept us in our clothes, ready to escape or take cover. If these be the birth pangs of liberation, I reflected, it's going to be a hard delivery.

Before daybreak the news reached us that the Germans had destroyed every bridge in Florence with the exception of the Ponte Vecchio. To prevent its use, however, at both ends they'd dynamited the houses into hills of rubble. The Germans had retreated to our side of town.

Over the thin breakfast Maria managed to provide, our talk was a mix of excitement and fear. Did blowing up the bridges mean the Germans were going to make a stand, or did they do it to gain time for an orderly evacuation? "Too late for that," one boy said with relish. "The partisans are just waiting for a chance to ambush them. The streets will be rivers of blood." Maria bitterly invoked the Madonna to be witness to the misery brought about by Germans and Allies alike, foreigners, all of them, who fought out their conflicting politics not on their own soil, but all over poor and ravaged Italy. Don Felicino said he hoped only that the Germans wouldn't turn the orphanage into a garrison, for which it was ideally suited. I thought the Germans wouldn't have deprived themselves of vital bridges if they felt they could hold the city.

"It might take weeks for the Allies to get across the river," I said, depressed.

"Not necessarily," Morino countered. "In Cyrenaica I saw Italian army engineers at work. Clever fellows. They put up prefabricated sections over rafts, rubber boats, barrels, anything."

"But what about artillery and tanks?"

"They roll right over those things," he explained, with a sweeping gesture.

I'd been impressed with Morino ever since the day he pried open Concetta's bread cupboard and turned it into a cornucopia from which he hurled life-sustaining loaves in all directions. His report on bridge-building was convincing enough for me. I was ready to believe any optimistic opinion. To speculate about failure would be unbearable. But we would have to be more cautious than ever, for, like wounded animals, the Germans were likely to be at their most dangerous.

CHAPTER THIRTY-THREE

Nothing seemed to change in the following days. There were rumors that the Germans were pulling out of Florence entirely. Willy and I stayed away from the gates and deserted street, moving only along walls and corridors to Maria's kitchen, then back to our room.

The German armed forces' radio station was no longer on the air. We heard convoys of trucks rolling through the night and sporadic bursts of machine-gun fire even during the day.

Where were those Allies? What was keeping them?

It was uncannily quiet. Perhaps the Allies were camped nearby and we could sneak over to them. Willy and I decided to detect their positions from the top of the *campanile* and map out an escape-route. By now, such plotting had become an automatic reflex. We pulled up the ropes and ladder, closed the trapdoor, and climbed to the bell's landing. We hadn't exactly expected Swastika and Union Jack banners to be arranged in neat, opposing lines, yet we were disappointed. No sign of anything unusual.

Across the street from the *campanile*, two German soldiers emerged from Via delle Panche near the grocery store. They stopped at the corner, arms at the ready. We jerked back and flattened out, peeking down from opposite rain gutter openings. They wore camouflage-spotted uniforms. One of them lit a cigarette.

Willy's excited and terrified whisper startled me. "Ludi, look, quick!" I slid over to his side. Five partisans crept through the field behind the church, approaching the Germans from the right. They opened fire but missed. The Germans took cover instantly and shot back, supported by unseen comrades farther down the street. We were caught in the middle and watched the encounter develop into a full-scale skirmish. Soon, the heavier German fire drove the partisans back. Some Germans pursuing them had already crossed to our side of Via delle Panche. A minute later there was an explosion that seemed right below us. Suddenly we heard a German soldier moaning. Frantic orders in German emanated from the church.

I knew we were doomed. They were going to come up the *campanile* to use it as a lookout. I rushed to pull up the ropes so we could swing ourselves down the outside of the tower, but Willy yanked them from me, arguing that it would be suicide. We waited in fear. No Germans came up. Shooting continued, and shortly after the partisans vanished. The quiet returned, but we remained in the tower another half hour before coming down.

The church door had been blown open, perhaps by a grenade. The walls were damaged, and there were large blood-stains on the floor. "That German must have been hit badly," I said. "They probably had to stretch him out."

"They may still be around. Let's get out of here."

We ran to the *rifugio,* out of sight, underground, to let our jarred nerves recover. Maria and a nun were there, trying to calm a young girl quivering and sobbing hysterically. Her dress was torn apart and I could see a blood-spattered breast. She'd been raped by German soldiers during a house search.

Chapter Thirty-Four

Two days later, walking into Maria's kitchen, I chanced upon the tail end of something Morino was saying: "...dancing and laughing, complete strangers hugging and kissing each other and soldiers. *Mamma mia!*" He crunched into an apple.

"What are you talking about, Morino?"

"The Allies are in Florence."

I couldn't swallow. "In Florence?" My voice cracked. "Where? How do you know?"

"I just saw them in Piazza Duomo. Nothing's functioning, no trams, no buses. I walked. Took me a good hour each way!"

Easy now, Louis, calm, calm. "Well, well, Maria, what do you say to that? Excuse me, may I have another *biscotto*?"

Maria said she would believe the *Inglesi* were here when she saw them, and, anyhow, English or Germans, it was all the same. She wanted a normal life again for her country.

"So, Morino, you actually saw them, huh?" I resumed as nonchalantly as I could.

"Yes, certainly."

"Weren't you afraid to go that far out in the open?"

"At first, yes. But I was careful. There wasn't a German in sight, so I kept going."

I made a casual exit from the kitchen, then ran to tell Willy the staggering news.

"Ludi, that means they'll be here today, tomorrow at the latest! *Mazel tov* and *Schechianou!** The nightmare's over!"

---

*"Congratulations." *Schechianou* is part of a Hebrew thanksgiving prayer.

I was afraid to succumb to the happiness that engulfed me. Would there be retributions for having rejoiced too soon? After all, I wasn't officially free yet. Just let me see a British or an American soldier, just one! I wanted to shake his hand, smell him, see what his uniform looked like, his boots and helmet, and hear him talk. I couldn't restrain my euphoria. I even flirted with the idea of telling Maria and the others I was *Ebreo*.* The temptation to see their faces was overpowering. "People, I have an announcement to make. I am not Nicola Capaldi. I'm not Italian, not French, not even Catholic. I'm Jewish!" I arranged and rearranged the scene to elicit from my listeners the most stunned responses to the *coup de théâter* I fancied my announcement would cause. However, common sense prevailed. It was too early.

No British soldiers showed up that day, nor the next, and I began to worry again. Normally it was no more than a fifteen-to-twenty-minute tramway ride into town. What was holding them up? Something must be wrong. Willy believed the Allies would first have to go after the bulk of the German army. But they would get to Rifredi eventually. Just a little more patience. "Willy," I said, "we're not on any main road. If we wait for freedom in an official ceremony, it might take weeks. The Germans could regroup and counterattack. I say we make our own way into town now!"

"Look, the war's been going on for five years, ten since we've been running from the Nazis," Willy answered. "What difference does another day or two make?"

"But Morino didn't see a single German!" I argued.

"That doesn't mean there aren't any. Besides, I bet there must be partisans behind shutters or on rooftops who would shoot at anyone not in Allied uniform."

*Jewish.

CHAPTER THIRTY-FOUR

We finally agreed that if no Allies showed up by the next morning, we would go. In truth, I was a little scared at my bravado. That night, I tossed the pros and cons around in my mind, frightened by dangers lurking in the no-man's-land out there, but my determination prevailed. Freedom was dangling so temptingly near that I felt a compulsion to touch it, breathe it.

The following morning, the same quiet. No voices, no animation, no clanking of military machinery to indicate our liberation had arrived. We decided to start out in full daylight, after lunch.

We told Maria we hoped to come back soon for our belongings. I asked her to not throw my notebooks away even if I didn't show up for a time. "Be careful, boys," she said.

The gate closed behind us and we remained motionless on the sidewalk. Left. Right. Nothing. Silence. We were alone.

Avanti! We started walking. It would be home territory until Piazza Dalmazia, having walked that stretch to Cinema Flora so often with the orphans. Later we would have to proceed by instinct in the general direction of Piazza Duomo. At first we'd thought of putting on the Orfanotrofio uniform as a safe-conduct, and then decided against it. From afar, a uniform is a uniform, and ours might easily have been mistaken for an enemy's.

We continued down Via delle Panche, keeping well away from the wall to show we had no hostile intentions. "Ludi," Willy whispered, "how's your English?"

"What? Have you seen Allies?"

"No, but suppose we run into General Eisenhower?" Willy was always the clown.

We heard faint steps behind us. We glanced back, relieved to recognize the grocer's wife at the end of the street. We turned left into Via Reginaldo Giuliani, leading to Piazza Dalmazia. No signs of life there, either. We hadn't gone far when we heard a shot. Frightened, we ducked behind the nearest open door. After an interval of quiet we continued toward the piazza. First we would have to cross Ponte Mugnone, a small bridge over the Mugnone River, which here was nothing more than a stream. As we approached the bridge we saw it had been dynamited. Large craters made vehicular crossing impossible. Some sections barely hung together. Willy pointed to what looked like a mine that hadn't been detonated.

We climbed carefully down the embankment and skipped across some stones to the other side. We slowed down as Piazza Dalmazia came into view. Surely someone would be there, civilian or military. We wanted to see before being seen. My heart beat faster. Would I see my first Allied soldier? I wanted to be ready for that great moment, remember every detail for the rest of my life. What would he say to us? What if he thought we were Germans in disguise? After all, our identity cards were forged. Never mind, it could all be straightened out. Let me just see my hero.

We were partially hidden behind a closed newspaper kiosk. We let our eyes pan around the piazza. Deserted. Eerie. A store's metal curtain had been bent open and gaped at me. A little farther, a cut telephone wire dangled from a pole, whipping it lazily. Near Cinema Flora, a barricade blocked the main street into town. From this distance it, too, seemed abandoned. We couldn't cross the vast open expanse without exposing ourselves. What to do? Suddenly something moved near the poster column across the piazza. I yanked Willy closer to me, and we riveted our eyes on the column. All was still again.

Had we been seen? I detected movement again. No more than a shoulder, but I was sure someone was hiding there. If it was a German, we still had a good head start to run away. We remained motionless, continuing to watch. Now and then the person behind it made slight movements, but I didn't get the impression he or she wore a German uniform. If only I were sure it was an Allied soldier or a partisan, I could come out and yell, "Hey, I'm a friend!" Another minute passed and I saw a bicycle wheel emerge, then an arm, then the black, flat hat of a priest. He limped as he wheeled the bicycle by his side, heading toward our side of the street. "Willy, am I dreaming? Don Giovanni? Yes, yes!"

"Don Giovanni!" we yelled, running across the piazza. Stunned, he let the bicycle drop and we fell into each other's arms. What were we doing out in the streets? Tired of waiting for the Allies, what else! His face changed. Were we mad? We had just crossed no-man's-land! He exhorted us to get out of there fast, hastily leading the way across the piazza to the barricade. It was manned by partisans. They let us pass without question. Previously, they had told Don Giovanni he could proceed at his own risk. Once behind the barricade, all of us started talking at the same time.

What was *he* doing here? He wanted to see how near he could get to the Orfanotrofio. He'd been worried about us, and the telephone lines had been cut. Rifredi was still in German hands because it lay on the path of their units retreating north. Was it true Florence was free? Yes. Had he actually, really, positively, seen Allied soldiers? Of course, for days! Where *were* they? Farther back in town.

"Can we go?"

"Yes."

"Now?"

"Yes."

"Then let's!"

Delirium!

There was only modest pedestrian and car traffic in the streets, and no Allied soldiers. We arrived at where the Via del Romito split in two. I stopped and stared, my heart pounding.

Two soldiers were sitting on a railing, nonchalantly watching the passing scene, rifles in their laps. I approached with trepidation.

"Excuse me—are you English or American?"

"English."

"Beautiful! Thank you, thank you for the liberation. I just now escape from the Nazis. I am a Jew," I said haltingly. Then I added, "Excuse me, please," and I kissed the nearest one on the cheek. Just as in my dream. He was embarrassed, yet allowed it with good humor.

"Good luck!" he shouted as I rejoined Willy and Don Giovanni. I was happy, but this long yearned-for event turned out to be less momentous than I'd imagined.

As we reached the center of town, the Allied military presence became increasingly evident. We saw our first Americans. Piazza Santa Maria Novella seemed to be a central dispatch area. We stopped to watch military personnel with their equipment, supervised by smartly dressed soldiers with the letters MP on their armbands.

We continued toward Piazza Duomo. There was no longer dancing or wild rejoicing in the streets. People had already recovered from their first outburst of exultation. But there was a festive air: happy faces, animated talk, expansive gestures, loud voices. I abandoned myself to the sensuousness of the atmosphere. I hadn't walked freely among people, openly in the streets, for five long years.

It was August 11, 1944

My God, I was *FREE*!

Chapter Thirty-Five

I was drunk with liberty. For the first time since I heard the name Hitler, twelve years earlier in Germany, I was experiencing something alien: a complete absence of fear. It would take some adjustment. Everything I saw and heard was a fresh and wonderful confirmation of my newfound freedom, contributing to my tipsiness. There was beauty in every detail: the national origins of soldiers (British, Americans, Australians, colonial Indians, New Zealanders, Canadians, Poles); the multicolored insignia on their sleeves (emblems of their regiments and armies); the aroma of Lucky Strikes and Navy Cuts; the styles of the uniforms (occasionally a Scottish kilt or an Asian turban); the music of English spoken in the streets; the mud-splattered Jeeps, the tommy guns, the signs pointing in all directions, often erected at the exact same spots where the Germans still had theirs; the profusion of Allied military departments' initials, including the word *billeting*, which I tried in vain to figure out (a billet, to me, was a ticket); even girls in uniform, beauties all, even the ugly ones. I followed them around a little to hear how English sounded with mellower voices.

Willy and I had our first taste of white bread again. I'd forgotten that bread didn't have to be gray. Don Giovanni took us to the Palazzo Vecchio to be legitimized as refugees. The clerk told us we were entitled to monthly living allowances. We spent the next few nights at Don Giovanni's house in Varlungo.

213

On my third day of roaming about town, still reveling in the sights and sounds, I came upon a line of women with buckets, receiving water from a military vehicle. The soldier supervising the distribution had a *Magen David* on his sleeve!

"Hello, I'm Jewish, too," I announced brightly, still amazed I could say such things openly. "Where are you from?"

"Eretz Israel," he replied, smiling. "From Kibbutz Ginossar."

I was awed and proud. A Jewish soldier from the Jewish homeland in the fight against the Nazis! He said the Star of David was the official emblem of his unit, composed entirely of Jewish boys from Palestine. I started to tell him about myself, but he interrupted. "Come with me. You'll meet the other boys."

He took me to a garage where the unit's vehicles were parked. It was the company base. He introduced me to his friends, his sergeant, and the commanding officer. "He's a genuine Jewish refugee. You should hear how he was saved by Catholic priests!"

When the officer learned I was alone in Florence, without means, news of my family, or fixed lodging, he said good-naturedly, "We'll adopt you."

The company was a water-tank unit of the British Eighth Army under General Harold Alexander. They had supplied water to troops in all the North African campaigns, and since the Salerno landing, throughout the battle in Italy. They were currently stationed in Florence, bringing water to the front and helping out the local population. The company also served as a central repair shop for disabled military vehicles.

The soldiers lived in a schoolhouse behind the garage. Willy stayed with the unit, too, and we were "billeted" in a classroom with eight others. They gave us cots, blankets, sheets and pillows, mess tins, cups, and overalls. We shined our shoes, made our beds the army way, stood in line for chow, learned to juggle both halves of the mess tin in one hand and a cup of tea in the other, and after meals dunked the utensils into barrels of boiling water. After a breakfast of porridge and orange marmalade, the twenty water-tank trucks rolled out to their assigned destinations. We worked a full day at the garage, got paid, and even enjoyed buying privileges at the company's NAAFI store (a store of Navy, Army & Air Force Institutes). On occasion, the boys smuggled us into theaters reserved for army personnel to see the latest films from America.

About ten days after we'd left, Rifredi was cleared of Germans and we returned to visit the Orfanotrofio. Padre Facibeni and a good number of orphans were already back. He was in fine spirits, and the orphanage was bustling with the new vitality of freedom. Unfortunately, during the last days before liberation, the Germans had used the *campanile* as a sniper's nest. We went up to look. Hundreds of empty cartridge casings littered the top landing. There was a large hole in the roof of our room, the result of a direct hit from a shell. The boys told us that the grocer's wife had been killed in Via delle Panche on the same day we'd left. That was the shot that had sent us diving for cover. It was futile to reflect on the quirks of fate.

The visit was unsettling. Memories crowded me uncomfortably. They were too raw and too painful. I was stepping over a threshold, back into my past, and I realized the monumental event of liberation had already made a clean cut from the long, sad chapter in my life. My past was really over.

We couldn't resist revealing our real identities to the boys. They'd been unaware of the persecution of Jews throughout Europe, therefore expressed only mild surprise. What really impressed them was that we weren't Mario and Nicola Capaldi but other people, with names, ages, and a national origin different from the ones we'd claimed.

"Then you speak German, too?" a boy marveled.

"Yes," I replied. "Even Yiddish."

"Say something in Yiddish!" another boy begged.

The strange-sounding words convinced them. I had said, "It's wonderful to have lived to this day to be able to talk to you like this."

Chapter Thirty-Six
WHAT I DIDN'T KNOW AT THE TIME

The northeastern Veneto region was still solidly in German hands after Florence's liberation in August 1944.

The school year over in Treviso, Don Angelo spent his vacation assisting Monsignor D'Alessi, who had been elevated from rector of the Seminario to bishop in Portagruaro, fifty-six kilometers away. Before leaving, Don Angelo had provided contingencies for the "Five French," including shoes for the children and a bicycle for errands. He instructed the Seminario bursar to notify him immediately of any emergency in Santa Bona.

One night in August, Aunt Sonia had a severe asthma attack, and Harry bicycled to the bursar at five in the morning. He came back an hour later with the doctor.

"There's really nothing more we can do for the signora here," he said, after examining Sonia. "She should go to a clinic."

Don Angelo arranged for "Maria Borelli" to be admitted to the private and expensive Monastier Clinic. He told the director to take good care of his "relative" and that he would pay for everything. After more than two weeks, Aunt Sonia's condition had not improved much. The director thought the best cure would be a stay in a drier climate, preferably in a sanitarium.

Don Angelo could only afford to place her with Sylvia in the convalescent home in Crocetta, where Miss Adler and Mrs. Schwartzwald had been living since they had left the Francescane convent. Higher up and farther inland, Crocetta enjoyed a healthier climate than Santa Bona.

There was no car available for the trip to Crocetta. Sylvia borrowed a bike, Harry a small donkey cart. He installed a fauteuil inside and tied the cart securely to his bicycle. The convoy set out. People along the way stared at the

217

middle-aged dowager enthroned on a donkey cart, holding an umbrella up against the sun while a puffing rickshaw boy wheeled her through the countryside and a maid pushed from behind, a caricature of bankrupt aristocracy.

En route, they came across the bodies of fifteen young men sprawled on both sides of the road. The Germans had shot them in reprisal for two of their officers who had been killed by partisans. The bodies had been left to rot as a warning. Partisan attacks on German convoys and supply depots had become more frequent, more effective, and more bold.

In early September Don Angelo left his post with Bishop D'Alessi to resume teaching. "I'd like to pay you for your services," the bishop said.

Don Angelo shook his head. "A father doesn't pay his son." He was already at the door when he suddenly remembered his Jewish refugees and the shrinking funds. He paused, then turned abruptly and said, "Please, I've changed my mind."

The students at the Seminario had been evacuated, as furious battles were expected to develop in northern Italy, gateway to Austria and, thereby, Germany. Don Angelo taught his classes in Merlengo, six kilometers away, but continued to live at the Seminario.

Don Angelo's mother, Henny Tarnover, and her two sons were in Ponte di Piave, a village on the northern bank of the Piave River. In the First World War, it had become the front line in fierce and prolonged fighting. In recent weeks a heavily defended bridge near the village had been attacked eighty-two times, and Ponte di Piave could fall into German hands while the Allies were still bogged down just north of Florence.

Aunt Sonia and Sylvia returned to Santa Bona at the end of September. In late October Don Angelo transferred his mother, the three Tarnovers, and household items to Fagare, a village south of the river, where a priest took them in. Don Angelo lent the "Five French" in Santa Bona his mother's pots, pans, dishes, and a small oven, which he installed with the pipe zigzagging up and out through the top windowpane.

Firewood was nearly unobtainable. "We still have a reserve at the Seminario," Don Angelo said. He told Harry to bring a big suitcase to a certain spot at nine the next evening. He threw some wood over the wall. Then he put the cost equivalent in the donation box. "I'm not stealing, you understand. Now you can stay warm and comfortable, and I can have a free conscience, too."

The storms of war continued to whirl over Europe and the Far East in December 1944. In Italy the Allies had been brought to a near standstill once more. For the holidays, Don Angelo bought the three youngsters fabric and sent them to a tailor to have clothes made. When Harry, Sylvia, and Renée went to show themselves to Don Angelo, he beamed, "Come sono contento!" and wrapped all three into his arms. He also sent along nearly unobtainable rations of flour, margarine, cacao powder, and a few eggs for the group to bake something festive.

Christmas morning, Mother kneaded the dough and spread out a chocolate layer while the children eagerly watched. Averting her eyes, she suggested they give the cake to Don Angelo as a gesture of gratitude. "At least, let us smell the dough," Harry pleaded. Mother passed the pan around from nose to nose. When the cake was ready, Harry dipped a match in whipped cream and wrote, "Al nostro Padre Don Angelo, Buon Natale da Santa Bona." Then he took the cake to Treviso. He waited until Don Angelo was in church, went up to his room, put it on his table, and left.

An hour later Don Angelo was already in Santa Bona. "But why have you made this sacrifice?" He insisted that they take the cake back, but Mother refused. "Then, share it with me." The group stood firm. Finally, they agreed to let him give the cake to Mrs. Glatt, who was still in the hospital with her spine ailment.

There was almost nothing left of the money Don Giovanni had given Don Angelo ten months earlier. Don Angelo went begging. In the afternoons after his classes he made the rounds on his bicycle. His group offered to take jobs in kitchens or factories to ease his burden. Don Angelo refused. "No, you would be exposed to all sorts of dangers. I've managed to pull you through safely this far, and as long as I can help it, we'll keep to our present arrangement."

Don Angelo received negligible donations: 200 lire, 150 lire. He considered revealing that he was helping Jews, but realized he could not involve others in his secret operation for fear of betrayal. He also used the little money he had of his own. Finally he turned to Baronessa Franchetti in Venice, a well-to-do woman whose father was Jewish. "I know your father is hidden in Crocetta. I've hidden two Jewish women there, too, and I'm taking care of others." He apologized for pressuring her, but said he had no choice. The baronessa gave him 6,000 lire and said he could come back when he needed more.

On December 27, 1944, the Allies dropped eighteen bombs on the Seminario in Treviso. Three more narrowly missed it. The vast and beautiful complex was almost destroyed. No other building was attacked. Several days earlier, German officers and trucks had been going in and out of the Seminario to requisition beds and mattresses for troops crowding into the area. Allied intelligence may have concluded that the Seminario was being used as a German headquarters.

After the bombardment, Don Angelo and other faculty members went to live at the empty Collegio Pio X. Its pupils had already been evacuated for some time with those from the Seminario.

There was only a modest coating of snow in January 1945, but the cold was severe. After nearly five years of war, coal was nonexistent, wood had disappeared from the open market, and Don Angelo had run out of supply sources. The children scrounged through the countryside for dead branches and old planks.

For weeks a layer of thick fog clung to the region, giving even the most familiar shapes a ghostlike and sinister appearance. At times, when the gray curtain drifted thinly before closing up again, a feeble sun eerily glimmered through without softening the frost on Santa Bona's windowpanes. There were not enough blankets to ward off the cold at night. Harry, Sylvia, and Renée huddled together under a spare mattress.

Harry helped out as usher at the local cinema, a large room on the parochial school's ground floor. That entitled him to free tickets. In exchange for them, he expected Sylvia and Renée to lend a hand with his chores, but they seldom did their full share. His position was simple: no help, no tickets. Before showtime, there was psychology at work on both sides, Harry hiding the tickets while the girls became anxious. "Oh, Harry, you know we love you. We'll help you next time. It's just that we were so tired. Girls can't be strong like boys, you know." Relenting, he reached into his pocket and handed them each a ticket. Confident *he had taught them a lesson, at thirteen he did not realize yet that, though it was said this is a man's world, it was a woman's universe.*

A unit of Mussolini's Black Brigades was headquartered outside Treviso. The unit moved into town in January after partisans had ambushed them on the open road. They took over the evacuated Collegio Pio X and erected a dividing wall through the entrance and its two wings. Don Angelo and the other priests were on one side, Fascists on the other. They did not know that Don Angelo was hiding an injured partisan at the Francescane convent next door.

*The SS and Fascist Brigades took reprisals against the partisans' sabotage with savage attacks and raids to flush them out of their hiding places. When a wave of Germans descended on Ormelle to comb the village for partisans, Mrs. Wolf slipped into nun's clothing and met the search party at the nursery with the ecclesiastic greeting, "*Laudetur Jesus Christus.*"*

Funds became scarce again and Don Angelo appealed to the bishop. His superior donated 35,000 lire and some clothing, saying, "My dear Don Angelo, I fear for you. What if they catch you? I wouldn't be able to help you."

"But, Your Excellency," Don Angelo replied, "should it happen, at least you wouldn't be ashamed of me. I would have saved lives instead of ended them."

In February, Don Angelo shifted his new class from Merlengo to Santa Bona. He taught in the only available facility, a bishop's mausoleum, located directly under the "Five French's" room in the parochial school next door to a family of Italian refugees.

Miss Adler and Mrs. Schwartzwald continued to live in quiet anonymity in Crocetta. In March they needed medical attention. The doctor who came to examine them was a Fascist. He told the convalescent home director, "I'm not fooled. Those women are Jewesses. Don't ask me to see that sort of person again. Just consider yourself lucky I don't denounce all of you."

Don Angelo hastily transferred the two women back to the Francescane con-vent in Treviso. For fourteen months, he had succeeded in protecting fifteen Jewish women and children without losing a single one.

Chapter Thirty-Seven

Willy had gone to join his father in Rome. We'd said our good-byes, with the hope that we would each find our families alive, and promised to stay in touch. All communication with Mother had been cut off since Florence's liberation. The Germans had established a strong defense line in the hills between Florence and the Treviso area.

I thought it my duty to go out and actively take part in the war. I was enjoying a cozy arrangement while others were fighting and dying in order to rid the world of the Nazi evil. There were rumors that the Germans had set up a systematic extermination machinery against the Jews of Europe and that Auschwitz was only one part of it. That chilled me to the marrow.

The soldiers of the Palestinian water-tank unit were brave young men helping to liberate Italy and humble the Nazis. And they were Jews! Warrior Jews! Unlike the refugees I'd known, meekly acquiescing to authority, always depending on others' goodwill, these free men could be proud of their heritage; proud of the land they called their own. I wanted to be one of them.

They tried to dissuade me from enlisting. They said I'd already suffered enough, that my duty was to my family. Nevertheless, I went to Allied military officers in town and asked for interviews. They always asked, "What's your nationality?" My parents had lost their Polish citizenship; we never tried to acquire the German; France wouldn't grant us theirs; and I wasn't Italian. Next: "What are your military qualifications?" It soon became apparent that no regular military corps of any country would take a stateless, inexperienced straggler into its ranks. The only other possibility was to join a group of partisans somewhere, assuming they would bother with a novice who wasn't even Italian. Finally, a Canadian intelligence officer offered me a job interrogating German prisoners near the front line.

My soldier friends argued with me. "Don't be a fool! You're not a Canadian national. They have no responsibility for you. If you got hit, do you think you would ever see your family again? No one would even know where you were buried. Come to Palestine. And why is interrogating prisoners more of a contribution than putting damaged military vehicles back into service?"

I guess I wasn't courageous or reckless enough. I remained working in the garage.

In the past, I'd been despondent over my awareness of the loss of time. Now free, I embarked on a frenetic catching-up program. I'd always been interested in cinematography, but in the chaotic aftermath of war I knew of no way to learn the craft. I tried anything to help me determine what other profession to follow. I learned all I could about cars, although injured hands, stubborn rusty bolts, and crank oil dripping in my face often made me curse that occupation. Three evenings a week at a nearby cinema, I learned to be a movie projectionist. I was also an apprentice in a dental lab. On weekends I visited Don Facibeni at the orphanage and Don Giovanni in his small house next to the Varlungo convent.

By winter I'd learned a lot from my stay with the unit, and not just about carburetors, broken axles, and Betty Grable. In the unit there were dark and olive-skinned soldiers, whose ancestors didn't speak Yiddish or any European language. I discovered that Jews can also originate from Erithrea, Iraq, or Yemen. From conversations and the letters and pictures my friends received, I began to get an idea of Jewish life in Palestine, of its cities, *kibbutzim,* and valleys. They talked of their home, this Promised Land, a place where the Star of David was an emblem of honor, not a mark of shame. I also learned that Jewish emigration to Palestine had been suspended for the duration of the war. Thousands of certificates issued by the British mandate had not been used and so were available again.

Even though I shared the life of the soldiers, I felt I didn't really belong. Our experiences had been too different. Their youth, although filled with trials, had been free of persecution. They had not been hunted down like animals. They'd grown up in a communal spirit of freedom and had formed friendships cemented through good and harsh times in Palestine, as well as through the vicissitudes of war. By force of events, I had developed as an awkward loner, learning to trust no one, and thus was deprived of social skills. I was worried mainly whether I would ever see my family again, and what direction to give my life, while those soldiers could enjoy a well-earned victory without qualms.

In the evening, Italian girls waited for them in front of our building. The soldiers came out well-dressed, showered, shaved, and "Old-Spiced." My closest friend was Herbert. He was quiet and pleasant, born in Germany like me. His parents had emigrated to Palestine as Hitler came to power. Our family also had had a chance to emigrate to Palestine in 1938, but Papa believed Hitler wouldn't last; eventually our emigration papers expired.

Herbert and I professed a dislike for the superficial and frivolous. We didn't hang up pinups, and found it demeaning to "conquer" hungry Italian girls with a few bars of chocolate. Instead, we preferred exploring Florence's art treasures.

We walked through the city, chatting in German. I bombarded him with questions about Palestine. Were there towns and theaters and cafés, or was it all a desert? He laughed and said

I had strange ideas. There were even paved streets and lampposts. As he talked, I became more convinced that this raw new country held the key to my future and a better life for my family.

A British soldier interrupted us and asked Herbert for a light. He brought his cigarette to Herbert's match and shot me a quick, penetrating glance, then thanked us and left. A few minutes later the same soldier stopped us again, this time accompanied by two military policemen. They asked for our IDs. I gave them a letter stating that the water-tank unit employed me as a mechanic. The MPs studied my paper and looked at each other; then one of them asked, "How come you speak German?"

Herbert said I was a Jewish refugee just liberated and didn't know English very well.

"Seems all right," the MP said finally. "Sorry, but we have to check these things, y' know. It's a shame, though. We thought we'd caught two German spies."

That night, asleep on my cot, I heard a door bang closed. I shot up, a knot in my throat, ready to run. Then I realized where I was.

The next morning I told Don Giovanni I was anxious to go to Palestine. "Maybe you should wait," he urged. "Your mother will probably be liberated any day now."

"But the emigration certificates are available now," I said, worried. "I want to establish myself immediately, so I can help bring the family there." I knew thousands of refugees were roaming all over Europe who didn't want to go back to the places where they were persecuted, just as I didn't want to go to Frankfurt, or even Paris. I explained to him how I had become disenchanted with France and its meaningless *"Liberté, Egalité, Fraternité,"* when so many French had been all too willing and eager to collaborate with the Germans to hunt down and capture Jews.

"You could stay in Florence and continue learning a craft. At least your family would know where to find you," Don Giovanni said.

I got up from my chair and started pacing. "But if I wait, the certificates may be gone. I don't want to lose the opportunity my parents lost. Papa will know where we are. On the train coming here, he gave me the address of friends in Tel-Aviv."

Resigned, Don Giovanni nodded.

I composed a letter to Mother and left it with him:

Dear Mutti,

Please excuse me for not waiting for your liberation. I hope you won't be too angry or upset, but I've received an emigration certificate from the British authorities, and I can't miss this opportunity for us. I will be leaving soon from Rome with a transport of Jewish refugees for Palestine— Willy and his father, too. I want to build a new life for us there. Twice I've seen Papa's efforts, sacrifices, and achievements for our family ruined because we established our lives on what turned out to be the wrong ground. In 1936, before the war, we had a chance to go to Argentina and in 1938 to Palestine, but we let it slip by when our emigration papers expired. Now I'm going because I think there has been too much misery for Jews everywhere else. The Jewish homeland is right for our future, so I'm going ahead to prepare for it. Please understand. Come and join me soon with Papa and Harry.

With many kisses, your Ludi.

I enclosed a beautiful Florentine mosaic bracelet, the first gift I was able to give to her since the liberation.

Chapter Thirty-Eight
WHAT I DIDN'T KNOW AT THE TIME

It was spring 1945. Paris had been freed since late August, the Americans had crossed the Rhine, the British were advancing on Hamburg, and the Russians were in Vienna. But the progress of the British Eighth and the American Fifth armies in Italy was slow, hard fought, and measured yard by yard against an enemy deeply entrenched in impregnable, natural strongholds.

Bologna, gateway to the great Po Plain, fell at last on April 21. It had taken the Allies more than eight months to cover the 107 kilometers from Florence. After Bologna, however, the Allies burst forth across the plain in pursuit of the Germans, who were rapidly retreating northward to make their ultimate stand in the Bavarian stronghold.

On April 26, the partisans caught Mussolini in Milan and hanged him in public. The Black Brigades disappeared from the Collegio overnight. They left behind piles of firewood, which Don Angelo and Harry Goldman loaded on a cart and wheeled by hand back to Santa Bona.

During the last days of April, red-kerchiefed partisans began to appear in the open around Santa Bona. German troops moved day and night throughout the region, while partisans waited in ambush. There was shooting only two kilometers away. Partisans scurried along Santa Bona's walls and manned strategic points, including the parochial school. Villagers took refuge in the church and in the school's upper rooms. As daylight faded, twenty people crowded into the "Five French's" room and slept on the floor. In the morning the news spread that the Germans had evacuated the entire area.

Don Bruno ran through Santa Bona, shouting, "The SS has abandoned the villa and left food! Quick, go get it!"

Harry was in a crowd of a hundred people, all yelling and shoving. While they snatched biscuits, canned goods, beans, flour, rice, and sugar, Harry's goal was a stockpile of empty sacks in a dark niche across the room. He quickly appraised them as more valuable than food and loudly announced, "This corner is mine!" Hailing a peasant with an empty donkey cart, Harry offered him a partnership in exchange for transportation. They loaded three hundred sturdy, jute sacks and brought them to the group's room. Villagers milled about in the streets, embracing, kissing, and slapping each other on the back. Wine circulated freely. Don Angelo hurried there from Treviso to share in the celebration. The next day the peasant brought a client for the sacks, but Harry refused to sell. The man bought only the peasant's share. A few days later, Harry found someone who paid him double, and the peasant shook his head in admiration and regret.

For the first time in five years, since the Nazis had invaded France, my family was free. But they, as well as everyone else in the village, were still afraid the Germans would return.

American armored cars arrived in Treviso's outskirts on the evening of April 29 and entered the city the next day. Units of the Palestinian Jewish Brigade were among the first Allied troops in Treviso. Some soldiers went to Santa Bona as soon as they heard Jews were there. The "Five French" introduced Don Angelo as their savior. The soldiers invited him to their barracks and presented him with a leather case and a bag of gifts. The inscription on the card read: "To a Friend of the Jewish People."

All German troops in Italy officially surrendered on May 2. On May 8 all hostilities ceased in Europe. Hitler and his paramour had committed a double suicide. Germany was finally defeated. But the nightmare the Nazis had created was over only for the dead.

First official reports appeared describing what the British had found upon liberating concentration camps such as Bergen Belsen, and what the Americans had found in Buchenwald and Dachau. More reports followed about gas-oven death factories. The enormity of the Nazi atrocities against the people of Europe and, in particular, against the Jews, ended all the years of mere rumor.

CHAPTER THIRTY-EIGHT

The annihilation was of unprecedented proportion in history. Generations of human beings had been murdered. Revelations that the Allies, and other governments, even the Vatican, knew about the genocide but failed to raise their voices to prevent or stop it came to us much later.

It is impossible not to ask why.

Chapter Thirty-Nine

~

As soon as communication was restored in northern Italy, Don Giovanni sent Mother a cable: "Ludi healthy in Palestine." She was stunned. Why had her eldest son not waited to hear if they were alive and well? But a few days later, my gift for her of the Florentine mosaic bracelet and my letter arrived.

After the initial shock wore off, Mother wrote that she cried when she finished reading it. Emigrating was not at all how she'd visualized our future. She had thought we would go back to our apartment in Paris to wait for Papa's return. My letter, however, had confronted her with a fait accompli, and she soon reconciled herself to following me. She wrote that she would go to Florence to arrange for emigration certificates, not only for herself and Harry, but for Renée, who now considered us her family—every member of her own had been deported. Aunt Sonia and Sylvia would be joining relatives in South America.

Now the group had to face separation from Don Angelo. They kept postponing it, the thought of leaving him painful because they had become so attached to him. When Mother finally got up the courage to tell him, he seemed stunned. "Can't you write to Florence?" he asked. "You could stay here until the papers arrive."

"Dear Don Angelo, you've done more than enough for us already! But we have to apply for our papers in person."

On the day of departure, a Jewish Brigade truck came to transport them to Florence. Don Bruno and many of the Santa Bona villagers and refugees gathered to say their farewells. Don

Angelo brought Don Bruno to Mother and said, "At last I'm able to tell you that these good people living in your parochial school for so long are Jewish."

Mother said Don Bruno was shocked, hurt to have been excluded from the secret. But Don Angelo explained, "I had no right to endanger you, too. If anything had gone wrong, you could always have said in all honesty that you knew nothing."

Don Bruno embraced Don Angelo and thanked him for his humane and courageous deed.

A flurry of kisses and good wishes followed. Don Angelo was pale and quivering as he shook Mother's and the other women's hands, then hugged Harry.

Running after their truck, he waved his arms and shouted, "Good luck, good health! May God protect you!"

They arrived in Florence toward evening and went directly to the Jewish Committee. There they received lodging tickets for an accommodation center that was filthy, noisy, and over-crowded; Mother told me later they were sorry for not having accepted Don Angelo's invitation. Harry and Sylvia went to Varlungo to see Don Giovanni, but he was out. They left word for him to meet them at a café in Via Cavour.

Don Giovanni arrived an hour later, as always, out of breath. It was an emotional reunion, the first time they'd seen each other since he'd had to leave Treviso more than a year earlier.

When Mother told him about the conditions at the center, he took them to stay with a Russian family he'd also helped dur-ing the German occupation. Mother and the other three women were given a room. Harry went back with Don Giovanni to Varlungo. The next day Don Giovanni transferred everyone to a *pensione*. They were able to pay for their lodging with their allowances from the refugee relief organizations DELASEM

(*DELegazione ASsistenza agli EMigranti Ebrei*) and UNRRA (United Nations Relief and Rehabilitation Administration).

The Italian owner of the *pensione* constantly hovered around Mother, offering her unlimited hot baths, and knocking on the door late at night with bowls of fresh fruit. His increasing ardor became such an embarrassment to everyone that Don Giovanni had to move the group to another *pensione*.

The group met several of "my" Palestinian soldiers and other Jewish officers from the American and British units in town, who often dropped in on the women, bringing them gifts of food and other items the public still was unable to obtain. These boys also brought gifts for Don Giovanni, who often lunched with them, still protesting and minimizing the importance of his part in saving Jews, which he said was only a natural, human thing to do. One soldier even sent him new bicycle tires from America. The *pensione* owners were impressed by the women. Who but "Very Important People" would merit such constant visits from the Catholic clergy as well as Allied soldiers wearing the star of David!

On Saturdays Don Giovanni came around and urged Harry and the girls, "It's *Shabbat*. Have you forgotten? Go to synagogue, go!" The synagogue the Germans pillaged in Via Farini had reopened. Don Giovanni and Don Casini, who'd returned to Varlungo from the countryside, were honored at its official rededication ceremony.

While the Palestine emigration certificates were being processed, Mother was still considering going first to Paris to await Papa and to salvage what she could of our possessions, although there was no way of knowing if there was as much as a toothpick left in the apartment. But Harry threw tantrums at any suggestion of delays, his usual—and successful—modus operandi. "We must go and join Ludi as soon as possible! You don't love him enough, or you wouldn't think of going back to Paris!"

Willy's brother Sigi arrived in Palestine a few months after Willy and I'd settled. He told us what happened at the Zecca garrison after Harry and I escaped its walls. The following morning he and Papa and about seven hundred other Jews captured in the raids were put into sealed boxcars. The train arrived in Auschwitz after eight days and nights, on Sigi's eighteenth birthday, November 15, 1943. On their first day in camp, Papa and Sigi were selected with twelve other men for a work squad.

An SS guard asked, "Anyone too sick to work?"

Papa spoke up: "I'm not sick but I'm recovering from surgery. All I need is a new bandage, please."

"Fine. Go stand over there with the women and children."

Sigi had remained in Auschwitz over six months before being transferred to another camp, but in that period he never saw Papa again. By then, everyone knew that all women, children, and sick men had been gassed.

I began to cry and couldn't stop.

Sick at heart, I wrote a letter to Don Giovanni to break the news to Mother.

As I was to learn later from my mother, at the *pensione* in Florence, the priests gave a farewell party for Aunt Sonia and Sylvia, whose papers had come through for Argentina. A mess chef baked the cake. Don Casini asked Renée to pick it up because he didn't want people to see him carrying the beribboned box and to start speculating whether he had a sweetheart.

Mother said that when Don Giovanni arrived she'd gotten one of her premonitions. He was wearing a new cassock for the occasion, but wasn't his lively self. After a few minutes he asked her if he could retire for awhile.

"Of course, please," Mother said, and opened the bedroom door for him.

"Is this your bed, Signora? May I sit on it?"

"Yes. Is something wrong, Don Giovanni?"

"I need to be by myself for awhile. Please call me when Don Casini arrives."

Puzzled, Mother closed the door and joined the others. Alone in the room, Don Giovanni asked God for strength in breaking the news to her. After Don Casini arrived, Don Giovanni came out and mingled with the guests, but seemed unusually quiet. Mother cut the cake, and everyone raised their glasses in toasts of good luck, bon voyage, and good health. Troubled by Don Giovanni's demeanor, Mother made a mental note to speak to him later. After the toasts Don Giovanni asked Sonia to come with him into the other room. Mother thought nothing of it. Her sister-in-law was leaving in the morning and he probably had something to say to her in private. Besides, there were the guests to look after, coffee and tea to serve. When Aunt Sonia returned with swollen eyes, Mother assumed Don Giovanni's farewell must have made her sad. Toward evening, guests and priests departed, Mother not having found a right moment to speak to Don Giovanni alone.

The following morning, Aunt Sonia and Sylvia left in an army car, their adieus filled with more tears than words.

Don Giovanni came back that afternoon. Mother made him coffee, but he barely touched it. She wondered why their conversation was dragging on so heavily. Don Giovanni glanced at her quickly, then studied his shoes. "I received a letter from Ludi yesterday," he said.

"And you tell me only now?"

"He saw Sigi in Palestine," he answered somberly.

"Sigi?" She stared at him. "Is my husband not here anymore?"

He shook his head sadly. "You must be strong for your children, Signora," he said. "They will need you now more than ever." Mother burst into tears. Don Giovanni got up, looked at her again, and left the room, painfully unable to say any more. Harry said comfortingly, "Ludi and I will take good care of you, Mutti, you'll see."

A short time later, Don Giovanni came back, having regained his composure. After the children had gone to bed, he kept Mother company a little longer, then clasped her hands in his, and left.

Mother stayed up, leaning on the windowsill, her memories wandering out into the night and the silent street below: married one day, the next fleeing to Germany with her Pinkus to avoid the anti-Semitic Polish army. A baby girl, dead at nine months from tuberculosis. Pinkus, traveling textile salesman, working, working, working. A nice home, a glimpse of happiness—then the Nazis shooting her brother in his home in Wiesbaden, a signal to flee again.

Illegally over the German border to France with the two boys, at night, waist-deep in water. Pinkus saying, "It's a free and humane country, Maniush. We'll be safe from persecution there." In Paris, no authorization to work and only a temporary permit to stay. "It'll be all right one day, Maniush, you'll see." A new, more-lenient government in power. A nice home again, again a glimpse of happiness. Hitler approaching Paris! Flee again!

"Just a few suitcases, Maniush. We'll be back soon." In the south of France, the word JUIF stamped in bold letters on identification papers. Pinkus chopping wood, leveling railroad beds, carrying heavy casks of grapes. Working too hard, smoking too much, coughing too much, but with the family together. "We'll pull through, Maniush. Don't worry." *Gendarmes* at the door. "Monsieur Goldman? Follow us!" The *gendarmes* back for the rest of the family. Taken to Agde, an internment camp. Reunion with Pinkus. Released! A miracle. A place of their own again, yet another glimpse of happiness. Then the Germans invading southern France! Escape to Switzerland!

"Just one suitcase, Maniush. It'll be easier to cross." In the forest at night, near the border. The group ahead caught by German shepherds. Back to the south, this time to the Italian zone. Forced residence, strict surveillance, but no camps, no deportations. "Here we'll be all right, Maniush." A little apartment, a new glimpse of happiness. Then Italy capitulates; the Germans taking over our zone! Quick, no time to finish the soup. Escape to Italy!

"Just a bundle, Maniush. Those are high mountains ahead, but no more Germans on the other side." In Italy, never a place to rest, never a glimpse of happiness. The hardships on the mountain, Pinkus's surgery, and right into the hands of the Nazis! Probably worrying about his family even on the way to Auschwitz.

And now she and her children would face a future without him. She broke down again.

Suddenly she noticed Don Giovanni coasting on his bicycle toward the house. He stopped under her first-floor window. "I thought I would circle around and see if anyone was still up. I was worried about you. The children?"

"They're asleep."

"Then go to bed, too, Mrs. Goldman. I beg of you." He rode off slowly.

Mother and Harry were informed that the Jewish Agency wanted Renée to go to Palestine by herself with the Youth Aliyah, an organization that rescued children from the Nazis and the aftermath of the war, and resettled them in *kibbutzim*. Harry went to see the agency representative. "She's our adopted sister," he said passionately. "My mother replaces hers. We are her only family. So we either leave together or not at all! Do you realize what it would mean for her to remain behind alone? She has endured enough suffering. Why do you want to inflict more?"

A week later the emigration papers came through, including Renée's. On the morning of departure, Don Giovanni arrived at ten, though they weren't due at the station until three. Mother was ambivalent about leaving. Don Giovanni had often suggested that they stay in Florence, promising to find work and an apartment for them. It was tempting, but Harry wouldn't hear of it. Palestine would be their home!

Don Giovanni looked at the old suitcases, held together with string, lined up near the door. He sighed softly, *"Ancora sfollati, sempre sfollati."** Mother overheard the remark and broke down weeping. Irritated with himself for having touched a raw nerve, Don Giovanni took Harry and left the house. They returned twenty minutes later.

Giacinto, the Varlungo convent's handyman, arrived and loaded the suitcases on a handcart. At the railroad station, when the inevitable moment came, the hustle and bustle of the crowd around them made it easier to let feelings show. Don Giovanni hugged Harry in a long, silent embrace, putting into it all the love and affection it would have been improper to demonstrate to the other two. Mother and Renée cried freely, and so did Harry. They exchanged good wishes and promised to stay in touch. Then Don Giovanni pressed the hands of both women and left.

---

*"Refugees again, always refugees."

The train started to move, for some reason was shifted to another track, then brought back to the same point of departure.

But Don Giovanni had not left. He sat on a stone ledge on the opposite embankment, watching his friends through the window of their compartment. They never saw him. That did not disappoint him. He had just wanted to be nearby as long as possible.

Three hours later, the train finally pulled away and Don Giovanni watched it disappear behind its black smoke.

Epilogue

Most of the men, women, and children the priests had saved gradually left Italy to start new lives in other lands, on other shores.

Mrs. Glatt and her daughter Ruth, Miss Sabine Adler, Mrs. Wallach, and Willy and Sigi's parents all came to Palestine, too. Mr. Wallach and Mr. Kohn, in the transport with Sigi and my father, died at Auschwitz.

Mrs. Grunewald and Diane, Miss Forscher, and Mrs. Tarnover with her two sons went to the United States. Schloime's circumcision finally took place in Florence, when he was nearly two. Mrs. Tarnover had wanted to give Don Giovanni the honor of being the *Sandek* at the *bris,* the man who holds the baby on his lap during the circumcision. In her eyes, no Jew deserved it more than he, but Don Giovanni declined it graciously.

Joseph Ziegler and all the other Jewish Committee members in Florence survived death camps, but Ziegler's entire family— wife, children, and mother-in-law—did not.

Rabbi Nathan Cassuto served briefly as a doctor at Auschwitz. As the Russians approached in late January 1945, he was marched seventy kilometers in the snow to Gross Rosen, where the Nazis murdered him to prevent his liberation by the Russians. He was thirty-four years old. His wife Anna survived the Birkenau labor camp and Theresienstadt, but her life also ended tragically. She'd settled in Jerusalem with her children and was working for the Hadassah Hospital. On April 13, 1948, Arabs ambushed the convoy of buses and ambulances in which she was traveling. She was killed with seventy others of the hospital staff.

Aunt Sonia and Sylvia joined their family in Buenos Aires. Uncle Jacob was never heard from again. Mrs. Wolf remained in Treviso. Other Jews I hadn't known, who'd also been helped by our priests, went to France. Some, incredibly, even returned to Germany.

Marco Ischio was tried for his crimes and sentenced to eight years in jail in Florence.

In 1946, Willy and I ran into Sandro, the boy from the Orfanotrofio whom we'd suspected was one of us. "Turns out you're Jewish after all!" I said.

"No less than you two."

"But you never knew we were."

"Oh, no? It was in your eyes." He told us he'd joined a group of new immigrants planning to found a *kibbutz* in the Judean hills. He didn't know what had become of the father and son from Fiume who'd worked as janitors at the orphanage.

In May 1948, Israel was officially declared a nation. It was immediately attacked by the armies of five Arab nations. The entire Jewish population numbered 500,000, and so every able-bodied citizen was mobilized in the battle for survival.

My brother Harry fell defending a strategic intersection twenty miles south of Tel Aviv, on the morning of June 11, two hours before the first cease-fire was due to go into effect. He was barely seventeen years old. Don Giovanni, Don Angelo, and Monsignor Facibeni were as shocked by his death as if he had been their own blood. They, who had spared no efforts to save his life, must have reflected upon God's unfathomable ways.

Our bond of friendship with the priests was never broken, despite the distances and passing years. We continued to stay in touch through letters and exchanged greetings on our respective holidays.

I saw the priests again in 1953. On a return trip to Israel from the United States, where I had finally settled and become a photographer, I made stops in Treviso and Florence. After getting his teacher's diploma, Don Giovanni had gone back to Treviso to teach philosophy and history while he continued his studies. He had obtained his doctorate in pedagogy in 1947. Had he not devoted his time to us during the war, he could have graduated three years sooner. Don Angelo had become professor of classical literature at the Seminario's high school.

In Florence, Monsignor Facibeni had grown thinner, further bent and weakened by his crippling diseases, but his eyes shone brightly as ever. He held me in a warm embrace and I got the old knock at the back of the head. I, too, had become one of the padre's older boys, an alumnus.

He continued to answer my letters but his handwriting gradually became illegible scribbling. I could see the suffering in every line. On a postcard of May 8, 1958, he made a special effort, "*Carissimo,* your constant souvenirs are a source of much consolation. I thank you. I think of you often and accompany you on your way with my poor prayers. Remember me in yours."

Three weeks later he was dead. His body lay in state in the Duomo Cathedral of Florence. Thousands of people came to pay their last respects to a man they'd regarded as a saint. Cardinal Dalla Costa celebrated the Pontifical Mass. Alumni carried the coffin on their shoulders through the city's thronged streets for burial in Rifredi. Traffic was stopped for the procession, comprised of many civilian and clerical dignitaries: the mayor, an army unit in parade uniforms, political leaders—including the Communists—and the head of the Democratic Christian government, Signor Adone Zoli.

An aide reminded him he had an important meeting in Rome that evening and suggested they leave. "Not until the procession is over," Signor Zoli said firmly.

"But you already attended the Pontifical Mass."

"You don't know what Monsignor Facibeni meant to us in Florence."

Perhaps my most enduring remembrance of the padre is his words in a note to me: "Let us hope that Man will come back to his senses and after so many horrors and cruelties finally understand that the only law of life is love."

As the years passed, all of us who were scattered around the world kept looking for a gesture with which to collectively express our gratitude to Don Giovanni, Don Angelo, and Don Casini. We finally agreed on a visit to the Holy Land.

Don Casini was busy sailing the seven seas as chaplain on Italian passenger boats. The other two priests protested that they weren't worthy of so great an honor and would feel guilty causing us such a financial sacrifice. I answered that they had no right to refuse us the pleasure of doing something nice for them, for a change.

Humbly they soon confessed that such a voyage had always been a cherished dream which, but for us, would have remained just that; they could never have afforded it. They would make the trip during summer vacation.

The extra time helped us to collect the funds. I calculated the costs, divided them equally among all participants, and set a deadline for payments. It was moving to see the money arrive from all corners of the world. When it was all in, I bought the tickets and sent them to Treviso.

Don Giovanni and Don Angelo arrived in Israel in July 1960. Mother, Miss Adler, Mrs. Glatt, and I greeted them. Fifteen years had passed since the women had seen the priests.

Mother put her small garden apartment at their disposal and moved in with a neighbor.

Their first visit was to Harry's grave in the military cemetery of Nachlat Yitzchak.

Each morning I escorted Don Giovanni and Don Angelo to a church in Jaffa for their prayers. We took them on tours of the country: the Sea of Galilee and the Mount of Beatitudes, the Capernaum Synagogue where Jesus had preached, Haifa, Nazareth, Acre, the *kibbutz* Enzo Sereni, settled by Italian Jews, Eyn Karem (John the Baptist's birthplace), Bethlehem, and Jerusalem. There, they also visited Yad Vashem, a memorial monument to the six million Jews killed by the Nazis. The priests' names were entered in the book of distinguished visitors.

We didn't publicize their arrival, knowing Don Giovanni and Don Angelo would be embarrassed. We also wanted our token of gratitude to remain strictly ours. But inevitably, officialdom learned of their presence. The Israeli Ministry for Religious Affairs was annoyed for not having been informed and sent a delegate to express the government's thanks. Reporters came and every major newspaper carried articles about and photographs of our heroes. A Yad Vashem representative arrived with a tape recorder. Mother spoke of the priests' rescue work. When she was finished, he said, "I've recorded many personal stories of the Holocaust. Most of them I wish I could forget. Yours is one we will all enjoy remembering."

The Italian ambassador held a reception for the priests and came to our farewell party.

On his sea voyages over the years, Don Casini also had reunions with his Jewish friends in Israel and other parts of the globe. Eventually, the title of monsignor was conferred upon him and also on Don Giovanni, who became rector of the Collegio Pio X. One day a letter from Don Angelo gladdened our hearts:

Dear Ludi,

It's fitting that I tell you a piece of news, even though you may know it already. A commission of the Yad Vashem Institute in Jerusalem has decreed to honor Don Giovanni, Don Casini, Don De Zotti, and me with the Medal of the Righteous among Nations for the help we gave you during the war.

I replied that if this had been decided twenty years ago, perhaps I wouldn't have accepted; to do so then would have seemed a vainglorious act. But now, in these times when there's still so much hatred and wickedness in the world, I accept the medal as an opportunity to point out that human fraternity is absolutely essential for mankind's future.

We'll be advised when to travel to Rome for the presentation at the Israeli embassy.

It's important for me that you, too, know I accept it in the spirit of which I wrote above. Because, as far as I'm concerned, you, my friends, each one of you, is the most beautiful medal.

Yours, Don Angelo

In 1973, the priests journeyed to Jerusalem, and in a moving tribute at the eternal flame of Yad Vashem, Israeli representatives expressed the gratitude of the Jewish people for their humanitarian deeds, a *mitzvah* in the truest Jewish spirit—a good deed done out of religious conviction. The ceremony was followed by the planting of trees in the Alley of the Righteous.

There, in the soil of Jerusalem, against a sweeping panorama and amid rows of trees each bearing the name of a Christian distinguished in aiding Jews during the Holocaust, three carob saplings are now growing.

They are named Monsignor Leto Casini, Monsignor Giovanni Simioni, and Don Angelo Dalla Torre. A fourth one, for Monsignor Giulio Facibeni, will be planted there soon.

He who saves a life saves the world.
—TALMUD: BABYLONIA BB, 11A

green
press
I N I T I A T I V E

Paulist Press is committed to preserving ancient forests and natural resources. We elected to print this title on 30% post consumer recycled paper, processed chlorine free. As a result, for this printing, we have saved:

7 Trees (40' tall and 6-8" diameter)
2,615 Gallons of Wastewater
5 million BTU's of Total Energy
336 Pounds of Solid Waste
630 Pounds of Greenhouse Gases

Paulist Press made this paper choice because our printer, Thomson-Shore, Inc., is a member of Green Press Initiative, a nonprofit program dedicated to supporting authors, publishers, and suppliers in their efforts to reduce their use of fiber obtained from endangered forests.

For more information, visit www.greenpressinitiative.org

Environmental impact estimates were made using the Environmental Defense Paper Calculator. For more information visit: www.papercalculator.org.